PENGUIN BOOKS

MOVIES TO SAVE OUR WORLD: IMAGINING POVERTY, INEQUALITY AND ENVIRONMENTAL DESTRUCTION IN THE 21ST CENTURY

Kenneth Paul TAN is a tenured Professor at Hong Kong Baptist University, which hired him under its Talent100 initiative in February 2021. He teaches and conducts interdisciplinary research at the Academy of Film, the Department of Journalism, and the Department of Government and International Studies. He is a member of the university's Smart Society Lab. Previously, he was a tenured Associate Professor at the National University of Singapore's (NUS) Lee Kuan Yew School of Public Policy. He was the school's Vice Dean during the most rapid and critical years of its growth and served in its senior leadership team for almost a decade. He has received numerous teaching awards over the years, including NUS's most prestigious Outstanding Educator Award. His books include *Singapore: Identity, Brand, Power* (Cambridge University Press, 2018), *Governing Global-City Singapore: Legacies and Futures After Lee Kuan Yew* (Routledge, 2017), *Cinema and Television in Singapore: Resistance in One Dimension* (Brill, 2008), and *Renaissance Singapore? Economy, Culture, and Politics* (NUS Press, 2007). He has also published numerous articles in leading international journals, reflecting an innovative and interdisciplinary research agenda that bridges Political Science, Public Management, Policy Studies, Sociology, Urban Studies, Cultural Studies, and Film and Media Studies. He is a member of the National Arts Council (Singapore)'s Arts Advisory Panel and the National Museum of Singapore's Advisory Board. He chairs the Board of Directors of theatre company The Necessary Stage (Singapore). He was also the founding chair of the Asian Film Archive's Board of Directors.

Advance Praise for *Movies to Save Our World*

Can movies build registers for bringing about social change amidst the devastating effects of neoliberal globalization and the global rise of authoritarian populism? Professor Kenneth Paul Tan, one of the most significant public intellectuals of Singapore, grapples with this vital question of our times, exploring the ways in which cinema can build our capacities for collective deliberation to build a just and sustainable world. The striking geographic expanse of the book and the brilliant analysis of the questions of poverty, inequality, massive ecological destruction, authoritarian populism and revolution offer conceptual fodder for exploring the ways in which the craft of moviemaking can connect audiences with their moral feelings and intuitions.

—Mohan Dutta, Dean's Chair Professor of Communication at Massey University, and Director of the Center for Culture-Centered Approach to Research and Evaluation (CARE)

In *Movies To Save Our World*, Kenneth Paul Tan explores how cinematic texts present poverty, inequality and environmental destruction in today's global world. Tan engages the films of Michael Moore and other major documentary filmmakers, as well as significant narrative fictional texts, to explore how cinema can help us see the problems, challenges, and inequities of the world, as well as possible solutions. The result is a probing and provocative text that enables us to envision the political possibilities of contemporary cinema.

—Douglas Kellner, Distinguished Research Professor of Education, Graduate School of Education and Information Studies, UCLA

Movies to Save Our World

Imagining Poverty, Inequality and Environmental Destruction in the 21st Century

Kenneth Paul Tan

PENGUIN BOOKS
An imprint of Penguin Random House

PENGUIN BOOKS

USA | Canada | UK | Ireland | Australia
New Zealand | India | South Africa | China | Southeast Asia

Penguin Books is part of the Penguin Random House group of companies whose addresses can be found at global.penguinrandomhouse.com

Published by Penguin Random House SEA Pte Ltd
9, Changi South Street 3, Level 08-01,
Singapore 486361

First published in Penguin Books by Penguin Random House SEA 2022

10 9 8 7 6 5 4 3 2 1

ISBN 9789815058314

Typeset in Garamond by MAP Systems, Bangalore, India
Printed at Markono Print Media Pte Ltd, Singapore

www.penguin.sg

Contents

For my mother,
Adeline Catherine Tan, née Francisco (1948–2021)

Preface

I love movies.

I wrote some parts of this book about movies over several weeks when I was quarantined alone in hotel rooms, when an endless stream of movies made its way to my always-on and always-charging iPad, allowing the time to pass quickly and pleasurably and keeping my imagination very much alive.

During this pandemic, cinemas have been closing everywhere. Box-office takings have been in significant decline globally. And blockbuster movie release dates have been postponed, often indefinitely. In the unforgettable words of Bette Davis in the 1939 film *Dark Victory*, when it comes to the movie industry's prospects, there could be 'a large order of prognosis negative'.

And yet, if quarantine, work-from-home, home-based-learning and safe-distancing arrangements are going to be the norm in our hyper-digitally connected post-pandemic world, then I think moviemakers, with all their creativity, ingenuity and determination, will find a way to flourish through independent and alternative modes of moviemaking and through new digital technologies that expand the cinematic experience beyond its physical limitations. Movies, more diverse and accessible, will become an increasingly important part of our daily lives, wherever we may be and whatever we might be doing at any moment.

If this turns out to be true, and movies come to play an increasingly significant role in shaping our individual and collective consciousness, then we need to pay more attention to how this is being done, by whom, for what purpose and to what effect.

In the light of such questions, this book provides critical analyses of more than seventy popular movies produced in the 21st century. Most of them were made in the United States, but a good number were produced in Australia and parts of Europe and Asia. Some of them enjoyed commercial success. Some received rave reviews for their artistic merits. Some earned prestigious awards. And some gained notoriety.

But all of them, I would argue, tell us in their own distinctive ways something important about poverty, inequality, environmental degradation, revolution and the dynamic relationship among them in the 21st century. Altogether, they help paint a bigger picture of how our world has evolved, especially since the 1980s, when the governments of many countries, starting with the US and the United Kingdom, began to embrace the logic and values of the free market. These countries opened their borders to the networks and flows of economic globalization. They yielded to the exacting demands of global competitiveness. They cut back on taxes and government spending, especially on welfare and social services. The impact of these global developments has been profound. Some people have gained tremendously by them, while many others have had to pay a heavy price. Since the 2010s, we have seen masses of aggrieved people, who were left behind, rise against the technocratic, liberal and globalist elite in their own countries, often led by charismatic and manipulative political leaders. What we are seeing today is tension between 'neoliberal globalization' on the one hand and 'authoritarian populism' on the other, two key and inter-related concepts that the first chapter of this book will discuss fully.

Chapter One lays out the broad conceptual framework that will serve as a kind of analytical scaffolding that supports our efforts to interpret these movies, identify their key messages, discuss how they might resonate with different audiences and uncover the conditions in which they are produced. This first chapter, not surprisingly, makes for some heavy reading. And while it is entirely possible to skip this chapter and go straight to the remaining chapters that deal with the movies more directly, much insight would unfortunately be lost by doing so. And so, I invite you, dear reader, to persevere with the first chapter, knowing that the investment of time and effort in it will pay off handsomely as you glide through the following chapters.

Chapters Two, Three, and Four make up Part One of the book, a section devoted to documentary movies. Many of the documentaries discussed here are structured rather like argumentative essays or research papers, advancing a central argument or thesis, through a systematic arrangement of smaller arguments supported by evidence, animated by real-life examples and strengthened by references to expert and reliable sources. Documentary-makers often use stock, archival and interview footage to present their arguments vividly and persuasively. The documentary-makers themselves sometimes appear in their own movies to influence, alter and directly intervene in the flow of events they depict. Some documentaries help to describe a complex problem by breaking it down into smaller, more easily digestible parts. Other documentaries help to join the dots so that we can see the big picture and appreciate the extent and urgency of the problem. Yet other documentaries set out a theory of the problem as well as practical steps for solving it. Part One offers analyses of American moviemaker Michael Moore's highly influential documentaries, as well as a range of other documentaries that deal with the more specific impact of corporate greed on health, education, racialized criminal justice, economic crises and environmental destruction.

Chapters Five and Six make up Part Two of the book, a section devoted to feature movies that, unlike traditional documentaries, gesture at 'higher truths' through the narrative telling of fiction rather than fact. Chapter Five offers a detailed comparative analysis of four successful feature movies—from the UK, the US, South Korea and Spain—that shine a light on the nature of poverty, inequality and revolution in different parts of the world. Chapter Six highlights two monstrous figures—the psychopath and the zombie—as cinematic metaphors for understanding the monstrous aspects of neoliberal globalization and authoritarian populism.

The closing chapter returns more pointedly to the question of whether movies can save our world. Moviemakers wishing to do so will be confronted with many more intractable problems in the foreseeable future, including profoundly disruptive technological changes, more frequent and less predictable occurrences of pandemics, more complex manifestations of global injustice and the rise of new autocracies around the world. If we do not come together and do something to stop our world from self-destructing under the weight of poverty, inequality and ecological degradation, it may become too late. Thus, the work of moviemakers to raise our collective global consciousness and optimism for positive change is urgent and vital. Movies can adopt a propagandistic approach to consciousness-raising, and this might, in fact, be necessary for urgent problems, but I want to argue that it is more sustainable for moviemakers, in collaboration with educators, to think of their craft as a means of raising the capacity and quality of collective deliberation, in part by expanding the language of deliberation beyond just the facts and figures of intellectual argumentation to include a connection with our moral feelings and intuitions.

This book was written during my transition from Singapore to Hong Kong, two historically important cities for movie production, populated by people who are noted for their love of movies. As I gave up a tenured position at the National University of Singapore (NUS) to take up a tenured professorship at the Hong Kong Baptist University, I also moved from teaching in a public policy school to an academy of film, in fact Hong Kong's flagship film school. This book, which has benefitted from conversations with my new colleagues and students at the School of Communication and Film, is produced at the confluence of my teaching and research interests in political science, policy studies, social theory, film studies and cultural studies. It also reflects my practical interest in nurturing wider public appreciation of movies, by helping to equip audiences with critical interpretation skills, without the need to acquire the sometimes-esoteric lattice of terminology that arises from film theory. In many ways, the book is a practical extension of my public outreach efforts as the founding chair (2005–17) of the Asian Film Archive, whose mission is to 'save, explore and share the art of Asian cinema'.

As always, there are far too many people to thank, so I will limit myself to just a few. First, the editorial team at Penguin, who were an enormous pleasure to work with. Second, my new colleagues at Hong Kong Baptist University, including Noit Banai, Cherian George, Huang Yu, C.K. Lau, Dorothy Lau, Ellen Seiter, Daya Thussu and Ying Zhu, for their truly stimulating company. Third, my friends Donald Low and Jennifer Chow, whose love of good food and conversation, of which hours and hours were spent talking movies, kept me energized. And finally, my wife Clara and my father Philip for their constant support, especially during these challenging last few years.

As I said at the beginning, I love movies. And so did my family. My late grandfather worked as the manager of Roxy Cinema, one of the oldest cinemas in Singapore. Many people from the generation that watched movies produced in the 'golden age' of Singapore cinema remember him fondly as 'John Roxy'. His daughter—my mother—also loved going to the cinema, especially as a child. And she fondly remembered doing that even towards the end of her life. She died peacefully while I was writing this book. It is to her that I lovingly dedicate it.

Chapter One

What is Wrong with Our World Today?

Peace, Prosperity and Progress

Our world seems to have become a better place, even though it may not appear that way, judging from regular news reports or the stories that show up on our social media feeds these days. We are more peaceful. We are more prosperous. We have progressed, as many have argued, both from factual observation as well as a philosophical point of view.

Through his impressive analysis of large quantities of data, for instance, Harvard professor Steven Pinker (2011) showed us that overt violence of all kinds has declined all over the world. This, he argued in his well-cited book, is true over the long arc of history. But it is especially true in our modern age, when now-familiar institutions such as the nation-state, judiciaries and trading systems have pushed us forward in a peaceful direction. This they did by drawing upon and thus strengthening those human motives that were to be found among an increasingly literate and human-rights-respecting people. These motives include empathy, self-control, moral sense and reason. The 'better angels of our nature', Pinker argued in ways that attracted a great deal of both scholarly praise and criticism, have gradually prevailed over our opposite inclinations towards violence.

Two decades earlier, at the momentous end of the Cold War, Francis Fukuyama (1992) had written what is probably still his most famous book, *The End of History and the Last Man.* In it, the prolific

American political scientist argued that History was coming to an end since, in the historical battle of ideologies, capitalist liberal democracy had emerged victorious over fascism and communism. The events of history (with a small 'h') would go on, of course. In our diverse world, the pace of liberal democratization would likely be uneven, as historical legacies and cultural-civilizational attachments could be deep, pervasive and unyielding. With the events of history, two steps forward could be followed by a step backwards. Overall, though, Fukuyama believed that the global progress to a capitalist liberal democracy was inevitable. All events that contradicted this megatrend were merely fluctuations and temporary departures that would eventually be dragged along by its irresistible current. Fukuyama, like many others at the time, was uplifted by the euphoria of the moment as the world witnessed the fall of the Berlin Wall and then of the Soviet Union.

Almost a century and a half before the publication of Fukuyama's remarkable book, a hugely influential German philosopher named Karl Marx and his collaborator Friedrich Engels had published *The Communist Manifesto*. In this polemically charged pamphlet, Marx and Engels (1848/1998) explained that the history of all societies that had ever existed was in essence the history of class struggle. According to this view, throughout history, there had always been classes of people who were dominant, oppressive and usually in the numerical minority, as well as classes that were subordinated, exploited and usually in the majority. These classes existed in formally unequal and hierarchical relationships with one another, mainly based on what the people of each class were able to own, buy, sell and invest. People from the different classes worked and lived under different conditions, not fully known to them. As some classes systematically prospered at the expense of others, a modern 'ruling class' was formed. Members of this ruling class actively shaped the common system of law and order, to maintain the advantage that they had been able to secure through exploitative economic and social relationships. They also manipulated the political system to control the political leadership and give exploited people the false belief that their interests were being safeguarded through a fair system of representative government. And, through its influence over institutions and producers of popular culture, the ruling class propagated a shared belief system that justified inequalities and made them tolerable and even acceptable by nearly everyone.

At critical junctures in history, however, the system ran into crisis. Marx observed a general pattern in the way crisis tended to play out in the capitalist stage of history. In its relentless exploitation of workers to do their jobs more efficiently and cheaply, the capitalist system overproduced and was unable to sell its products back to the impoverished masses. Workers from among these masses then lost their jobs, which brought even more hardship to their families, locking them and their children into endless cycles of poverty and misery. When their lives became unbearable, they developed consciousness of their identity as a systematically exploited class, whose potential for economic and social advancement had been stymied. More contemporary examples of economic crisis, such as the Global Financial Crisis (GFC) of 2007–2008, which is the subject of several movies discussed in this book, may not have played out in the same ways as Marx had theorized. Yet, in common with Marx's explanation is the basic idea of a destructive and ultimately unfeasible system, driven by insatiable greed, human ingenuity and a loss of empathy.

According to the pattern that Marx observed, intellectual leaders emerged from among the masses, helping them understand and think critically about their exploited condition. These intellectuals also developed a language for not only expressing this condition but also forging solidarity among the exploited, whom the capitalist system had alienated, atomized and therefore weakened as a political force. With political leadership, such class-conscious solidarity would become the basis of revolutions that could lead to fundamental social reconstruction, and not just reform.

Among these intellectuals today are the moviemakers. They seek not only to make beautiful and marketable works of art, but also to hold up a mirror to our society, reflecting with clarity the good and the bad, to shape our conscience and provoke necessary action, including action to save our world. Other moviemakers may, in the popular culture they produce, intentionally or unintentionally reinforce the shared belief system that normalizes, obscures or justifies exploitative relations. In practice, each movie is likely to have both revolutionary and reactionary elements.

Over the centuries, as slaves revolted against their masters, serfs against the feudal aristocracy and the working class (or the 'proletariat') against capitalists (or the 'bourgeoisie'), history progressed in stages towards greater equality and freedom for humankind. Marx's History exceeded Fukuyama's capitalist liberal democratic end point, evolving further into a classless, propertyless and stateless society. This was the ideal—some might argue fantasy—of communism, where everyone could, at least in theory, have everything that they needed and would give back to society whatever they could.

Pinker, Fukuyama and Marx all belong, broadly speaking, to an Enlightenment tradition of thought, which took an optimistic view of History as an unfolding of reason through the myriad events over time and space. These events may seem random to the unphilosophical eye, but they, in fact, lead progressively to the enlightenment and emancipation of all people. All three owed an intellectual debt to the great, 18th-century, German philosopher, Georg Wilhelm Friedrich Hegel (1807/1997), who developed and advanced a view about universal History as continuous improvement over time, resulting from ideological development through a series of clashes between old and new ideas, and the supersession of the former by the latter. Through this continual conflict of ideas, we become self-consciously more knowledgeable about ourselves and the world we live in. We also become freer human beings able to build free social institutions. And thus, the true meaning of human History, what Hegel called its 'Spirit', is revealed. Hegel also identified an intrinsically human desire and struggle for recognition that made social hierarchy fundamentally unstable and, therefore, impermanent. Thus, at the end of universal History, when all contradictions are resolved, Hegel expected to find universal equality.

Marx accepted Hegel's notion of conflict and resolution as the dynamic principle that drives human History forward, but he replaced Hegel's focus on ideas with a primary concern over the evolving material and technological conditions that shape the tense and contradictory relations between classes. These contradictions are finally resolved in a communist world, the final stage of history when everyone is a creatively autonomous worker and there is plenty to satisfy the needs of all.

Fukuyama adapted Hegel's idea about the fundamental human desire and struggle for recognition as one important driving force in all human History, a force that interacts with two others that he derived from the ancient Greek philosopher Plato: the capacity to reason and the need to satisfy our desires. Science, technology and industry are about how we use our collective brainpower and ingenuity to turn the resources of the natural world into things that satisfy our needs and appetites. And the market or the economy is a mechanism for coordinating our various needs and appetites with what others have produced through a system of exchange signalled by prices. Science, technology, production, consumption, exchange, prices and markets are the basic components of capitalism, which developed over history alongside liberal democracy as a political mechanism through which autonomous individuals enjoy equal recognition through the distributed power of the vote. Thus, the interaction of reason, desire and recognition—Fukuyama's three fundamentally human forces—drives History towards its capitalist liberal democratic conclusion.

The death of communism at the end of the Cold War was, for Fukuyama, a historic opportunity to bury Marx and his ideas once and for all, as French postmodern philosopher Jacques Derrida (1994/1993) observed critically. With the events of history on his side, Fukuyama was triumphantly able to declare the ultimate pre-eminence of capitalist liberal democracy as the only viable socio-political system at the end of History. Only that system—and not communism as Marx had argued—could potentially satisfy everyone's material needs and ensure universal and reciprocal recognition. Pinker, two decades later, would provide a wealth of empirical evidence to support a similarly progressive narrative that takes us to a liberal endpoint, not unlike Hegel's or Fukuyama's, where conflict and violence will have been replaced by peace and plenty.

So, if Hegel, Fukuyama and Pinker—the liberal strand of 'optimists'—were right, our world has been moving towards a state of greater material equality, mutual recognition and peaceful stability, whether we have noticed it or not. Our destination is a combination of global capitalism, liberalism and democracy.

However, the end of the Cold War has not brought History to an end. Instead, we are seeing a decline of Western societies in many respects. Political commentator Ross Douthat (2020) described the US as a decadent society, a victim of its own success and paralysed by economic stagnation, cultural-intellectual exhaustion and institutional decay. A 'new Cold War' has emerged, where the US—hobbled by its domestic politics, economic stasis and unaffordable military commitments around the world—is struggling to retain its pre-eminent global status. Meanwhile, China has risen in stature, poised to overtake the US and replace Pax Americana with a new Pax Sinica, one that is not necessarily capitalist, liberal or democratic as we know it. And the US, under President Joe Biden, is determined not to let that happen ('Joe Biden is determined', 2021).

Poverty and Inequality in a World of Abundance

Today, we live in a world of abundance. Much of this has indeed been the result of the immense productive power of capitalist liberal democracy, which Fukuyama theorized as the best system to facilitate the relentless drive of human ingenuity to satisfy our needs and ambitions through science, technology and industry. Although Fukuyama and others tried in the 1990s to bury Marx under the rubble of historical communism, the relative peace and prosperity of 21st-century capitalism have been haunted by Marxist critique, aimed primarily at new forms of social injustice associated with what has come to be called 'neoliberal globalization'.

Neoliberal globalization is a broad theoretical framework that exposes and critiques the excesses of capitalism, as it pervades all parts of the world through economic globalization—the profound opening of national and city borders to inward and outward flows of goods, services, capital, technology, information and people. Since the 1970s, a neoliberal policy consensus has grown around the desirability of removing national barriers to free up movements of goods, services and capital; of reducing taxes and government spending especially on the welfare system; and of selling off state assets in a strategy of privatization. The goals of neoliberal policies have been to establish macroeconomic stability, cut back on government budgets, privatize government operations, charge users for public services, reduce trade tariffs, promote exports, facilitate foreign capital flows and reduce worker protections through flexible labour markets (Klees, 2008).

Although 'neoliberal globalization' is often used as a pejorative term, neoliberal reforms in moderation can be progressive. Cutting back on government spending, letting the private sector take over the provision of some essential services, loosening government regulation of businesses, and opening the economy to international competition can have the positive effect of forcing a bloated and bureaucratic public sector to become leaner, more cost-efficient, accountable, responsive and focused on performance and results. These reforms can help to expand the private sector, encouraging competitiveness, innovation and a spirit of enterprise. They can also improve the customer service experience of citizens, encouraging them to be self-reliant and less parochial in outlook. Neoliberal globalization makes economies around the world thoroughly interdependent. There is, of course, much to be gained materially and culturally from global openness.

However, without adequate restraint, these gains can come at a severe cost. Local identities could be fractured. Local cultures could be devalued and even destroyed. Moral solidarity and democratic capacities could be degraded. What we might be left with is widespread social injustice, where massive wealth is concentrated and expanded in the hands of the few at the expense of the many, whose lives become increasingly precarious. And all of this could happen alongside a systematic destruction of our habitat through the collective lack of restraint that we exercise over our unbridled economic demands. Whether the system will benefit or hurt us individually, our collective human security will be threatened in the long run. Contrary to the singularly progressive vision of History articulated by Hegel, Marx, Fukuyama and Pinker, this existential threat suggests that our world is cultivating the seeds of its own destruction beneath the veneer of progress and success. For us as a species to do anything about this, we need critical thinking to understand what is going on underneath this veneer.

Thinking critically makes us appreciate more seriously the fact that, in this neoliberally globalized world of abundant resources, poverty and inequality continue to be among the most intractable problems today. The United Nation's Agenda for Sustainable Development asserts that

> . . . eradicating poverty in all its forms and dimensions, including extreme poverty, is the greatest global challenge and an indispensable requirement for sustainable development.

Ending poverty and reducing inequality within and among countries by 2030 are part of the UN's seventeen 'Sustainable Development Goals' (or 'SDGs'), formally launched in 2015 ('Transforming our world', 2015). Prior to the SDGs, the UN had put in place a global plan of action called the 'Millennium Development Goals' (or 'MDGs'). Of its eight goals, the first was to eradicate extreme poverty and hunger by 2015 ('We can end poverty', no date). There have been many criticisms levelled at the MDGs and their successor the SDGs, questioning their rigour, legitimacy, implementation and record of success.

Bent Greve (2020a), a Danish scholar of welfare systems, acknowledged the fact that many people have been lifted out of absolute poverty since the 1990s, particularly in China and India. And yet, in some parts of the world, such as the sub-Saharan region, extreme poverty remains rife. A report by the World Bank (2020) noted that poverty reduction, which had seen progress from 1990 to 2015 thanks to collective global effort, was slowing down and stalling even before the COVID-19 pandemic struck in 2020. This was especially so in the case of extreme poverty. The report also noted that gains in what it called 'shared prosperity' were uneven and, like poverty reduction in general, had also been slowing down and stalling even before the pandemic. Shared prosperity measures the extent to which relatively poor people can participate in and benefit from their national economic growth. Thus, it can be a measure of economic inequality. The report concluded that the COVID-19 pandemic and its associated economic crisis have reversed any improvements in poverty eradication, economic inclusion and inequality reduction. The situation is expected to worsen, with armed conflict in some of the poorest and most fragile parts of the world as well as the unequal effects of climate change. Not surprisingly, it is the poorest in the world who are the worst hit, with COVID-19 pushing 100 million people into extreme poverty in 2020 alone. And out of this expanded class of chronic poverty, a new profile of the global poor has emerged: urban and educated, working in the informal sectors and living in middle-income countries.

The fact thus remains that poverty and inequality have continued to be on the high-profile global agenda for a long time. And yet, we seem helpless to do anything about it. This indicates not only the resilience of poverty and inequality, but perhaps also the depths to which the problem is embedded in the system itself. Nothing less than a change in the system will create the conditions of possibility for reducing and eliminating poverty and inequality.

Survival of the Fittest

The fact that 'liberal' appears in the word 'neoliberal' would suggest commonality or continuity between the two. Indeed, one could think of neoliberalism as a renewed vision of the freedom that lies at the heart of classical liberalism. Individual freedom serves as the basis of social good. Maximize every individual's freedom, and society will flourish.

However, neoliberal freedom, unlike the freedom of classical liberalism, is achieved almost entirely—and almost obsessively—through the market. At one level, the market is viewed as morally neutral since its mechanism is simply about the efficient coordination of countless individual transactions to ensure that the prices of things reflect what needs to be produced to satisfy every individual's desires. Markets, in other words, sort out a whole lot of things according to what's available and what's desired, without making subjective judgements about their moral value. Hence, if this morally neutral machinery for material exchange could be expanded to include all human interactions in society, then it could provide an impartial means of adjudicating among all differences, especially in plural societies, where people hold diverse views, perspectives, values and interests. In this way, an expanded market can coordinate and resolve all kinds of differences and disagreements within a diverse global society, without having to make subjective judgements about what or who is right or wrong.

Neoliberalism goes further than simply promoting the expansion of market neutrality into all spheres of social living, although that is usually how things are explained. It also promotes substantive (and therefore hardly neutral) values arising from the logic of economics. According to this logic, all things are measurable by the common denominator of money. Our actions should therefore be informed by a properly standardized accounting of the monetary costs and benefits of the various options available to us. A multifaceted mode of reasoning that includes philosophical, moral, political and aesthetic dimensions has no place in this universe, flattened to the one-dimensionality of monetary value.

Harvard political philosopher Michael Sandel (2012), by no means a Marxist, has argued that such pervasive market logic and the values that form around it end up debasing other authentic domains of our lives, including the social, moral and aesthetic domains. Moral limits are crossed without any discomfort, to the point where morally repugnant acts are neutralized by their thoughtless conversion to monetary equivalence. Sandel proposes that the market is not amoral and, as its values become ubiquitous, we increasingly lose our moral compass, our collective sense of right, wrong and every nuance in between. From a communitarian vantage point, we lose what it means to share or even care about a common good, on which we can build a collective sense of responsibility for one another.

A basic assumption of classical economic analysis is *homo economicus*, or 'economic man', the individual whose calculative actions within conditions of perfect knowledge are aimed at maximizing personal satisfaction. The neoliberal primacy of the market not only relies upon such a caricature for many of its theories to work, but also normalizes such an idealized individual so that it becomes what people think they should be. If others behaved this way, and you did not, then in the competition of life, you would always stand to lose. Taken to its extreme in neoliberal globalization, the 'economic man' is the hyper-individual who is responsible for no one other than himself and who competes incessantly in an atomized society, where community and the possibility of moral solidarity are severely limited and replaced by self-interest and greed.

Critical scholar Henry Giroux (2019) identified economic Darwinism as one of the pathological features of the neoliberal America of Donald Trump, where fascist potential has been unlocked. Here, society, consisting of self-interested atomized individuals, celebrates the more entrepreneurial among them, those who are most able to conform to market values. Economic Darwinism upholds the idea of personal responsibility for success and failure. It obscures the social, cultural, economic and other institutional factors that may create systematic advantage for the 'successful' and the limited opportunities for those who 'fail'. Economic Darwinism goes even further than that, demonizing the disadvantaged by placing the blame for failure squarely on their lack of effort and ability, often using derogatory and even inflammatory language to suggest the threat they as a 'class' pose to society by being a drain on its resources and vitality. Narcissists thrive in this neoliberal society, celebrating greed, boasting about their predatory accomplishments and using muscular, demeaning and bullying language, sometimes to compensate for their own insecurities.

Whether the critiques come from a Marxist such as Giroux or from a communitarian or civic republican such as Sandel, neoliberal globalization—even as it held promise of reforming bureaucracies, energizing economies and globalizing mindsets—is undesirable for the way that it undermines communities, moral solidarity, responsibility for one another, the public good and the possibility of a more equal society free of domination and exploitation.

The Neoliberal Elite: Technocrats and Corporate Capitalists

For the market to be freed up, expanded and promoted, one might think that neoliberalism requires the state to be diminished: bigger market, smaller government. However, there was not necessarily a rolling back of the state. Governments sometimes became stronger and 're-regulated' the markets in new ways to serve the interests primarily of corporate capital. Technocrats obscured the political function they played in neoliberal globalization by disguising themselves as 'pragmatists'. By claiming to be above the dogmatic rigidity of ideology and the chaotic irrationality of politics, they focused on achieving results in the most technically efficient, effective and impactful ways. They often justified their pro-corporate capitalism policies in terms of a largely discredited theory that the benefits of looking after the rich and powerful would 'trickle down' to everyone, even the least advantaged in society.

Since the 1980s, technocratic governments in countries such as the United Kingdom, the United States, Australia, New Zealand and Singapore have adopted a highly managerial style of government, focused on performance management, bottom lines, customer-orientation and key performance indicators, while anathematizing politics and devaluing social participation in governance. This movement, known in the public administration literature as New Public Management, was revolutionary in the 1980s in the way that it disrupted bureaucratic dysfunction everywhere by reforming public service to be more de-centralized and business-like, treating citizens as customers and public servants as public managers and policy entrepreneurs, incentivized to do more with less (Kapucu, 2006).

The illusion of economic, political and cultural liberalization enabled by a more business-like government that was receding from its dominant central role obscured what was, in fact, a more sophisticated and nuanced control over society, especially the labour force. Labour unions were politically neutered, either by quashing or corporatizing them, leaving workers increasingly exploitable and precarious as they had to compete fiercely for their livelihoods against one another. This was really a new level of authoritarianism, much less overtly brutal but even more insidious in its deep internalization (Scholte, 2005).

This new authoritarianism was also insidious for its corrosive effects on democracy, so profoundly mistrusted by the neoliberal elite consisting mainly of technocrats in government and corporate capitalists. Mark Purcell (2008), a professor of urban politics, argued that more substantive practices of democracy that give people a say in questions of social justice, beyond just periodic voting in elections, has diminished. This has happened because of the neoliberal shift of power from the state to the highly mobile corporate capital. Professor of sociology Colin Crouch (2004) argued that our neoliberal world is a 'post-democratic' one, where a decline of progressive social forces and the rise of global capitalism have both enabled a relatively unconstrained concentration of real power in the hands of the political and business elite. The procedural aspects of democracy such as free, fair and competitive elections—what people seem to pay more attention to—have turned into mere spectacles of public life, masking the absence of substantive democratic discussion where egalitarian and socially progressive goals may be properly pursued.

In these conditions, the state pulls back its welfare and social services expenditure, reducing overall taxation and shifting its burden from corporations and wealthy individuals to ordinary people through regressive tax reforms. These moves are explained in terms of cost-cutting efficiencies favoured by New Public Management and the 'trickle down' idea at the heart of neoliberal globalization. So as these societies become wealthier, they also become less democratic and more unequal. Reagan's America, depicted in several movies discussed in this book, is a good example of social disinvestment leading to rising inequality and poverty and democratic decline.

French economist Thomas Piketty (2014/2013), in his magnum opus *Capital in the Twenty-First Century*, argued that there has been an increasing concentration of wealth at the top, resulting from the rate of return on capital exceeding the rate of economic growth over the long run. Over time, inherited wealth will result in extreme inequality and socio-economic instability. A global wealth tax is Piketty's recommendation. But this is a utopian fantasy in a world lacking global leadership and governance.

As income inequality rises and wealth is increasingly concentrated at the top, an underclass has emerged out of the working class, impoverished and disenfranchised, often also humiliated and ignored. In times of national crisis, when neoliberal policies are at their harshest, the likelihood of social unrest is very high. To keep a disgruntled working class and a growing underclass in check and to deal with a breakdown of popular consensus over the desirability of neoliberal globalization, the neoliberal elite turn to its traditional instruments of repression, such as the military, the police, the courts and the prisons, using fear and brutality to cow the disgruntled into obedience.

In normal times, however, what Italian political theorist Antonio Gramsci (1971) wrote in his *Prison Notebooks* remains as true today as it did in the 1930s. To maintain this exploitative socio-economic arrangement, the neoliberal elite would actively need to propagate the ideology of neoliberal globalization, not only to normalize it as 'common sense' but also to make it appear as the only game in town that one has no choice but play to win. Thus, even more important than economic and political coercion is the ideological work that is done, especially within civil society—including families, schools, trade unions, churches and so on—under the intellectual and moral leadership of the neoliberal elite. Through this work of cultural hegemony, consent is achieved through the alliances and compromises that are made between the neoliberal elite and the various social forces at play.

Marxist professor of geography David Harvey (2005) argued, for example, that the neoliberal project often requires nationalism. The neoliberal elite employs an exclusionary language of nationalism and heightened patriotism to generate emotionally satisfying illusions of external threat and national unity, as well as the strong leadership required for the nation's protection. Singapore, as Harvey also pointed out, is a case in point. In this island-nation, which achieved political independence in 1965, one would today find a neoliberal market comfortably combined with an authoritarian state that periodically exerts highly draconian powers over its citizens, while invoking national solidarity against enemies and threats and speaking a moralistic and sometimes chauvinistic language of Asian—at one time even Confucian—values.

The neoliberal project has also been sustained by a popular belief in meritocracy. Sociologists Jonathan Mijs and Mike Savage (2020) noted that meritocracy is a 'deeply elitist project', opposed to discrimination but not to inequality. They pointed to research showing that at least two-thirds of people from every country in the West believe that individual hard work counts towards success, so much so that as income inequality rises, they become even more convinced of the meritocratic basis of success. Even the most precarious and insecure, this research shows, have deeply internalized the meritocratic logic that it is one's own effort, rather than structural forces, that determines one's fortunes in life. I have argued, in the case of Singapore, that meritocracy—once able to hold together the logics of equality of opportunity, allocative efficiency, competitiveness and reward—has since the 1990s lurched towards a focus on rewards, now understood as elite entitlement (Tan, 2008). Unlike the West, Singapore—a high-trust society—is witnessing growing scepticism, even cynicism, towards meritocracy and the national leaders that it is designed to identify and promote. In Singapore, rising inequality suggests a dysfunctional meritocracy, whereas in the West, it reassures people that the meritocratic system is working as it should.

Neoliberal Welfare

Data from surveys conducted in the last couple of decades show that Americans have had a rather ambiguous view about poverty and welfare (Howard et al., 2017). They believe that policymakers should place a high priority on poverty reduction and that government spending to help the poor is too low. However, Americans are also suspicious about welfare, concerned that it can induce over-dependency on public programmes, which have not generally been, in their view, effective. Many Americans also blame the poor for their own misfortune. This is consistent with the meritocratic notion they favour of individual effort, rather than structural factors, as the key reason for success or failure.

Many also believe that African Americans, in particular, do not really need welfare. Political scientist Sanford Schram (2019) argued that race has become a social marker of the innocent and the guilty, of the deserving and the undeserving. The persistence of racial disparities did not indicate neoliberal failure, but provided justification for neoliberal poverty management, a system of exploiting racial divisions to justify advanced marginality among low-income people from racial minority groups. Schram asserted, the neoliberal relations of poverty are highly disciplinary.

The idea of 'responsibilization', the insistence that individuals take personal responsibility for their well-being, ends up blaming individuals for making bad choices that lead to adverse circumstances, as if they enjoyed the full range of choices to make. Responsibilization pathologizes the poor as individuals who do not want to do better for themselves, who cannot even plan for their own future, as if these were capabilities that they could readily afford.

Schram noted a shift in efforts to understand poverty from studying an individual's background including their personality, psychology and behaviour; to the social-structural factors that keep them in poverty; and more recently to thinking about poverty in relational terms. What is the relationship between the poor and those who have more autonomy over their life chances? What is the relationship between the poor, who are welfare recipients, and the state actors assigned responsibility for managing, monitoring and disciplining them into market compliance? The neoliberal welfare system focuses on enhancing the motivation and ability of welfare recipients to be re-incorporated into the job market. As such, it is an instrument of the market rather than protection against its excesses. An important goal is to run welfare programmes as cheaply as possible and—in the case of private-sector companies appointed to run these programmes—even to make a profit.

The Temporary Assistance to Needy Families (TANF) was established in 1997 as a US federal assistance programme based on the principle of moving people from welfare to work. Labour economist Janice Peterson (2020) observed how a programme like this, which eliminated entitlement to cash assistance and put in place mandatory work requirements, succeeded when the economy was strong. However, over a longer period, and especially in a weakened economy, employment was volatile and much harder to maintain, and low wages with long hours of work made recipients financially paralysed. Peterson cited studies that showed how TANF ended up exacerbating deep poverty rather than reducing it. For instance, the Center on Budget and Policy Priorities (CBPP) reported in 2017 that, for every 100 poor families, only twenty-three received cash assistance from TANF. In 1996, that number was sixty-eight (Floyd, Burnside and Schott, 2018). Poverty researchers Kathryn Edin and H. Luke Shaefer (2015) found a sharp increase in the number of households with children that reported incomes below US$2.00 per person per day. Noting how narratives of successful poverty elimination in the US were grossly exaggerated and diverged from what was observed in real life, Peterson argued that such false narratives were a pretext for reforming welfare further along neoliberal lines, which stigmatized the poor and the programmes that they really needed.

So, what we have in our neoliberally globalized world is hyper-individualistic competitiveness, increasingly precarious working-class lives, the replacement of substantive democracy with the mass-mediated spectacle of electoral politics and the continuous ideological efforts of the technocratic and capitalist elite to garner buy-in from all, especially those who have the most to lose from neoliberal globalization. In these circumstances, the capacity for personal and collective critical thinking and moral judgement has diminished severely. There is moral numbness in the private and public spheres, creating conditions that are ripe for the emergence of authoritarian populism as a grotesque reaction to the unbridled capitalism of neoliberal globalization.

Populism on the Road to Tyranny and Totalitarianism

Populism is very certainly not a new, or even modern, phenomenon. At its most general level, populism is a politicization of 'the people' as an idea that is contrasted against the idea of an elite. This can range from a politics of promoting the interests of the people over those of the elite, to protecting the people from the corruption, exploitation and manipulation of the elite. Often, populism is used as a pejorative term.

Foundational texts in political philosophy such as Plato's (1941) *The Republic* already recognized populism as a central problem of politics and society. You might even say that *The Republic*, in seeking an answer to the question 'What is justice?' is a philosophically elaborate argument against populism. A just man, Plato argued, is wise in being able to know what is best for all parts of his soul. He is courageous in defending and pursuing what he has rationally come to know and value. And he is temperate in subjecting his ambitions and appetites to the rule of reason. The mind should rule over the heart, the stomach and the sexual organs, so to speak. Correspondingly, a just city cultivates and educates a class of philosophers, people who can think and arrive at the knowledge of the true essence of things, especially the knowledge of what 'goodness' itself means. A just city nurtures a class of warriors who must act courageously in the interest of the city's preservation and ambitions. And all classes in this just city—the philosophers, the warriors and ordinary people—agree that it is the philosophers who should be their leaders, even though (or precisely because) philosophers in their thirst for knowledge tend to shun the world in favour of a quiet life of contemplation.

Plato then went on to illustrate how this 'aristocratic' ideal of a just city could degenerate in the real world. In times of war, military generals will rise in prestige and start to dominate the ruling class, forming what he called a 'timocracy'. Then, as generals become rich and fixated upon their property, military honour is replaced by wealth as a ruling virtue, and timocracy breaks down into an 'oligarchy'. The accumulation of wealth by the powerful few worsens material inequality in the city and provokes the eventual revolt of an underclass. As hierarchies break down and people do as they please, the city becomes what Plato called a 'democracy'.

According to our modern understanding, democracy can mean many different things. But Plato was highly sceptical of this kind of democracy, viewing it as a society that, in the name of equality, gives free rein to everyone's desires and appetites. People quickly become disengaged from their society and its norms, as they erode over time. In a democracy that is more licentious than free, popular impulses are raw, undisciplined and lacking in structure, leadership and purpose. Easily manipulated, democratic society very readily descends into mob rule. In these circumstances, a demagogue—a charismatic political leader, for example—can easily exploit mass aimlessness, fears and insecurities to seize power and become a tyrant. Tyrants are ruled not by wisdom but by base desires. They crush their opponents and all that is wise and good. They consolidate and magnify their power through constant warfare. Plato's account presented populism as a significant moment on the path to tyranny, where the rule of wisdom is gradually replaced by ambition, greed, envy, disorder, purposelessness and terror.

A political theorist of the 20th century who drew heavily on the thought of ancient Greek philosophers such as Plato was Hannah Arendt. A Jewish intellectual, she fled Nazi Germany in 1933 and eventually emigrated to the US in 1941, where she became a celebrated and controversial university-based political thinker. Arendt (1951) was interested in making sense of the rise of totalitarianism in Western civilization, which—for all its attention to enlightenment, emancipation, freedom and equality—made possible such human atrocities as the Nazi holocaust and the Stalinist gulags. Arendt's (1958) key to this puzzle was an idealized model of direct democracy associated with ancient Greek cities. Citizens directly and actively participating in public life—rather than the Platonic aberration of people going about their private lives doing whatever they pleased—was a vital aspect of ancient democracy and, in fact, the very basis of what made them human. Man, as the Greek philosopher Aristotle (1998) famously taught, is by nature a political animal.

Modern liberal democracies, on the other hand, 'liberate' citizens from their daily responsibility to deliberate on matters of public importance. Modern citizens, for the most part, merely cast their votes in periodic elections designed to appoint representatives who will act on their behalf in the public realm. Even then, voter turn-out is typically low. Citizens retreat into the private realm where they can focus on work, enjoy whatever their salaries buy them and reflect on their individual lives. They labour to satisfy their biological needs and work to produce material and cultural objects that make up our world. But politics as the highest form of human activity—what Arendt called 'action'—is quite simply absent for most of the modern citizenry. The political realm itself has been degraded into what is in effect a bureaucratically administered space that attends to individuals' basic biological needs, above all else. The modern welfare state, especially when transformed under New Public Management reforms, is an example of how the administration of individual well-being—and thus their sedation—has taken over the great words and deeds of political debate in the public sphere. Disinterested, rather than self-interested, debate of this kind is what makes us human and gives us our identities.

American sociologist Richard Sennett (1977), whose thinking Arendt had greatly influenced, described a very similar idea in his eclectic and idiosyncratic analysis of how secularism and industrial capitalism, among other things, have brought about the fall of what he called the 'public man'. Citizens today focus too much on their private lives. Whatever is left of the public sphere, furthermore, is degraded by a general interest in intimate matters that properly belong to our private lives. The elevated concerns and deliberations of the public sphere—which make us large-minded, political and therefore human, as Aristotle and those influenced by him have argued—now have been replaced by a mere semblance of public discussion and debate. Whether it is the sensationalist and combative news shows we watch regularly on television, or the scandals of politicians and celebrities that dominate the headlines, or the gladiatorial excitement of flame wars on social media, the public sphere today—or what's left of it—has disintegrated into a form of entertainment. The agora of ancient times has today become much more like a television talk show: the more it lacks civility and appeals to our voyeuristic and exhibitionistic pleasures, the more we are lured into it out of the comforts of our private lives.

What would a properly functioning public sphere look like? Arendt, who was deeply wary of technocratic assertions about objective truth and the dangers of politics in modern times, believed that the public sphere presented a necessary opportunity for opinions to be validated and new ideas birthed through face-to-face discussion and debate. This was politics. And politics was valuable. And only in the public sphere could valuable politics of this kind thrive. The plurality of ideas, perspectives and interests to be found there can exercise and build up the individual and collective capacities for active thought, judgement and creativity. The physical spaces of the public sphere allow citizens to present themselves openly to one another, exchanging great ideas and deeds that could be held in the collective memory. On this basis, reciprocal relations and a sense of solidarity can be fostered to build up civility. As citizens in this political realm, we would learn collectively how to forgive so that we can be freed from the legacies that divide us. And we would learn how to make and keep promises so that trust and reciprocity can be built as we try to anchor the uncertainty of our collective future.

The general absence of this in the modern world gives rise to mass society. Citizens have become individuals who are disconnected, lonely and disengaged. Self-interest, economics and administration have replaced public deliberation and destroyed the plurality of ideas. What we are left with is a collection of atomized and dehumanized individuals without a sense of identity, memory, values and imagination.

Arendt (1963) is perhaps most famous for introducing the phrase 'the banality of evil', which is the subtitle of her book based on what she observed of the high-profile trial in Jerusalem of Adolf Eichmann. Eichmann had been a relatively senior Nazi official responsible for organizing the logistics of transporting Jews to extermination camps in Eastern Europe. What people expected to see being held to account behind a glass cage in court was a monstrously evil persona, full of 'satanic greatness'. Instead, what they beheld was a most unremarkable technocrat, who spoke remorselessly in clichés that reflected mediocrity, and intellectual and moral shallowness. Moved by this observation, Arendt theorized evil not as some fearsome demonic force, but as the result of very ordinary people simply wanting to fit in, join the right group, do the job they've been tasked to do, follow orders, avoid responsibility and do whatever is required to advance their own careers. Such people surrender their responsibility to think critically and exercise judgement in the course of their work. They are thus complicit in some of the most unspeakable acts in modern human history.

They are a kind of zombie—although Arendt never used this metaphor—moving mindlessly in throngs and seeking human flesh to consume and infect, dead on the inside and terrifyingly apocalyptic.

In his account of tyranny and its evils, Plato mistrusted the democratic popularization of politics into a sort of individualistic liberality where anything goes, insisting that a just city must ensure that only the philosophically reasonable should formally take charge and define for the people the good life that they should lead. But in the real world, aristocratic de-politicization of this kind is necessarily fragile and, by his own admission, cannot last. Arendt, on the contrary, argued for the re-politicization of the modern world. By reinvigorating the public realm, citizens can become equal, free and active when they debate among themselves, drawing upon a plurality of ideas and points of view. In the process, they also develop their identities, values and capacities for critical thinking and judgement. It takes all of this to stand in defiance against the banality of evil that we see everywhere in our technocratic world today, the same banality that countenances—in fact, exacerbates—unconscionable levels of extreme poverty and inequality in a world of plenty.

Authoritarian Populism

Plato, Arendt, Sennett, Sandel and several others were responding in very different ways and for very different reasons to what they observed as the degeneration of the public realm. For Plato, it was the shift from a system of government by an intellectual and moral elite to one taken over by leaders of baser instincts, resulting eventually in a licentious society of aimless individuals ripe for political manipulation by an emerging tyrant.

For Arendt, the modern world has seen an eclipse of the public realm, where collective deliberation among citizens who present and debate different ideas and points of view on matters of the highest importance is what makes them all truly human. As modern citizens retreat into their private affairs and ignore their political responsibilities, the public realm is left vacuous and becomes the site of often thoughtlessly technocratic administration of the most basic biological needs. Sennett described this as the 'tyranny of intimacy' and the fall of public man. For Arendt, without the public realm, we stop being able to think critically and make careful judgements, passively and thoughtlessly adopting the routines, norms and expectations of a highly administered and self-interested life. Collectively, this can amount to the kind of evil that may be banal in its origins, but whose consequences can amount to some of the most serious crimes against humanity in the 20th century.

Sandel also valued the public realm of collective reason and the Socratic role in it of a public philosopher such as himself. The public philosopher's role is a pedagogical one, constantly questioning our assumptions and leading us in thinking together about the important and hard questions that should concern us all. Sandel was critical of the way that such questions have been approached, formulated and answered almost entirely these days by an appeal to the logic and values of the market. There are some things, he insisted, that money simply cannot buy. And our collective inability to exercise moral reasoning over difficult political and policy questions leaves us vulnerable to the excesses of capitalism and populism, which divide and polarize in ways that further erode any possibility of civic life.

These arguments are relevant once again in the 21st century, perhaps even more so. The civic impoverishment of the public sphere and its domination by the logic and values of the market have intersected with the trajectory of neoliberal globalization discussed earlier.

The 21st century has witnessed the rise of a particularly authoritarian form of populism around the world. Populist parties and social movements have garnered widespread support. They are led by authoritarian leaders, often the charismatic demagogues that Plato warned against more than two millennia ago. Populist leaders claim to speak for 'the people' and to protect their interests from the neoliberal and globalist establishment elite, whom they portray as corrupt and exploitative. By doing so, populist leaders can mobilize mass support. 'The people' is, of course, for the most part an ideological and highly emotive construct, summoned at politically critical moments to connote authenticity, purity, innocence, hard work, community, common values, authority, vulnerability and the power to revolt against. 'The people', is therefore, a powerful ideological resource for populist leaders who seek power by channelling an exaggerated in-group sense of identity against 'outsiders' such as migrants, ethnic minorities and potentially any minoritized people who, as a class, can be portrayed as a threat to mainstream ways of life. Thus, populist leaders can provoke and galvanize rage against social diversity, multiculturalism and the plurality of ideas and values that this usually brings (which Arendt, of course, considered crucial for the public realm).

A report by the Tony Blair Institute for Global Change made a few important observations about populism from a global perspective (Kyle and Gultchin, 2018). Between 1990 and 2018, there were forty-six populist leaders or political parties holding executive office across thirty-three countries. During this period, the populists who were in power around the world increased from four to twenty. Populism spread in regions such as Western Europe and Asia, alongside the more traditionally prone Latin America and Eastern and Central Europe. Populists have also been gaining power, not only in emerging democracies where they have traditionally thrived but also in more established democracies such as the US, Italy and India. From being primarily anti-establishment in character, populism has shifted to being primarily nativist. 'Cultural populists', as they are called in the report, regard themselves as the 'true people' and they view outsiders such as immigrants, minority groups and cosmopolitan elites with great suspicion, even hostility.

In their study of Trump's America, 'Brexit' in the UK and the rising support for populist parties in Europe, US-based political scientists Pippa Norris and Ronald Inglehart (2019) argued that populism, as manifested in these cases, has more to do with culture than economics. The material gains from decades of globalization have not been evenly distributed. Neoliberal elites and their corporate partners have benefitted a great deal more than ordinary people, many of whom have been severely disadvantaged in economic terms and have had to bear the brunt of the austerity measures implemented in times of economic crises. These are, no doubt, grounds for explaining populism as resulting from material inequality, poverty and the blame that people can be persuaded to place on the neoliberal establishment elite as the cause of their troubles.

However, in their analysis of the data, Norris and Inglehart argued that the rise of populism has had more to do with people's heightened discomfort with social and cultural change and the increasing presence of immigrants in their midst, which signal a formal acceptance of multiculturalism and cosmopolitanism. The 'counterculture' in the 1960s, for instance, has accelerated long-term transformation in American society, leading to greater tolerance of diversity and inclusion, and the institutionalization of this tolerance. However, as these changes threaten the perspectives, values and prospects of those who were once privileged and dominant, conditions become ripe for a 'cultural backlash' and the manipulative manoeuvres of charismatic leaders eager to galvanize a 'majoritarian' sense of victimhood in support of their power.

A year before Norris and Inglehart published these observations, UK-based political scientists Roger Eatwell and Matthew Goodwin (2018) published their book on what they termed 'national populism', which they described as a 'revolt against liberal democracy'. They argued that economics and socio-economic status were much less important for understanding the primary causes of national populism, compared to the decreasing levels of trust in political institutions and the establishment, the breakdown of community and identity due to globalization, the relative deprivation experienced in a society made more unequal by neoliberal economics, and the weakened identification with political parties and what they stand for.

Before Eatwell, Goodwin, Norris and Inglehart made their arguments that cultural factors more than economic ones provide a stronger explanation of contemporary authoritarian populism, Harvard professor Dani Rodrik (2017) had made a convincing case for taking economic impact seriously. He described much of what we understand to be neoliberal globalization as 'hyper-globalization', against which right-wing populism was, in his view, a political counter-reaction. There are, of course, many gains to be had from globalization, especially from trade and commerce, as Pinker demonstrated in his account of human progress. But there also need to be significant redistributive efforts on the part of national governments so that those who find themselves worse off from globalization, and there are many who do, will not have to suffer and can, in fact, benefit from it. Instead, neoliberalism has diminished comprehensive state welfare systems that tax the rich and subsidize the poor, leading in effect to social disinvestment and the dismantling of social safety nets—the opposite of what is required to help globalization's victims. So, globalization makes possible great national wealth, but can also bring economic disruption and dislocation, instigating structural change that can polarize the labour market and diminish the availability of good middle-class jobs. Longer-term technological trends, including automation, artificial intelligence and the internet of things, have exacerbated these problems. As have neoliberal policies of deregulation and the decline of labour unions.

These economic dislocations have also aggravated the pre-existing cultural divides that culturalist explanations of populism focus on. Amid economic hardship, people are more likely to be mistrustful and resentful of outsiders, including immigrants and other minorities. They become increasingly receptive to politicized explanations of their misery that point the finger of blame precisely at these outsiders. Cultural resentment is linked to underlying economic dislocations.

Populist parties and demagogues seize the opportunity to harness the social undercurrents of xenophobia, racism, sexism and homophobia, among others. As Greve (2020b) explained, welfare chauvinism, a nativist view that welfare benefits and services should only be available to national citizens, fuels the policy agenda of right-wing populist parties that advocate for an overall reduction in taxation and size of the welfare state. Populist parties and leaders who may themselves benefit from neoliberal globalization are keen to distract the people from the economic causes of their hardship. This is achieved often through the redirection of their anger and hostility away from neoliberal economic policies and towards scapegoats, the 'folk devils' of moral panic.

Folk Devils, Moral Panic and the Policing of Neoliberal Crisis

When public dissatisfaction with the debilitating effects of neoliberal globalization lacks theoretical and ideological sophistication, it accumulates, festers and is exposed to the vulnerability of manipulation by ideologues and demagogues. Typically, demagogues appeal to the unhappiness, hardship and sense of righteousness of the aggrieved masses. By using inflammatory language, charismatic demagogues can galvanize and channel these angry energies not towards the heart of neoliberal globalization, from which they, in fact, profit, but towards at least two visible targets. First is the establishment, made up of elites and their institutions that are described as out-of-touch, disdainful, corrupted, corrupting and exploitative. Second are the minoritized people, including foreigners, who are portrayed as disloyal, immoral and dangerous 'others' within the nation, always a threat to national order and its way of life. This is essentially authoritarian populism, a perversion of democracy, which it often mimics grotesquely. This is 'mob-ocracy' that vilifies and victimizes minority groups, experts and institutional figures of authority, under the manipulative spell of charismatic demagogues.

Authoritarian populist attacks on the neoliberal establishment elite and minoritized communities often take the form of moral panic, of which sociologist Stanley Cohen, in his pioneering work on deviance and youth subcultures in the early 1970s, has provided the most useful definition.

> Societies appear to be subject, every now and then, to periods of moral panic. A condition, episode, person or group of persons emerges to become defined as a threat to societal values and interest; its nature is presented in a stylized and stereotypical fashion by the mass media; the moral barricades are manned by editors, bishops, politicians and other right-thinking people; socially accredited experts pronounce their diagnosis and solutions; ways of coping are evolved or (more often) resorted to; the condition then disappears, submerges or deteriorates and becomes more visible. Sometimes the object of the panic is quite novel and at other times is something which has been in existence long enough, but suddenly appears in the limelight. Sometimes the panic passes over and is forgotten, except in folklore and collective memory; at other times it has more serious and long-lasting repercussions and might produce such changes as those in legal and social policy or even in the way society conceives itself. (Cohen, 1972)

Sociologists Erich Goode and Nachman Ben-Yahuda (1994) updated this definition in the 1990s, presenting moral panic as a model involving a sequence of five elements or stages, each a criterion for identifying whether a moral panic has occurred.

1. At the first stage, there is heightened public attention and concern formed around a person or group, whose behaviour is viewed as a threat to mainstream society's values and interests (such as immigrants, ethnic minority groups, LGBTQIA+, single mothers and the 'strawberry generation').
2. At the second stage, there is increased hostility towards these deviant groups, whose members are stylized as 'folk devils'. The amplification of their deviance and the cultivation of fear are often achieved through the production and circulation of negative stereotypes in the mass media, including movies.
3. At the third stage, politicians, religious leaders, news producers, experts, opinion leaders and civil society activists work to secure and reinforce consensus in mainstream society on the reality, extent and cause of the threat. Mainly through mass

media platforms, this consensus forms a moral barricade that starkly divides 'us' and 'them'.

4. At the fourth stage, public reaction grows in ways that are disproportionate to the reality that it refers to.
5. And at the fifth stage, the intense concern and hostility towards folk devils, having erupted so suddenly and fiercely, recede just as abruptly. Moral panics are volatile, but they can have significant and long-lasting repercussions on culture and the institutions of society and politics.

When considering the significance of moral panic within the dynamic tension between neoliberal globalization and authoritarian populism in the 21st century, it becomes clear that moral panic is part of a larger policing mechanism that helps to maintain the hegemony of neoliberal globalization, threatened in times of crisis. Stuart Hall and his colleagues (1978), pioneering cultural studies scholars in the UK, argued in the late 1970s that consensus is complex, dynamic and contested in modern capitalist society, even with the active complicity of the political and administrative elite, police, courts, legislature and mass media. Folk devils, the manufactured spectacle of threat to mainstream society, help to secure hegemony by creating the fear-driven conditions within which it is easier to obtain broader consent and support for a politics of law and order and a culture of surveillance to 'police the crisis'. Thus, elite interests can be protected and the stability of the capitalist system restored, without radical change to the laws and regulations that sustain the exploitative nature of modern capitalism.

Moviemakers as Public Intellectuals in the Global Culture Industry

In a world that is increasingly driven, structured and controlled by the logic and desires of global markets, where partnerships between technocratic and corporate elites concentrate power and wealth in an ever-decreasing proportion of the world's populations and where the increasingly left-behind masses are readily manipulated by populist leaders who are able to channel their frustrations towards both the establishment as well as minoritized scapegoats, how can a critical consciousness be nurtured as a precondition for orienting the world towards more progressive directions? This book will explore the idea that 21st-century movies have the power to generate critical consciousness about poverty, inequality and environmental degradation.

In the very first episode of the Brazilian original Netflix series *3%* (2016), for instance, a group of hopeful young people from the poorer sections of an unspecified future country gather for 'The Process', a rite of passage through which impoverished 'Inland' youth compete to be the top 3 per cent who get to advance into an affluent society called 'Offshore'. The charismatic head of 'The Process' launches it with these words:

> 3%. Only 3% of you candidates will become the select group of heroes heading to the Offshore, where the Founding Couple created the perfect world, where there is no injustice. Everyone gets an equal chance and the place they deserve. Offshore or Inland, or as some call it, 'their side' or 'our side'. This Process ensures that only the best among you will enjoy life in the Offshore. As I'm sure you're aware, envy and resentment have led to the rise of opposition groups who, in the name of a false and hypocritical equality and by disseminating populist ideas, aim to destroy everything we've achieved. But they have always failed and will continue to fail . . . Remember, you each create your own merit and no matter what happens, you deserve this. This is a good time to express your gratitude. Repeat after me: We are grateful for the chance . . . for a better way of life . . . and so we thank you.

Almost immediately, the grateful candidates—already brainwashed to treat this as the opportunity of a lifetime—are subjected to intense interviews, designed to test not only intelligence, originality, honesty, but also political conformity. They are then put through a practical puzzle-solving challenge, which tests for technical ability, speed, ingenuity and cunning. The challenge seems to focus on results rather than process. The evaluators turn a blind eye to whether the candidates were helpful to one another or cheated to get the desired result. The audience is immediately given a sense of what this elite Offshore society values and looks for in its 'best'.

The series, which ran for four seasons on Netflix, was beautifully directed by *City of God* (2002) cinematographer César Charlone and his team. The characters were well-developed and the plot intriguing. The first episode alone was able to bring the audience into a brand-new world whose rules were uncannily like our own. And against the strangeness of this reel world, the meritocracy that we celebrate or criticize in our real world appears starkly open to philosophical questions about merit, arbitrariness, fairness, social mobility, individual responsibility and so on. The clarity gained from seeing something so familiar in a setting so unfamiliar can help us rethink the complex circumstances of our own society, to better understand where meritocracy fails in practice or lacks legitimacy in theory and even to perceive the kernels of a better world that we can strive for.

Another similar example is *The Hunger Games*, director Gary Ross's 2012 box office success and the first in a franchise of four movies. A fictional nation called Panem, which is divided into twelve numbered districts governed tyrannically from the Capitol, uncannily evokes the tension at the heart of US federalism as we know it. The movie's visual language—from the imperial scale, structures and symbols of the Capitol to the rural poverty of coal-mining towns in the districts—also evokes the varied landscapes of the US and the vast asymmetries of power they represent. Every year in Panem, each district is required to send a teenage boy and girl—picked by lottery—as tributes to the Capitol, where they all fight to the death, until only one survivor is left triumphant. Originally instituted as brutal punishment for a failed uprising against the authority of the Capitol, the Hunger Games—as it is now called—has become a prestigious national ritual of unity, performed in an annual gladiatorial spectacle. Spectacle, of course, distracts from injustice and is therefore extremely useful to sustain the ideology of the ruling class, elevating terror and obedience to the sublimity of achievement. The mass media plays a key role in the production of spectacle, manufacturing celebrity and entertainment through the manipulation of image and narrative to satisfy the voyeuristic and sadistic fantasies of a morally and aesthetically numb mass audience.

The Hunger Games are essentially a mechanism for divide-and-rule politics. Democratic antagonism towards the tyranny of the Capitol is deflected so that districts become antagonistic towards one another instead. Individual tributes become antagonistic towards one another too, in a grotesque performance of the survival of the fittest. In this meritocratic battle, only one can win. Victory is glorious, but defeat is death. And the victorious, grateful to and flattered by the system, are rendered susceptible to co-optation by and into the same elite circle that had abused them.

The audience is compelled to confront their own reflections in movies like this. In real life, do our elite seem always too ready to sacrifice the young and the poor for their self-interests? Do the elite glorify barbarism in a hypocritical language of honour, pride, patriotism and the greater good? How easily do we get absorbed in the public adulation and material reward of a brutal game, playing not only to win but also to secure its legitimacy so that the glory of our victory might be ever magnified? How easily do we repress our fear, ambition, greed, lust and aggressiveness beneath a celebrated image of dignity, grace and heroism?

Another brutal mechanism for elite control over the masses is the intriguing premise of a franchise of five movies and two seasons of a television series, beginning with the movie *The Purge*, directed by James DeMonaco and released in 2013. The franchise features a near-future America that celebrates an annual holiday when, for a twelve-hour period overnight, it is legal to commit all crimes, including murder. Having its origins as a social experiment to reduce crime and poverty, the Purge became an annual ritual of national catharsis, believed to make the remaining 364 days of the year more peaceful and freer of crime. Not all believe in the virtues of the Purge, giving rise to ideological and political division, not unlike the left–right divide that has paralysed public life in the US today. For instance, no amount of gun violence, including the numerous episodes of school shootings, seems to be able to break the impasse between opposing pressures for gun control and gun rights today. And the political outcome on gun violence, regardless of whether the Republican Party or the Democratic Party is in ascendency, has in large part been strongly influenced by the National Rifle Association, a powerful lobby group.

The Forever Purge (2021), the fifth movie in the franchise and directed by Everardo Gout, takes us to a future America that has just reinstated the Purge, following an eight-year ban by a more liberal government. During the ban, anti-elite, racist and anti-immigrant sentiments were building up, leading to the re-election of the fascistic New Founding Fathers of America. On the night of the new Purge, a television news anchor announces, 'The national holiday celebrating our American freedom is finally back.' But when the twelve-hour Purge is lifted this time, a new authoritarian populist movement continues the deadly violence in a 'Forever After Purge' to purify the country, primarily of immigrants. In this 'United States of Hate', political manipulation has activated and unleashed the fury and rage of the 'left-behind' masses, that—as if infected by a virus—throng the streets violently and out of control to spread death, just as zombies do. *The Purge* movies are like zombie movies in many illuminating ways.

The Forever Purge did not fail at the box office, but it did receive numerous negative critical reviews. Critic Anya Stanley (2021), for instance, described it as

> . . . a story that a battered nation has heard a lot—a sermon of immigration and class warfare that's too heavy-handed to say anything its prospective audience hasn't been told on countless social media feeds over the last few years.

Insofar as *The Forever Purge* closely mirrors Trump's America, down to the odious populist rhetoric that was being repeated and commented on almost every day in the mainstream and social media, the movie does not add much critical insight other than to emphasize the horror and terror of elite manipulation in authoritarian-populist America.

Neill Blomkamp's *Elysium* (2013), a less impressive follow-up to his highly successful feature debut *District 9* (2009), points to an even more distant future in which Earth has become over-populated, diseased, polluted and crime ridden. The wealthy and powerful have escaped to an orbiting space station named Elysium, where they reproduce their affluent ways of living, own healthcare machines that repair their bodies for health and longevity, and defend its borders fiercely against the intrusion of the left-behind slum-dwelling poor on Earth. In Greek mythology, Elysium was the blessed home of the righteous and heroic who had been immortalized by the gods. In the movie, Elysians are wealthy capitalist shareholders of exploitative businesses on Earth, where workers are mistreated as disposable factors of production drawn cheaply from an army of surplus labour. In Elysium, there is corruption at the highest levels. Against the orders of Elysium's president, the ultra-right-wing secretary of defence engages mercenaries on the ground to brutalize immigrants from Earth whom she and her followers regard as criminal and dangerous. She successfully bribes a sadistic CEO to reboot Elysium's operating system that his company had manufactured, so that she can replace the relatively more liberal president in a political coup. This form of authoritarian populism focuses on how a powerful neoliberal elite—formed around a corrupt partnership among technocrats, corporate interests and criminal elements—can gain political ascendency by manipulating the middle class through a nativist agenda.

All four works, and the worlds they have invented, have something important to tell us about meritocracy and its relationship to poverty, inequality and ecological degradation. In *3%*, people revere the meritocratic system, for all its defects, as a legitimate one-time opportunity for everyone to move up in society. In *The Hunger Games*, the poor are forced into a fatal meritocratic competition with one another at the prime of their lives, an insidious means of controlling oppositional energies and inventing honourable traditions to obfuscate the vulgar brutality of elitism. In *The Forever Purge*, the poor are also violently pitted against one another, one ceremonial day each year, to reduce their number and vitality. The rich can afford security. And when populist leaders encourage an emotionally charged rhetoric of racism and nativism, the ritual goes out of control. In *Elysium*, there is not even a pretext of meritocracy and social mobility, as the wealthy have insulated themselves in an orbiting space station away from the impoverished inhabitants of an apocalyptic Earth, which they had played a part in destroying. The only way to move from poverty to a good life in Elysium, where all diseases and injuries are curable, is to employ life-risking illegal methods of emigrating from Earth.

All four movies are also examples of what digital culture scholars Tanner Mirrlees and Isabel Pedersen (2016) have described as 'critical dystopias'. *Elysium* could be classified under this science fiction sub-genre because it speculates about the future in a different non-existent world, whose fictional content is derived from real material conditions and the social conflicts they give rise to in our time. Mirrlees and Pedersen argued that dystopian science fiction tends to contradict the neoliberal ideology of universal human progress and the role that the minimal state, free markets and new technology play in its achievement. Dystopian science fiction can show vividly how the persistence of neoliberal globalization can lead to grossly undesirable futures. Critical dystopian movies critique the existing world by telling stories about severely dysfunctional future worlds, magnifying the dangerous defects of capitalism, identifying oppositional possibilities for new political activism and offering hope for change that can lead to a better world. This is true of *3%*, *The Hunger Games* and *The Forever Purge* as well.

While movies can shed critical light on our understanding of social, spatial and climate injustice, we need to remain conscious and critical of how they are also produced within a culture industry, neoliberally upgraded in many global cities to a 'creative economy' that is increasingly global in scope. For example, as Mirrlees and Pedersen noted:

> To appeal to as many viewers as possible, and collect optimal box office receipts across borders, global Hollywood designs de-nationalized science fiction films that often address planetary hopes and fears of about (sic) the world system.

In criticizing facets of neoliberal globalization and authoritarian populism, movies may—perhaps inadvertently—also be reinforcing other forms, modes and practices of exploitation, domination, subjugation and injustice. After all, movies are often themselves the products of conditions that they seek to criticize. For example, by indiscriminately embracing globalization, movies can devalue authentic local cultures, even wiping them out in favour of superficial and condescending world-class imagery and trends. As local culture and art forms become more crudely commodified by a culture industry eager to mass-produce and soothe through entertainment, people become more intellectually, morally, politically and aesthetically numb and then dumb, easily accepting conformity and conventional wisdom.

Even as early as the 1940s, neo-Marxist critical theorists Theodor W. Adorno and Max Horkheimer (2002/1944) observed how popular culture was really an industrialization of culture, to mass produce standardized cultural goods, whose purpose was not only profitmaking but also the manipulation of consumers into passivity, conformity, docility and contentedness. Their real interests as an exploited class of workers were distorted by mass entertainment and advertising, which generated a false need for the products of capitalism. In the 21st century, the situation may have worsened. Critical inquiry is dampened in what Giroux (2014) described as a 'neoliberal culture of idiocy and illiteracy'. In such conditions, audiences can be overcome by a sense of inefficacy and learnt helplessness.

Movies, in these circumstances, may themselves turn out to be symptoms of moral panic, amplifying public concern and hostility towards the establishment elite as well as minoritized groups. Why, one might ask, does *Elysium* present the rogue politician as a French-speaking short-haired woman, the brutal mercenary as having a South African accent, the meek and ineffectual president as having an Indian name, and the hero and his community as speaking either American English or Spanish? By riding on the latent energies of moral panic, using the stereotypes and folk devils that are central to it, moviemakers may more easily achieve commercial success and perhaps even critical acclaim. How can movies, moviemaking and moviemakers transcend the conditions they purport to criticize if these are often the very same conditions that bring them success?

In the chapters that follow, we will explore the potential of movies to save our world from poverty, inequality and ecological degradation, three particularly worrying conditions in the 21st century that are constantly being shaped by a dynamic tension between neoliberal globalization and authoritarian populism.

The movies selected for analysis are produced in the 21st century. Most of them are popular movies, sufficiently successful in commercial or artistic terms for a big enough international audience to have watched them in cinemas and festivals, or on television and streaming devices. Intentionally or unintentionally, many of these movies enlighten us in some way or other, making visible and clear our undemocratic conditions of social injustice. A few of them, mainly documentaries, even make suggestions for what we can do to be emancipated from these seemingly debilitating conditions.

We will explore how movies can form an important part of our cultural infrastructure to enrich the public realm with a plurality of ideas and perspectives that help us become more effective citizens and thus resist the modern tendencies towards thoughtlessness, tyranny and totalitarianism.

We will explore how moviemakers can be public intellectuals, providing ideological, moral and political leadership to disrupt and fracture the hegemony of neoliberal globalization and all its debasements. Through their work, moviemakers can help shape the thinking and values of the public, predisposing them to the kind of progressive and radical changes that are necessary to save our world.

Part One

Documentaries

Chapter Two

The Populism of Michael Moore, Working-Class Hero

Not surprisingly, neoliberal globalization and its more pathological facets have attracted the attention of numerous documentary-makers who are especially critical of the corrupting and destructive impact of profit and greed on the world we live in. What audiences get out of watching these documentaries is a reasonably coherent popular theory of our dysfunctional world. Many of these documentaries are at least implicitly utopian in the way they project a desirable vision of a progressive future and what it would take to achieve it. Thus, watching them together with critical dystopian movies, such as the ones discussed in the previous chapter, can have an 'inter-textual' effect of mutually drawing out the potential meanings and implications of one through the logic of the other. In attempting to conscientize their audiences, project a desirable vision of a progressive future and spell out practical steps that everyone can take to move in the direction of the change that we need, some of these documentaries may depart from or even abandon the conventional view that documentaries must seek to be objective, unbiased, non-partisan and completely factual. A call to action, based on a strongly argued thesis and artistic devices aimed at generating active discussion, is what many of these documentaries really are.

Can these documentaries collectively transform popular consciousness in ways that challenge the neoliberal hegemony, preparing the ideological and political ground for reform and more progressive revolutionary change? Or do they, in fact, summon the more regressive forces of political society, inadvertently strengthening the currents of authoritarian populism that have already been gathering momentum?

Documentaries to Change the World

The documentary as a movie genre began with public education as its primary purpose. It was a kind of propaganda. The moviemaker who coined the term 'documentary', John Grierson (1966), described this propaganda as the 'creative treatment of actuality'. The movie medium itself was simply the 'most convenient and most exciting available' at the time to create an immediate sense of urgency leading to desired action.

No longer a marginal genre, documentaries have risen in popularity and importance in the 21st century, not least because of the expanded possibilities of digital media. Documentaries have been enjoying increasing viewership, with an expanding number of specialist channels becoming more widely available. Much more commercially viable these days, some documentaries are even managing to make impressive box office profit. Several of them, such as *Bowling for Columbine* (2002) discussed in this chapter, *Super Size Me* (2004) discussed in the next chapter and *An Inconvenient Truth* (2006) discussed in the chapter after that, have received critical acclaim. And there are many festivals around the world dedicated to this genre or some aspect of the multi-faceted professional and academic interests that have evolved around it.

The documentary form itself has diversified in practice, extending beyond orthodox ideas about objectivity and verisimilitude into more subjective, innovative and participatory approaches that take a less narrow view about 'truth'. American film theorist Bill Nichols (2001) usefully identified six modes in documentary filmmaking.

1. The first, what he called the 'poetic' mode, is—like modernist art—more concerned about creating mood, tone and affect in fragmented and non-linear compositions than in establishing truths through evidence and rhetoric.
2. The 'expository' mode aims to advance a strong perspective or set of arguments on a subject, through the careful assembly

of footage, including stock and archival footage. Through commentary delivered via titles and voiceovers, expository documentaries address the audience directly and from a position of authority. They make use of persuasive rhetorical devices to anchor audience interpretation to the documentary-makers' intention while, for the most part, projecting authority and objectivity.

3. The 'observational' mode aims to reveal a kind of anthropological truth by unobtrusively filming the subject's real life in all its uninterrupted spontaneity. And in all of this, the documentary-makers are deliberately hidden from view.
4. The 'participatory' mode, in contrast, foregrounds the documentary-makers, their interaction with the subject, their experience of the situation and even how they themselves may have evolved while making the film.
5. The 'reflexive' mode foregrounds the documentary-makers' role in the process of moviemaking, revealing the artifice that is involved in such a creative process and outrightly raising questions of representation. In so doing, reflexive documentaries de-familiarize what audiences have taken for granted in their everyday lives, including the very form of the documentary.
6. The 'performative' mode emphasizes the subjective and affective aspects of movies, by addressing audiences emotionally and expressively. By being vividly responsive, the performative documentary-makers animate their audiences' responsiveness too. Such documentaries often give an active voice to those who are under-represented or misrepresented. Documentary-makers do not speak for minorities and those who are marginalized. Instead, they are given their own voice to speak about themselves and their experiences.

While these documentary modes may be thought of as individual sub-genres, it is more likely that a documentary today will comprise a combination of these modes, with one more dominant than the others. Quite aside from lowering the cost of production significantly, which is by itself a game-changer, digital media technology has also blurred the lines between movies and other artistic genres and disciplines, between reality and representation and between the filmers and the filmed. This blurring has led productively to more experimental, participative and democratized practices of documentary production, empowering voices that are usually silent or silenced. With the power to speak for themselves and through novel ways, the marginalized may reclaim their agency. Scholar-activist Thomas Waugh (2011), who wrote a 1984 article titled 'Why documentary filmmakers keep trying to change the world, or why people changing the world keep making documentaries', has been an influential advocate of documentary production whose commitment to ongoing political struggles extends to working with the people engaged in those struggles and, in fact, giving them the power to make these documentaries themselves.

Since 2011, the PUMA Impact Award has been recognizing documentaries that have had a positive social and environmental impact through public-awareness raising; capacity-building; and changes that are political, corporate and behavioural in nature. Morgan Spurlock, who made *Super Size Me* (2004) and *Super Size Me 2* (2017), documentaries discussed in the next chapter that are critical of the food industry, was a juror for the 2011 award. He asserted:

> There's real power in a documentary, and there's real power in movies to begin with. Movies transcend culture; they transcend countries, and to be able to have something that can create global awareness is necessary today. (Quoted in Jones, 2011)

Documentaries today have, it would seem, enormous opportunity and even greater potential for social impact. However, several media scholars have been critical of this kind of optimism. Brian Winston, Gail Vanstone and Wang Chi (2017) warned us, quite rightly, against exaggerated claims about the popularity, artistry, innovation and impact of documentaries today, and that we should view these developments with a sense of proportion and a critical eye. Otherwise, we might miss the underlying scientism of objectivity, eurocentrism and patriarchy that have propped up the hegemony of western documentary-making.

Pooja Rangan (2017) described participatory documentaries as insidious when the disenfranchised represent or are made to represent themselves with what she calls 'immediacy', which produces a sense of directness and urgency to evoke actuality that can obscure the fact of their creative artifice. This appearance of truth is yet another form of 'othering', this time through the invitational gestures for inclusion, participation and empowerment. In short, one should be alert to documentaries—or movies in general—that advance a progressive agenda yet exploit their subjects to motivate public action and to achieve critical acclaim and commercial success. Bearing Rangan's critique in mind, how should we view documentaries by Michael Moore, who often invites his subjects to express their hardship and struggles vividly, sometimes through performative gestures that Moore himself designs and the licence he takes with time and space to suggest not only strong causality, but immediacy and urgency as well?

Michael Moore, Working-Class Hero

Perhaps the most commercially and critically successful documentary-maker in the 21st century is American activist Michael Moore. His documentaries are among the most profitable in the US, with *Fahrenheit 9/11* (2004) earning well over US$220,000,000 worldwide, making it the highest-grossing documentary of all time. That documentary also won the top award at the Cannes Film Festival that year. His *Bowling for Columbine* (2002) won an Academy Award for Best Documentary Feature. To explain Moore's success, critical media scholar Douglas Kellner (2010) described him as

> . . . a populist artist who privileges his own voice and point of view, inserting himself as film narrator and often as the subject of his films' action. Moore plays the crusading defender of the poor and oppressed, who stands up to and confronts the powers that be. He uses humor and compelling dramatic and narrative sequences to engage his audiences. Moore's films deal with issues of fundamental importance, and he attempts to convince his audience that the problems he presents are highly significant and concern the health of U.S. democracy. Moreover, despite the severity of the crises he portrays, the films and filmmaker often imply that the problems can

> be subject to intervention, and that progressive social transformation is possible and necessary.

In an interview for a Channel 4 News (2018) podcast series in the UK titled *Ways to Change the World*, Moore was asked, 'So you make movies, don't you, to change the world, to change the way people think?' He replied:

> I make movies . . . for a number of reasons . . . I want people to think about things. I want them to maybe consider a different way of looking at something. But . . . I'm a filmmaker so I know they've worked hard all week and I'd like them on a Friday or Saturday night to be able to go out for a couple of hours, sit in a movie theatre, and after two hours leave there and say to each other wow that was really something . . . So many documentary film makers believe they have to bludgeon the audience over the head like somehow that would . . . make them come around, . . . all that makes them do is wanna go get a drink to take care of the headache you've just given them. So you come to my films, yes I use satire and humour as a vehicle through which to explain what I think is going on.

No matter how entertaining or compassionate they might be to his audience, Moore's documentaries have clear 'expository' elements, advancing a strong, polemical and often controversial argument against the evils of global capitalism by mustering the most vivid evidence to support his many provocative claims. Often, his voice provides authoritative commentary on the events they feature, posing rhetorical questions that provoke outrage.

Moore's documentaries also have 'participatory' elements. He himself often appears on screen directly interacting with ordinary people. He participates in their activities, interviews them and leads them in outrageous and provocative stunts to draw public attention to injustice. Moore's persona is an integral part of the narrative. He fits in very naturally with the working-class communities that he depicts and engages with. In many of the documentaries, there are important references to Flint, Michigan, his hometown in America's industrial heartland and one of the poorest and most-exploited cities in the US.

Ravaged by globalization and deindustrialization, Flint is a striking example of how the 'American dream' has turned into a nightmare. And out of this nightmare, Moore has emerged as a working-class hero, an organic intellectual who uses his success and celebrity to shape and sharpen the critical consciousness of his working-class community and to influence the values and decisions of those parts of the political elite that have not been irredeemably corrupted by corporate America.

In his Channel 4 News (2018) interview, Moore acknowledged that he was exactly

> Trump's demographic . . . an angry White guy over the age of 50 with a high school education.

He noted that the US President had not attacked him as he had done so fiercely in the case of his other adversaries. One reason for this, Moore conjectured, could be that Trump did not want to upset Moore's working-class audience and supporters, who overlapped with his own working-class Republican voter base. In some rather unexpected ways, this observation reveals how—at least superficially—the two are mirror images of each other.

Trump and Moore are both 'working-class heroes', but for very different reasons. Moore is an organic intellectual, emerging from within the working class and rising to a position of cultural leadership from which he could help articulate the experiences of the working class and their exploitative conditions. Trump did not hide his very privileged background but used it to project an image of meritocratic success in capitalist America, claiming to champion the interests of working-class Americans who, he claimed, had been exploited by the Washington elite and hoodwinked by the mainstream media. Trump took great pains to differentiate himself from this elite in the minds of his working-class base.

In the Channel 4 News interview, Moore criticized the Democratic Party elite for their inability to communicate with the working-class voters. They

> . . . can't say a simple sentence to the American people like Trump does.

Instead, their messaging has been formal, technical, nuanced, guarded, even timid. Film academic and critic Sergio Rizzo (2005) observed that when Moore positions himself

> . . . as the working-class outsider, he alienates mainstream Democrats (often accusing them of being 'wimps' and 'sellouts') and those to the left of the Democratic Party as well.

In this sense, Moore was like Trump in his criticism of the arrogance, emotional coldness and reticence of the Washington elite. But unlike Trump, Moore also attacked big corporations, CEOs and billionaires, their insatiable greed and their relentless control over the political elite. In an interview on ABC News (2018), Moore noted how Trump had been a CEO and a billionaire before becoming president, and asked:

> . . . how many CEOs of corporations that you know that believe in democracy? They don't run their corporations like a democracy. They run it as a dictatorship. I'm in charge. Do what I say or leave. And also, they end up making the most money. So [Trump] likes that idea of the few making the most money, while everybody else works their butts off working longer hours than people ever had before. Many people working two jobs . . . he wants to be able to say this is the way it's going to be.

Though critical of the Democratic Party, Moore was supportive of a younger wave of its leaders who identified as democratic socialists and were set to reinvigorate the left-wing politics of Democratic Senator Bernie Sanders. Trump, instead, pushed through policies that were strikingly advantageous to big corporations and at the expense of the working class. He was able to do this mainly by distracting them, using the language of fear, hate and intolerance to generate moral panic.

Without doubt, both Trump and Moore are populists. Both are charismatic and highly skilled communicators, able to mobilize support, explain complex phenomena in a language that the working class can relate to, energize their audiences, unleash popular feelings of outrage and villainize the enemy in dramatic contrast with working-class decency. What Trump can achieve through his mass political rallies, Moore can also do through his movies, which have a very pronounced performative element, activating the emotions and subjectivity of his audience by centring his own emotions and subjectivity as a personal witness to and crusader against the world's corruption and as a provocateur of change.

Kellner (2010) described Moore's documentary style as 'unique' in the way it

> . . . combines partisan and interventionist cinema with his personal voice and vision, combining the personal with the political, pathos and humor.

Moore is certainly confrontational in his style, often performing outrage at what he depicts as the unconscionable behaviour and actions of those who benefit from and perpetuate capitalist injustice. He sometimes takes liberties with the smaller facts to arrive at the larger truths. Moore's sense of humour is irreverent, iconoclastic, satirical and even buffoonish. Its effect is to deflate the puffed-up sense of importance that the neoliberal elite usually project in their public image, thus exposing their egregious behaviour and the hypocrisy that conceals it. In all of this, Moore's highly—almost excessively—personal, confrontational and humorous performative mode makes his documentaries very entertaining, one of the main reasons for their commercial success. Their viewership and outreach give these kinds of political documentaries an unusual opportunity to change minds, actions and thus, the world.

What differentiates Trump's authoritarian populism from Moore's left-wing populism is the former's propensity for folk devilling Muslims, Mexicans, the Chinese, Hollywood liberals, journalists and so on, as threats to the well-being and way of life of decent, White, working-class Americans. Trump does this by making dog-whistle comments that seem to have the effect of inciting racial supremacist and other hate groups to violence. While Moore may seem to also direct criticism and working-class hostility towards the neoliberal class of CEOs and billionaires, his provocations are peaceful and focused on radical change, sometimes through mutual understanding, but more often through satirical ridicule.

Roger & Me (1989)

Moore made at least four movies before the 21st century, the most well-known being his first, *Roger & Me* (1989). The documentary explored the devastating economic and social impact of the closure of General Motors (GM) factories in Flint to open new factories in Mexico where lower-waged workers could be hired. Flint, a city in the US state of Michigan, the birthplace of the US automobile industry and Moore's hometown, depended profoundly on GM for its economy and livelihood.

The documentary's premise centres on Moore's largely unsuccessful attempts to interview Roger Smith, GM's Chairman and CEO. Moore used irony heavy-handedly to reveal the moral failings of the wealthy class and corporate elite amidst vast economic and social inequalities. Images of high-class neighbourhoods filled with mansions were juxtaposed against dilapidated and rat-infested working-class neighbourhoods and downtown areas, where rows and rows of boarded-up homes and stores were the backdrop to a rise in violent crimes. In this city, workers were being laid-off and evicted from their homes, while the elite attended outlandish events such as a 'Great Gatsby' party, where people were hired to be human statues, or a fundraiser in which the attendees paid US$100 to stay overnight in a jail cell just for fun and an unusual experience. When interviewed, the elite downplayed the devastation that Flint was undergoing, blaming the poor and unemployed for not picking themselves up. Through their influence over the entertainment industry as well as the churches, the elite were able to send out hollow and condescending messages of hope that things would get better.

Although the movie was heavily criticized for factual inaccuracies, which was also the fate of Moore's subsequent documentaries, Miles Orvell (1994), a professor of American studies, argued that the movie should be viewed as a 'documentary satire', a hybrid form from which the literal truth should not be expected. Instead, its value should lie in the satirically oblique truth that critically reveals the world in an exaggerated, telescoped and tragi-comical way. In other words, we should not be obsessed about every little detail that Moore gets wrong, such as the sequence of actions and events, the time lag between them and the assertions of causality. Instead, we should pay attention to the larger point being made about the vastly different worlds that the rich and the poor live in, the attitudes that the former display towards the latter and the destructive consequences of self-interested decisions made by corporations and their CEOs.

Towards the end of the movie, Moore's voice announced,

> As we neared the end of the 20th century, the rich were richer, the poor, poorer . . . It was truly the dawn of a new era.

Indeed, some of Moore's most powerful work emerged in this markedly new era, as he witnessed the intensification of neoliberal injustice in the 21st century.

Bowling for Columbine (2002)

In the first of these, *Bowling for Columbine* (2002), Moore took on the powerful National Rifle Association and the pro-gun lobby in a sprawling documentary about violence in the US. In his characteristic 'foot-in-the-door', 'vigilante journalism' style, noted by film programmer Spiro Economopoulos (2003), Moore confronted, embarrassed and even harassed his interviewees to create sensationalist moments in the movie. Putting the frequent occurrence of school shootings in the US under the spotlight, Moore looked for deeper explanations in the nation's history, attitudes to individual rights, the industrial production of military weapons of mass destruction, defence and foreign policy, deep-seated racism, a culture of fear, the easy availability of guns, popular cultural influences, mental health and rising unemployment and poverty. Sociologist Bernard Beck (2003) described the documentary as

> . . . a collection of filmed essays exploring different aspects of a common topic . . . an anthology of commentaries rather than a unified visual ethnography.

While the documentary remained inconclusive, it did suggest that at the root of the problem was poverty, arising from the lack of a comprehensive system of state welfare, making everyone feel insecure, mistrustful and fearful of one another. Poor parents who were forced off welfare to take up jobs in faraway locations had to commute long distances. As a result, they had much less bandwidth for paying attention to what their children got up to.

The movie also suggested that it was in the interest of the pro-gun lobby to sustain a culture of fear to justify the need for guns in society as the best form of self-defence. One segment of the movie showed how, shortly after the Columbine High School massacre, public attention was re-focused on goth singer Marilyn Manson. According to media reports, the shooters had listened to Manson's hard rock music before they went out to kill their schoolmates. Many 'experts' were called upon to make claims about the negative influence of this genre of music and their satanically styled performers. This contributed to a moral panic that served to distract the public from the NRA's culpability for school shootings as well as the troublingly resonant observation that the US government had ordered its most massive bombing of Kosovo, controversially justified as a 'humanitarian intervention', that very same day.

Americans often justify their right to gun ownership in terms of self-defence, an argument that seems more compelling when there is a perception of rising crime rates. Where there are strong undercurrents of racism that disproportionately associate crime with Blacks and Hispanics, moral panic is easily triggered. In the documentary's concluding scene, when Moore got to interview then NRA President Charlton Heston, the Hollywood actor answered a question about why the US had such a terrible record of gun violence by pointing to its history of bloodshed. When Moore pointed out that countries such as Germany, Japan and Great Britain did not have such a record despite their equally violent histories, Heston turned to ethnic diversity as a possible reason. The scene ended with Moore, who had earlier gained Heston's trust by showing his NRA membership card, questioning Heston's decision to lead pro-gun public rallies in cities where school shootings had just happened. Unable to answer this question adequately, Heston walked out of the interview as Moore invited him to look at a large photograph of a six-year-old girl who had been shot dead in school by a six-year-old boy. Moore excels in these performative moments, when he can provoke audience emotions in the most vivid ways.

In another scene, Moore visited the Kmart headquarters with three survivors of the Columbine shooting to ask the giant department store chain to tighten its rules on selling ammunition, since the Columbine shooters had obtained cartridges from a Kmart store. Not getting the response they wanted, the group went to one of its stores and got a minor among them to purchase, without any difficulty, more than 700 rounds of ammunition. They returned to the headquarters the next day with a group of reporters to confront and embarrass the corporation with the ammunition they had bought. In response, a senior spokesperson came out and read a press release announcing its decision to phase out the sale of handgun ammunition in all its US stores within the next ninety days. The result was 'more than what we asked for', Moore was heard saying. The scene served to demonstrate how the actions of ordinary people, with a bit of ingenuity and the cooperation of the media, can make a surprisingly impactful change.

As a sprawling collection of 'filmed essays' on a complex topic, *Bowling for Columbine* may be difficult for many among the audience to understand intellectually. Communication scholars Brian L. Ott and Susan A. Sci (2015) offered a different view, that the movie's

> . . . 'argument' is activated affectively, that it is experienced sensually, felt viscerally.

Moore, they claimed, takes the audience through a sequence of moods, from irony and curiosity, to terror and sublimity, to fear and loathing, to cool rationalism and finally to mourning and melancholia. For many, it is the experience of the documentary and the sensations it produces that matter most.

By this time, Moore's movies were already having an impact on documentary-making. Communication scholars Thomas W. Benson and Brian J. Snee (2015) praised him for helping to

> . . . put documentary film back at the center of political debate, acting as filmmaker, participant, and reflexive interrogator of his own method.

They observed:

> Moore's films helped revive attention to the documentary mainstream once again and helped create a market for his successors. Films by others, like *Super Size Me* (2004) and *An Inconvenient Truth* (2006), got onto theater screens and found a broad audience, possibly because of the visibility and profitability of *Roger & Me* and *Bowling for Columbine* (2002). Moore's commercial and financial success may have given producers, distributors, and exhibitors renewed confidence in nonfiction film as a marketable commodity. Furthermore, his work reminded audiences that documentary and entertainment are not exclusive categories.

Fahrenheit 9/11 (2004)

Fahrenheit 9/11 (2004), Moore's next documentary, was daringly critical of the Bush presidency's first term. In a sharply accusatory style, *Fahrenheit 9/11* began with an assertion that George W. Bush had stolen the presidential election in 2000, winning the crucial Florida election after its governor, his brother, connived to purge many Black Democrat voters from its rolls. The documentary then proceeded to narrate a devastating sequence of events, including the 9/11 terrorist attacks on the World Trade Center and the Pentagon, the US retaliatory attack on Afghanistan and its subsequent invasion of Iraq. Its aim was to suggest that the so-called 'war on terror' was connected to shady business dealings involving the Bush family, their government associates, the defence industry, corporate interests and Middle East oil, centred on the family of Osama bin Laden.

In his critique of the Patriot Act, which was controversially enacted in 2001 to give the government wide-ranging powers to intercept and obstruct terrorism, Moore returned to the theme of America's culture of fear, violence and their connection with authoritarianism. Through the manipulation of fear, the government justified going to war in distant lands and recruiting young American soldiers especially from impoverished neighbourhoods in cities like Moore's own Flint. In a highly performative scene, Moore and a young Black soldier went to Washington, D.C. to ask congressmen on the streets if they would volunteer their own children to enlist and fight the war in Iraq.

The movie helped the audience to see clearly how the interests of the mostly White US elite were advanced by a war based on a lie that Iraq was manufacturing weapons of mass destruction and fought by working-class American youths, many of whom were killed in battle or badly injured. Continuous war, senseless as it was, served as the means of keeping the whole structure of society intact.

The picture that Moore painted of the US elite was thoroughly cynical and remarkably sordid. G. Thomas Goodnight (2005), a scholar of rhetoric, noted how the movie

> . . . packed the wallop of a satire, which in the political realm licenses the artist to treat a subject roughly, bringing the mighty low.

It was calculated to help defeat President Bush in the 2004 elections, in no small part by vividly presenting voters with a narrative of how the president and his administration had given misleading information to the public to buttress reasons for going to war with Iraq. Moore was deliberate in including as many scenes as possible of Bush behaving in a buffoonish manner, relaxing when he should be working, tripping up his words and—most damning of all—smirking during the most inappropriate moments. His post-9/11 popularity in decline, Bush still managed to win, but by a narrow margin of the electoral votes. At the end of the movie, audiences were urged to 'Do something: www.michaelmoore.com'.

But what was the impact of *Fahrenheit 9/11*? Film scholar Robert B. Toplin (2006) described it as a movie that 'divided a nation', provoking controversy like no other movie had done. Several documentaries were produced to critique and rebut Moore's arguments in this and his earlier movies. Scott Krzych, a film and media studies professor, described them as

> . . . hysterical discourse.

Making personal and professional attacks on Moore, these reactionary documentaries

> . . . misconstrue, mischaracterize, and seemingly misunderstand Moore's respective critiques . . .

deploying

> . . . the formal appearance of political debate for a contradictory end: to deny outright an encounter with political difference and thereby to refuse any serious consideration of the issues, ideas, or arguments expressed by a political opponent.

Communications scholar Natalie J. Stroud (2007) conducted a national survey and found that where *Fahrenheit 9/11* was concerned, there was selective exposure. Those who were already more liberal in their ideological outlook and who already held negative views about Bush were more likely than others to intend to go see Moore's movie. And those who viewed the movie became significantly more negative towards Bush than those who intended to view the movie but did not. Viewing the movie may have inspired more political discussion, but discussions with friends and family did not moderate the movie's effect. From this data, you could say, very broadly speaking, that *Fahrenheit 9/11* was able to politicize a self-selected audience, reinforce rather than moderate or change their political views and polarize society even more sharply along the liberal-conservative spectrum, and more specifically, the anti-Bush and pro-Bush divide. Goodnight (2005) discussed the impact of *Fahrenheit 9/11*, a 'wartime' movie, on deliberative democracy, where the power of celebrity advocacy in a presidential election year generated controversy in the public discourse, especially in the talk shows on television. Film scholar Richard Porton (2016) observed that the movie was

> . . . stirring up debate (of an often quite ferocious variety) at dinner parties, multiplexes, office water coolers, and public meetings. Whether you love, loath, or feel ambivalent about Michael Moore, it's obvious that more than a few minds have been changed.

Sicko (2007)

Moore went on to make *Sicko* in 2007, a documentary about the dysfunctional healthcare system in the US. A large part of the movie documented the tragic stories of ordinary Americans who had not been able to afford adequate healthcare in a system thoroughly captured by profit-driven corporations such as hospitals, health insurance companies and pharmaceutical companies. Fifty million Americans were without health insurance. Those who had insurance were subjected to the unsavoury practices of many insurance companies. Moore had put out an advertisement inviting people to send him emails if they had had problems with their health insurance companies. Within a week, he received more than 25,000 responses. Many had horror stories to tell. These companies maintained long lists of pre-existing conditions through which they were able to reject applicants or deny payment to claimants disqualified on technicalities. To help them minimize payment and thus maximize profit, insurance companies employed investigators and medical directors who were handsomely rewarded if they could come up with technical reasons for rejection. The documentary showed how hospitals abandoned their own patients on the streets when they were unable to pay. This included an elderly woman who was left wandering the streets, disoriented, in a bad neighbourhood. In an emotional voiceover, Moore asked:

> Is this what we've become? A nation that dumps its own citizens like so much garbage on the side of the curb because they can't pay their hospital bill.

Even volunteer rescue workers, the heroes who persevered in the rubble of the collapsed twin towers following the 9/11 terrorist attacks, found themselves ineligible for government medical support. Many of these volunteers had developed serious respiratory and other medical problems.

In the documentary, Moore travelled to Canada, the UK and France. He asked people who lived in these countries, including Americans, if what the US politicians and conservative media often said about the evils of 'socialized medical care' was, in fact, true. What he learnt was that in these countries, where there was free universal healthcare, people did not need to pay very much—usually nothing at all—for the care that they received. They did not have to wait long to receive treatment. Doctors were well remunerated. Taxes were high, but people could easily afford to live very comfortably, with decent working hours, generous leave entitlements and inexpensive childcare of high quality—all without having to carry the personal burden of debt that too many Americans must live with.

Typical of his performative style, Moore expressed utter disbelief when told that the purpose of a cashier's counter in a UK National Health System hospital was not to collect payment for hospital bills—since nobody needed to pay anything—but to disburse payment to discharged patients for whatever transport costs they might have incurred. He performed even more disbelief when he learnt that government doctors made house visits in France, responding very swiftly to phone calls and without charge. And when women had children in France, they were entitled to receive help from government workers who visited their homes regularly and even did the laundry for them, also without charge.

Two important ideas emerged from these comparisons. First, democracy—whether through the popular vote or the culture of protest—forced the governments of these countries to pay attention to ordinary people's needs and to be responsive to them. Second, the people of these countries accepted the principle that those who were better off should help pay for those who were worse off. And this was the basis of their moral solidarity. In comparison, the US seemed grotesquely undemocratic and selfishly individualistic.

Many Republican politicians and media personalities in the US crudely describe such systems as 'socialist' or even 'communist', terms that are used in the most pejorative sense to stir up populist fears to distract people from making demands for policy changes that would disadvantage the neoliberal technocratic and corporate elite. Moore returned to his theme of American authoritarianism, which was dependent on sustaining a culture of fear and, in this case, keeping ordinary people working long hours, living stressful lives, becoming dependent on opioids and generally being too unhealthy to pose a democratic threat to authority. Meanwhile, American politicians, regardless of party affiliation, were being successfully lobbied by corporate interests able to buy their support for policies that continued to allow these interests to prosper at the sometimes-fatal expense of ordinary Americans.

In one of the most performative segments of the documentary, Moore took his group of 9/11 heroes—the neglected rescue workers—on a boat trip to Guantanamo Bay, where suspected terrorists were detained by the US government and apparently provided with 'top-notch' medical care. Moore highlighted the irony of the detention camp as

> . . . one place on American soil that had free universal healthcare.

From the boat, he called out to the guards asking if his group could get some of the medical treatment that the Al Qaeda detainees were enjoying.

The group then sailed into Cuba—a Marxist-Leninist socialist republic and demonized enemy of the US—to see if they could get some medical treatment. Moore and his group discovered that Cuba not only provided free universal healthcare for everyone, but also had one of the best healthcare systems in the world. Cuba was among the most generous countries sending doctors and equipment to other developing countries. The American heroes finally got the medical treatments they badly needed but could not afford to purchase in their own country.

This scene deflated the image that many Americans had of themselves as the greatest country in the world. Evoking sadness and shame, such a scene could motivate audiences to demand change, or it could instigate defensiveness and even more cynicism about Moore's work as socialist or communist propaganda. Moore concluded the movie with a shot of himself walking up the steps to the US Capitol, carrying his basket of laundry. He had just aired the dirty laundry of the greatest country in the world. In a voiceover, he reflected:

> No matter what our differences, we sink or swim together . . . They [the other countries visited in the documentary] live in a world of 'we', not 'me'. We'll never fix anything until we get that one basic thing right. And powerful forces hope that we never do and that we remain the only country in the western world without free universal health care.

Ernest Callenbach (2008), American author and film critic, praised the movie with characteristic eloquence:

> … here comes Moore, lumbering and low-class, slapping his films together with a fierce and shameless humor, impatient, openly disrespectful of what used to be called The Power … while embodying the outraged decency of the ordinary American, [he] has been cataloguing the cruelty, the perversity, the crass inhumanity of our society: the heartlessness of its industry leaders, the fear and hair-trigger violence of gun-crazy adults and youth, the shameless lying of our government, and now the painful inadequacy of our medical system. / Having shoved the specter of single-payer universal healthcare onto the public agenda, Moore will probably move on . . . to another critically ill American institution. Now it is up to us to see if we can find a cure for this one.

Slacker Uprising (2008)

The next critically ill American institution that Moore moved on to after *Sicko* was the institution of democratic elections. Produced in the style of a 'concert movie', *Slacker Uprising* (2008) was released the following year as a record of Moore's 'shadow campaign' in the 2004 presidential elections. In support of Democratic candidate Senator John Kerry and against the incumbent George W. Bush, Moore toured college campuses in more than sixty cities. These 'slacker uprising' rallies, targeted mainly at college students who were often demeaned by conservatives as lazy and irresponsible, included live music performances by Steve Erle, REM, Tom Morello and Joan Baez; stand-up comedy by Roseanne Barr and Moore himself; and appearances by other celebrities such as Viggo Mortensen, who in a speech at one of these rallies said:

> When we as Americans see ourselves as different and superior to other peoples and other nations, as George W. Bush with his go-it-alone agenda would have us do, we are not freeing ourselves or anyone else. We are not respecting ourselves or anyone else. We are rather enslaving ourselves by willingly building the walls of our own prison with one ignorant brick after another.

Also invited to speak at these rallies were veterans and relatives of soldiers killed in battle. In emotional speeches, they thanked US soldiers for their service. They expressed sympathy for all families of dead soldiers as well as the Iraqi people who suffered from the US invasion. They called for US troops to be sent home. They wanted Bush and his administration to be held accountable for lying about the weapons of mass destruction as a pretext for waging war and incurring hardship on lower-income Americans. They accused corporate interests of profiteering from the war. Generally, they supported their country and those in military service, but not President Bush and his bellicose policies.

Moore accused the mainstream media of being a propaganda arm of the Bush administration when it participated in deceiving the American public about such things as weapons of mass destruction manufactured in Iraq. Though ready to acknowledge the polemical nature of his work, Moore described his own documentaries as 'anti-propaganda', poised to create a more informed public, without which democracy would cease to exist.

The Republican Party and its supporters opposed Moore very strongly, recognizing—as Moore claimed—the power of movies like *Fahrenheit 9/11* to influence swing voters. They accused him of having a 'hidden agenda', of making documentaries based on untruths and misrepresentation, even though most admitted to not even seeing the documentaries. They argued that controversy was not what college students needed, called him a 'communist' and urged that he be shipped off to Iraq and 'blown up'.

But Moore had the support of the students, who treated him like a rock star. Republican attempts to cancel Moore's campus rallies nearly always failed. Bribes offered to the students by local business Republican supporters also failed. In one case, when the university authorities disallowed the event, the students moved the rally to a venue that could accommodate an audience many times larger. Republican efforts backfired. Moore's visit to Kent State University was especially poignant and resonant. In 1970, this was the site where four students were killed and nine wounded by the National Guard. The students had been protesting the expansion of US presence in the Vietnam War. In the 2000s, 'slackers' were still protesting US aggression in so many parts of the world. What would be their fate?

Moore's message was loud and clear. Everyone should go out and vote. And everyone should volunteer to encourage everyone they know to go out and vote. In the end, Bush still managed to win his second term, but by the smallest of margins. Moore believed that Kerry had got the youth vote, but their parents continued to vote for Bush. A decade later, in a talk show interview on ABC News (2018), Moore admitted:

> I don't know how much hope I have left to be honest . . . hope is going to be the death of us if we just sit around hoping. We need action. No more time to hope. Don't sit there and hope that the midterms will go well. Or hope that the Democrats will run somebody in 2020. It is going to take actual physical action. Everybody has to get off the bench. Everybody in the pool. Everybody, this is your country you cannot call yourself an American if you don't participate, because America implies a democracy and it's not a democracy if more than half the people stay home on election day.

Capitalism: A Love Story (2009)

In his next documentary, Moore shifted his political attention from the electoral front to corporate power. In the immediate aftermath of the Global Financial Crisis of 2007–2008, *Capitalism: A Love Story* (2009) targeted the banking system, which he considered to be at the heart of what was rotting in American capitalism.

In the opening credits, we were shown clips of bank robberies, which were meant to set the stage for the irony of how, today, ordinary people are being 'robbed' by the banks. We then heard an account of how the mighty Roman Empire fell. Juxtaposed with images of America today, this account of a decadent empire highlighted parallels in history. To Moore, capitalism was a radical evil that could not be regulated but must be eliminated and replaced by democracy.

The documentary observed the plight of working-class Americans who were forcibly evicted from their homes after they were unable to pay their mortgages in an economy that benefitted capitalists and CEOs, whose opportunistic actions impoverished the middle class, leaving many unemployed. For example, without any moral compunction at all, the boss of a company called Condo Vultures seemed to take great pride in his ability to 'take advantage of others' misfortunes' during an economic crisis when massive numbers of working-class homes were being foreclosed.

Moore's main target in this movie was Wall Street. While earlier American presidents such as Franklin D. Roosevelt and Jimmy Carter had already anticipated the corrupting influence of unbridled capitalism, Moore pointed to the Reagan presidency from 1981 to 1989 as the start of a profound rot in the system. Reaganomics, together with Thatcherism in the UK, is often tied to the rise of neoliberalism worldwide.

Reagan appointed the chairman and CEO of investment and wealth management giant Merrill Lynch to serve as treasury secretary and then White House chief of staff. With this influence over the president, the country was increasingly being run like a corporation, where there was wholesale dismantling of infrastructure, job losses, the weakening of labour unions, middle-class wage stagnation and the rise of middle-class indebtedness, bankruptcies, unaffordable healthcare and incarceration. Meanwhile, the stock market and CEOs prospered.

At the centre of the financial crisis were derivatives and other complex financial instruments that Wall Street manufactured and sold to working-class people, who did not understand what they were buying with their hard-earned savings. Moore's documentary explained in the simplest and clearest terms what these financial products were about. He described them as 'complicated betting schemes', purposely designed to be confusing, so that the corporate and technocratic neoliberal elite could take advantage of the masses. They, of course, rarely read or understood the fine print. For instance, elderly people were tricked into refinancing their homes and then losing them when they could not repay, often after the terms were adjusted to be much less favourable. As more and more Wall Street capitalists joined the ranks of the government and neoliberal policies prevailed, financial regulation was effectively destroyed. Unbridled greed led to financial catastrophe. But it was ordinary people who paid for it through the foreclosure of their homes, the loss of incomes and jobs, and the government bailouts that corporations 'too big to fail' felt entitled to. Politicians and the pro-corporate capitalist policies they supported were rewarded with campaign contributions made from within Wall Street. The economic and political elite, in partnership, were complicit against ordinary people, who tragically bore the brunt of financial and economic meltdown.

While the social injustice of the corporate bailouts in 2008 were the highlight, Moore's documentary also showcased the many less spectacular though no less important examples of systematic profiteering and exploitation. For instance, Moore exposed the financial incentive for judges to 'funnel' young people into privatized juvenile homes for the most trivial offences. He pointed to the danger of paying airline pilots salaries that were so low that some of them had to live on food stamps and donate their blood plasma just to make ends meet. He also exposed the grotesque practice of companies that took out insurance policies on their employees, often without their knowledge, to make a profit out of their deaths. Known as 'dead peasant insurance', this product gave companies a handsome pay off when their employees died but left the family of the deceased with nothing.

Just before the GFC, Citigroup had published its infamous 'plutonomy' memo that described how the US was no longer a democracy, but a plutonomy, where the rich accounted for a vastly disproportionate and still-increasing share of income and wealth in the economy. Indeed, CEOs, billionaires and their financial managers were celebrating the end of democracy and its replacement by an extreme form of oligarchy. The memo, however, warned of a 'political backlash' stemming from the 'one person, one vote' basis of democracy. This could take the form of populist demands for higher taxation on corporations and the wealthy, more protection for local workers and a movement against economic globalization. As discussed in the previous chapter, Plato had already philosophized about this in ancient times, warning that oligarchy can easily slip into a populist form of democratic revolt.

Moore did not share Plato's pessimism for democracy and populism. His political agenda was to return power to the people by re-energizing American democracy. To convince his audience, Moore adopted several rhetorical manoeuvres. Firstly, nostalgia. Moore presented a surprising picture of the post-war years of affluence, when tax rates on the wealthy could go as high as 90 per cent. The state was able to finance public infrastructure and a welfare system that made even single-income middle-class families feel secure. He included archival footage of

President Roosevelt sending in his National Guard to protect workers on strike and reading out a proposal for a Second Bill of Rights that would ensure every American, regardless of race, had a decent job, liveable wages, universal healthcare, education, a home, paid vacation and an adequate pension. Tragically, Roosevelt died before this could be enacted. Kendall R. Phillips (2015), a communication scholar, analysed the rhetorical force of nostalgia in *Capitalism: A Love Story*, where images of the 1950s are invoked to ground Moore's moral critique and provide coherence to his arguments. Nostalgia can frame our affective relationship to the past, usually an idealized past, in order to serve the needs of the present through a sense of collective loss.

Secondly, Moore invoked religious morality. As someone who had once considered the priesthood, he interviewed Catholic priests and a bishop for the documentary. Their message seemed to be that capitalism, as practised in the US, was radically evil and contrary to the teachings of Christ. Capitalism had hijacked Christianity, forcing its teachings to be compatible with and even supportive of capitalist orthodoxy and excess.

Thirdly, Moore challenged the inevitability of capitalism and offered democratic alternatives, such as workplace democracy. He presented the case of a democratically run company, where profit and personal enrichment were less important than the value of fairness and dignity. Every worker, regardless of role and hierarchy, received the same share of the profits. Peer pressure and embarrassment, it was thought, prevented people from acting out of greed. In the end, the company was able to make more money. Moore gave a second example of highly productive people who were clearly not driven by greed. Jonas Salk, the inventor of the polio vaccine, for instance, did not patent his vaccine as he wanted the benefits of his research to be widely shared. And yet, in financial terms, he made enough to live a reasonably comfortable life.

Fourthly, Moore tried to change American audiences' prejudiced view of socialism. Republicans, the Right more generally, and their media mouthpieces regularly used 'socialism' as a bogeyman, subjecting to this scare tactic any politician who argued for spreading national wealth more evenly, including of course President Barack Obama. Moore observed that this scare campaign was becoming less effective. The weaponization of the word socialism, he claimed, made Americans—especially younger ones—more curious about what it really meant. Popular support for Senator Bernie Sanders signalled a rise in its popularity. People were also becoming aware of the painful irony that rich and powerful fear-mongers did not exclude themselves from benefitting in a kind of 'socialism' for the banks and corporations through government bailouts when they failed.

Fifthly, Moore encouraged people—no matter how powerless they might feel—to fight back. He identified examples of popular protest as a signal that Americans were already starting to turn against the rich, as their belief in the 'American dream' of success had weakened profoundly. He noted how small-town police officers had started to put a stop to foreclosure and how people had started to liberate their foreclosed property. At the advice of more progressive politicians, people became squatters in their own foreclosed houses, successfully hanging on to them despite being bullied by the banks. Laid-off workers were organizing strikes with greater support from community, religious and national leaders. Moore wondered rhetorically whether this was the beginning of a workers' revolt against Wall Street.

In a typically performative scene, Moore undertook to reclaim money that Wall Street had stolen from working-class people by threatening to make a citizen's arrest of the corporate elite. He placed a crime scene tape around Wall Street buildings, declaring: 'I refuse to live in a country like this and I'm not leaving.' However, in the final words of the documentary, he urged the audience to hurry up and do something, as he did not think he could do this for much longer.

Movie critics and academics were not hugely impressed with Moore's performativity. Leslie Felperin (2009), a critic, noted how even audiences who agreed with Moore's politics might find it difficult to

> . . . stomach his oversimplification, on-the-nose sentimentality and goofball japery.

Critic Wendy Ide (2010) was more complimentary:

> Like the complacent clown prince of agitprop, Moore hectors Wall Street doormen and security guards, while the company bosses

> remain in their fortress made of money, blissfully unaware of the fat man making a scene on the street far below . . . But for all his cheap tactics, Moore mounts a persuasive case that something is rotten in the current economic system.

Film educator Andrew J. Douglas (2010) criticized Moore for touching on

> . . . all of the major populist hot buttons, including Walmart, Wall Street, and home foreclosures, [without] investigat[ing] them in a constructive way.

Moore does not, for example, engage with alternative theories. An anonymous reviewer in *The Economist* criticized Moore for seeing 'conspiracies everywhere':

> The $700 billion bail-out after Lehman's collapse was no genuine attempt to stave off depression, but a financial coup d'etat, staged by big banks. Like nefarious screen villains, the bankers 'had a simple plan: to remake America to serve them.' ('False profits or false prophets?', 2009)

In an interview, several years later, on a UK-based talk show Good Morning Britain (2016), Moore argued that you could not defeat Donald Trump by

> . . . trying to be smart, trying to be logical.

Moore believed that

> . . . satire and ridicule is what is going to be used to destroy him.

In 2018, HBO (2018) talk show host Bill Maher introduced Moore as 'the people's comedian', able to 'make what's important interesting and compelling'. For the most part, those who expect Moore to make a factually accurate, tightly logical and comprehensively argued documentary will be disappointed, while those who understand and accept the political purpose of his movie and its satirical dimension will be more laudatory.

Fahrenheit 11/9 (2018)

Almost a decade later, Moore pivoted his struggle back to the more immediately political front. In *Fahrenheit 11/9* (2018), he turned his critical attention to Donald J. Trump, whose presidency was announced on 9 November 2016 (hence the movie's title). The documentary began with Trump's 'shock' victory over the liberal favourite Hillary Clinton, who—it was thought—would surely command the votes of women, LGBTQIA+ and Black Americans to become the first female US president. Trump had, however, attracted what appeared to be the votes of enough working-class Americans, mostly demoralized White males, who responded enthusiastically to his 'Make America Great Again' slogan, words that had been spoken before by former presidents Ronald Reagan and Bill Clinton, but in a very different socio-political context.

Moore observed that even Trump's team looked surprised and almost sad to win, having run a fake campaign that was aimed—he claimed—as a publicity stunt to boost his television ratings. And when that stunt backfired, Moore argued, Trump was eventually attracted to the adulation of crowds and became emboldened to embrace his new role as 'King of the World'. Before long, the mainstream media, for whom Trump was the most profitable thing to fall into their lap, started to feel the heat as he demanded only positive coverage and loyalty, or else face the full force of his attack on 'fake news'.

Moore's documentary highlighted Trump's very worst features. He was shown to be a sexual predator and pervert, behaving inappropriately with his daughter Ivanka in public and bragging openly about how he would purposely walk into contestants' changing rooms at the Miss Universe pageant, which he owned for many years. He was shown to be a racist; practising discrimination against Black tenants in his properties; demanding the execution of five innocent Black people; and—in what has come to be called the 'birther conspiracy'—constantly questioning Obama's citizenship, birthplace and therefore eligibility for the presidency. Trump was also depicted as 'treasonous' in his affection and support for autocrats such as Russian President Vladimir Putin, Philippine President Rodrigo Duterte, North Korea's Supreme Leader Kim Jong-un and—at times—China's President Xi Jinping.

Moore went back to Flint, his impoverished hometown, to expose yet another terrible injustice, this time the devastating effect of profiteering by the neoliberal elite on the quality of something as basic and essential to life as water. The Michigan government had decided to build a lucrative but unnecessary water pipeline from the polluted Flint River to supply households. As a result, residents were ingesting lead. Their hair fell out. They were developing skin rashes. The children got seriously sick. Over a longer period, IQ levels dropped. People had problems with memory. These effects were potent and irreversible. And when Flint water started to corrode the equipment of General Motors, a big political donor, the state government decided to divert clean water from Lake Huron to GM only, while the people still drank poisoned water from Flint River. In a typically performative gesture, Moore tried to make a citizen's arrest. He challenged the governor's communication director to drink a glass of Flint water, which he, of course, refused to do. Moore then went to the governor's mansion and hosed it down with Flint water. While the methods may seem buffoonish, the message was grim. The American dream had become a nightmare for Flint and, across the country, there were different Americas, one for the affluent and one for the down-and-out.

Moore questioned the emerging conventional wisdom that 'real America' had become conservative, tired of being neglected by an increasingly elitist Democratic Party and now naturally supportive of the Republican Party and a strongman leader like Trump. One after another, Moore produced poll numbers that showed how 'real America' was quite liberal, a legacy of the counterculture in the 1960s. The mismatch between majority values and choice of leaders seemed to arise from a presidential electoral system that was designed to be indirect, which in effect often meant that the candidate who got the highest number of popular votes did not necessarily win the presidency. Over the decades, there has also been an increasingly large non-voting majority, whose support had not traditionally been sought by either party. This majority, Moore argued, could be enthused not by someone such as Hillary Clinton—the Democratic Party elite's candidate of choice—but by the likes of Senator Bernie Sanders. Sanders, a long-time democratic socialist who wanted to take on the billionaire class and redistribute wealth and opportunities more equitably, had become something of a threat to the liberal establishment. Moore claimed that Sanders had, in fact, won the popular vote in the Democratic Presidential Primary Elections, but the system was rigged by the party elite and so Hillary Clinton instead was declared as the Democratic nominee. Increasingly, the working class felt ignored and betrayed by the Democratic Party. They left the party, their faith in democracy seriously diminished. This opened the way for authoritarian populism.

In fact, Moore's documentary explicitly compared Trump's America to Hitler's Nazi Germany. To create ironic resonance, he juxtaposed video footage of Hitler and the Nazi regime with audio of Trump making a speech. The similarities between both leaders and regimes were uncanny. Trump's dog-whistling and bullying rhetorical style, conveyed almost every day in the media across the ideological spectrum, encouraged and empowered explicitly racist and xenophobic behaviour everywhere. Through mass rallies, he energized his voter base made up mainly of evangelical Christians and rifle-owners, secured their loyalty and got them to believe in him rather than in the truth, whenever the two diverged, which was often. Through the right-wing media, such as Fox News, he mobilized popular disgruntlement against the arrogance and disrespect of the liberal elite. He made every effort to discredit anyone or any institution courageous enough to challenge his political legitimacy.

But Moore argued that it was not because of Trump that the US has shown fascistic qualities in more recent years. Instead, we need to think of Trump as a product of a longer-term development in the US towards authoritarianism. To substantiate this argument, Moore highlighted several policies of Democratic presidents such as Bill Clinton and Barack Obama that were not so different from Trump's own policies.

> Evil is a slow-moving organism . . .

Moore said in a voiceover near the end of the documentary.

> By the time it coalesces into one giant terror, it is too late.

The 'whole rotten system' that produced Trump needed to be dealt with.

Compared to his earlier documentaries, *Fahrenheit 11/9* offered more optimistic reasons for positive change. It highlighted the efforts and early success of a new generation of younger, more grassroots-connected and highly energetic women leaders in the Democratic Party, such as Alexandria Ocasio-Cortez (or AOC) and Rashida Tlaib, who became the first Muslim woman in Congress. The documentary also showcased the plight of teachers in West Virginia, whose salaries put them below the poverty line. Let down by their union leaders, the teachers organized their own strike, inspiring other exploited school workers to join. This growing solidarity led to salary increases for teachers, bus drivers and canteen servers. As word of their success spread to other counties, working-class people similarly came together and managed to push for positive change. The documentary also featured the impressive work of young school-aged activists, who—following the Stoneman Douglas High School shooting in 2018—were able to organize a national walk-out day in schools around the country to protest the US government's inaction and its politicians' capture by the National Rifle Association. They continue to organize marches and demonstrations at various scales. The image of children rebuilding a world that their parents' generation had destroyed was a powerful one.

Amidst the optimism and the argument that the system rather than the president was the fundamental problem, Moore nevertheless acknowledged Trump's resilience and what his movie was up against:

> No matter what you throw at him, it hasn't worked. No matter what is revealed, he remains standing. Facts, reality, brains cannot defeat him. Even when he commits a self-inflicted wound, he gets up the next morning and keeps going and tweeting. (Merry, 2017)

Faith in the Democratic Ideal

On his *The Late Show* (2018), host Stephen Colbert asked Moore,

> What is the end game here? Because you don't want to end this in anything violent or some sort of really revolutionary confrontation. You want a political change at the end of this. Do you have any hope for that?

In his reply, Moore argued that most Americans were liberal on most issues and so the Democratic Party should be their natural choice. His most important goal, it would seem, was to reform the US electoral college system, so that the choice of president would better reflect the popular vote and therefore be more aligned with the democratic principle of one-person, one vote. In the absence of such reform, he wanted his movies to motivate people to 'get off the couch' and 'put our bodies on the line'. By this, he meant going out to vote in full force and encouraging others to do the same. This seems a rather modest goal, much less radical than socialists would want but certainly not an easy goal to achieve in practice. Moore ultimately has faith in the principle of American democracy. What he wants to do most is not to provoke revolutionary change that involves the violent seizure of wealth and power from the neoliberal elite. He wants mainly to fix the machinery of American democracy to be more aligned with its principle and to motivate citizens to take their vote seriously and act accordingly.

Moore's critique of Trump's authoritarian populism and its role in sustaining the interests of a corporate America that continues to exploit working-class people finds resonance in other parts of the world. In an interview with Piers Morgan on television show Good Morning Britain (2016), Moore expressed great admiration for European social systems, but warned that the UK was becoming so much more like the US, to its detriment. Brexit, the UK's withdrawal from the European Union, is another oft-cited example of the rise of authoritarian populism in the 21st century. When Moore was asked in the Channel 4 News (2018) interview to comment on this, he explained:

> They had every right to do it. They had a righteous anger. It was justified. Acknowledge that to them and then tell them look . . . I'm speaking out for the Labour Party and I will speak to the people who voted for Brexit. I understand why you did it. We broke faith with you. We stopped being the party of the people. We took this country to a war that the United States started. We've been snipping away at the social safety net, the very thing that has made Britain so different from other countries, that we try to make sure that nobody falls in between the cracks, and we've been taking that away bit by bit. And we haven't stood up for you. And we've heard your message loud

> and clear. And we apologize and now we're . . . going to fight for you every step of the way. That's what needs to be said and I think people will go OK.

Just as in the American situation, Moore has faith in the democratic ideal in Europe, even if the system and practice do not always lead to the desired outcomes. His approach to change-making is to use empathy and persuasion, rather than brute force. This is reflected in his documentaries in so far as they treat his exploited and marginalized subjects with empathy (though, some have argued, also with a bit of condescension and moral superiority). They also engage the audience in a highly performative act of persuasion.

Michael Moore's documentaries are powerful. He has an impressive ability to clarify complex relationships and to communicate them in the most vivid, convincing and unforgettable ways. He does not simply observe and capture 'reality' as it is, but actively creates situations that the audience can relate to. Often, he himself appears in these situations, seeking the truth, reacting to injustice, learning from others and pushing for change. He creates dramatic and provocative situations, taking some liberties with the hard facts, to draw strong reactions from the audience, rarely allowing them to stay neutral and uninterested. His cinematic palette includes parody, satire, slapstick, melodrama and styles from a range of genres, even as his own stylistic signature remains unmistakable. The world he paints is starkly black-and-white. It is a world of victims, villains and heroes. Victims are sensitively humanized, their tragedy emphasized. The villainous neoliberal elite are dehumanized and often shown to be perverse and criminal. Moore himself appears as the working-class hero, emerging out of and always returning to Flint, one of the most traumatized places in the US, its people the victims of gross injustice perpetrated by greedy corporate interests in partnership with corrupt politicians. His documentaries encourage everyone to be heroes too, showcasing examples of small and big acts that decent ordinary folks—the 'small guy'—can do in their everyday lives to bring change. This is because his message—a higher truth as it were—is urgent: that America and the world are in deep trouble, trouble of our own making and we all must act now before it is too late.

Chapter Three

Corporate Greed: Health, Education and Criminal Justice

At the end of Michael Moore's movie *Roger & Me* (1989), the prolific documentary-maker announced 'the dawn of a new era'. He could already see, in 1989 when the movie was released, that the 21st century would be an era marked by an ever-widening gap between the rich and the poor. At the heart of this dystopian vision was a self-interested and manipulative neoliberal elite comprising a technocratic government and corporate power that ultimately controlled it. So exploited, disempowered and deceived were the masses that they often ended up making decisions and acting in ways that ensured their own continued immiseration.

In this 21st-century era, documentary movies have enjoyed greater popularity, especially those that reflect, critique and provoke collective action against the dystopian conditions of capitalism. This chapter focuses on several of these movies. You could say that most of them were built on the foundations of Moore's holistic critique of anti-democratic capitalism in America, caused and then exacerbated in large part by Republican neoliberal policies since the time of Reagan. Some of these movies attempted a broad diagnosis of American and global capitalism in crisis. Others were more focused on the pathological effects of capitalism on specific domains such as health, education and crime. Yet others zoomed in on the corporate greed that motivates so much of what happens in Wall Street, to the detriment of the rest of society and, through neoliberal globalization, the world. In terms of style, *Super*

Size Me (2004) and its sequel come closest to the performative gestures of Moore's documentaries that aim to elicit highly emotional responses from the audience through exaggeration, theatricality, buffoonery and big personalities. To some degree, *Inequality for All* (2013) and *Saving Capitalism* (2017), featuring the larger-than-life personality of Robert Reich, also bear this stylistic resemblance with Moore's documentaries.

Capitalism in Crisis

Robert Reich is the central figure in two US documentaries that attempt to diagnose the crisis of 21st-century capitalism and suggest ways of restoring it to health. Reich was in public service during the Ford, Carter and Obama administrations, but most notably as the Secretary of Labour under President Bill Clinton. He is currently a public policy professor at University of California, Berkeley. His teaching on social-justice issues and democracy extends beyond the classroom through videos popular on social media as well as two movies *Inequality for All* (2013) and *Saving Capitalism* (2017), both based on books he had written, the former directed by Jacob Kornbluth and the latter, by Kornbluth and Sari Gilman.

Carole Cadwalladr (2013), a journalist at *The Observer*, described *Inequality for All* as

> A really astonishingly good movie that takes some big economic ideas and how these relate to the quality of everyday life as lived by most ordinary people. The love and care and artistic flair that Kornbluth brought to it is evident in every frame. It was really really hard work … to make something look that simple.

Kornbluth told Cadwalladr that he had grown up poor and had always been sensitive to the inequalities of society. Therefore, the movie's emotional centre, not surprisingly, is filled with the 'human stories of working American families struggling to cope'. In the question-and-answer session, a third of the audience at the movie's Sundance premiere admitted to having teared up at some point in the movie. *Inequality for All* is revolutionary in intent but directed with a light touch and gentle humour. Putting Reich at the centre, Cadwalladr argued, is a 'stroke of brilliance'.

Like Moore, Reich is a charismatic figure of the political left in a neoliberal America that has learnt to fear and hate the idea of socialism. But unlike Moore, who comes across easily as a populist working-class hero who can connect on a folksy level and who pulls buffoonish stunts for dramatic effect, Reich plays up his academic and policy-elite credentials. His on-screen persona speaks passionately, with great clarity and without condescension about his pet subjects, including more technical ideas from economics, his primary field of expertise. The *New York Times* journalist David Gelles (2017) gave him a much tougher description, as

> . . . a multi-platform attack dog of the far left, a verbose gadfly who can be counted on to deliver withering critiques of Republicans, Democrats, lobbyists, lawyers and even former colleagues.

Though professorial in tone, on-screen and off-screen, he appears to have an engaging, even poetic, pedagogical style and a respectful and self-deprecating manner that can disarm his opponents on the right. In the documentaries, he is shown trying to have respectful conversations with those who identify with the Republican Party, even though Gelles (2017) reported that

> . . . Republicans disagree with Mr. Reich on just about everything. His arguments, they say, oversimplify the legislative process, misrepresent the true effects of some laws and ignore the ways in which big business has benefited workers and consumers.

Like Moore, Reich is idealistic about democracy, believing that people must be active citizens for democracy to work. Without a well-functioning democracy, the rich and powerful would systematically bully the poor and weak. Democracy fails to function when the capitalist elite give in to their greed and use their power and wealth to accumulate more power and wealth. Reich personalizes this idea by drawing upon three life narratives. First, he describes how he volunteered to be an intern for Robert Kennedy during the years when American politics was characterized by charismatic leadership, democratic high-mindedness and a can-do spirit. Second, he describes how he became a 'pain-in-the-ass' as a cabinet member in the Clinton administration, trying his best to push through reforms such as the elimination of federal tax subsidies for corporations. He eventually resigned from the position disappointed that not enough had been done. In subsequent years, inequality worsened and his 'failure' has weighed heavily on him. And third, he describes how he has suffered since childhood from a disease that made him much smaller than other children. To protect himself from bullies, he made alliances with older boys. One of them, a civil rights worker, was later murdered by the Ku Klux Klan for helping to register African American voters. This inspired him to dedicate his life to fighting the bullies and defending the powerless and the voiceless. Reich's self-deprecatory manner, specifically about his diminutive size, serves symbolically to reinforce the message that the 'small guy' can fight the big bullies in the system, a message that Moore—a physically much larger man—also conveys in his movies. What both Moore and Reich want to do is to teach people how to mobilize, organize and energize other people for democracy to function again.

Inequality for All and the Netflix Original *Saving Capitalism* are similar in content, the latter in many ways a reinforcement and elaboration of the former, but also an extension of the arguments to consider the Trump era. Both are thoroughgoing critiques of contemporary neoliberalism in the US, but they both also acknowledge that capitalism and post-war economic growth are not in themselves immoral and have, in fact, generated a lot of benefits. In this way, Reich has a more generous view of capitalism than Moore, who in *Capitalism: A Love Story* (2009) advanced the argument that it is radically evil. In Reich's view, capitalism degenerated once the system started to benefit only some at the expense of the many others, leading to vastly unequal outcomes that subverted the proper functioning of democracy and its corrective power. It all started in the 1970s, with Republican President Ronald Reagan's neoliberal policies that included tax and spending reforms, deregulation and an assault on the labour unions, all of which celebrated the ideal of a free market without government intrusion. In fact, the government turned out to be more intrusive in its enforcement of new rules that protected and advanced the interests of corporations and the wealthy. Reich observed how wages, from this time, started to flatten out: the middle-class share of the national income declined, and money rose to the top as the wealthy elite effectively influenced these rules in their favour. By the 1990s, the middle class was hollowing out, the salaries of CEOs and the financiers of a deregulated Wall Street shot up, and taxes on the richest Americans were being significantly reduced with each new presidency, regardless of party. Meanwhile, globalization, technological change and the decline of labour unions saw job losses and wage reductions, just as the cost of housing, healthcare, childcare and a college education rose steeply.

Reich argues that capitalism cannot survive without a strong and vibrant middle class that constitutes the main source of consumer spending in the US economy. Although many Americans would describe themselves as middle-class, those who are still employed often have dead-end jobs with incomes that have stagnated and even declined to such an extent that many struggle just to make ends meet. Noting such high levels of insecurity and anxiety in a rich country like the US, Reich asserted that,

> Nobody should be working full-time and not making it.

Meanwhile, the top 1 per cent of Americans are earning multi-million-dollar incomes each year, without spending proportionally as much as the middle class would have done. Their concentrated wealth, it turns out, does not generate sufficient economic activity in the US but ends up as part of global capital markets. The neoliberal tax system, which is tilted against the middle class and buttressed by trickle-down economics justification, means that not only do the wealthiest Americans contribute insufficiently to the generation of economic activity, but they also grossly under-contribute to the national budget with horrendous implications for the state's ability to finance healthcare, education, infrastructure and other socially necessary public goods.

Reich argues that inequality would not be such a problem if there were sufficient opportunities for people to succeed in society whatever their starting points. He illustrates this historically through a post-war virtuous cycle that had led to the rise of a prosperous middle class. As wages increased, workers were able to buy more and companies could hire more people. Tax revenues increased, giving governments the ability to invest more, including investments in the education of workers, which then led to productivity gains and an expansion of the economy. The problem since the 1970s has been the lack of upward mobility for the aspirational middle class. Reagan's policies had instead set off a vicious cycle. Wages started to stagnate. Workers could buy less. Companies had to downsize, raising unemployment. As tax revenues decreased, governments cut their programmes, which meant that workers became less educated and less productive.

Inequality and social immobility serve to undermine democracy. The billionaires, Reich argues, abuse their wealth and influence to lobby the government for tax policies and regulations that are favourable to themselves and for bailouts when their exploitative schemes fail. In the US democratic system, politicians need massive campaign financing to be successful. Thus, politicians, including the president, can be bought through campaign contributions, and are highly susceptible to the combined lobbying efforts of public relations firms, think tanks and research institutes. Many politicians themselves become lobbyists once they are out of power. This gives rise to 'crony capitalism'. And those who seek to reform the corrupt system are accused of peddling 'class warfare' and of being 'socialists' or 'communists', both dirty words in neoliberal America.

Democracy has failed the Americans who are left behind. There is hardly any productive democratic outlet for their anger and frustration. Their preferences have almost no impact on public policy. In a speech given as Labour Secretary, Reich noted how

> . . . We are on the way to becoming a two-tiered society, composed of a few winners, and a larger group of Americans left behind, whose anger and whose disillusionment is easily manipulated. Once unbottled, mass resentment can poison the very fabric of society, the moral integrity of a society, replacing ambition with envy, replacing tolerance with hate. Today the targets of that rage are immigrants, welfare mothers, government officials, gays, and an ill-defined counterculture. As the middle class continues to erode, who will be the targets tomorrow?

Reich was cautioning against the rise of authoritarian populism in the US. He explained that populism is not necessarily a bad thing, given that it is 'a reaction against those in power in favour of the broad public'. Populism can take the form of 'Occupy Wall Street', a left-wing protest movement against economic inequality by those who called themselves the '99 per cent' or of the 'Tea Party Movement', a right-wing movement within the Republican Party demanding lower taxes, decreased government spending, reduced national debt and smaller government. There are left-wing populist leaders such as Bernie Sanders and right-wing populist leaders such as Donald Trump. Clearly, Reich was gravely concerned about the right-wing variety. America, Reich believed, is at a crossroads. Mass anxiety welcomes the strongman as the leader, who happily exercises authoritarian methods of control, galvanizes mistrust and hostility towards democratic institutions and scapegoats minorities to drum up more support. Or America could choose a reformist populist agenda: restructure the system so that it better reflects the needs of ordinary people. In such a restructured system, corporate power can be countervailed by democratic institutions, admitting popular participation and citizen engagement.

While the situation may look hopeless, Reich maintains optimism throughout the two documentaries, believing that history is on the side of positive social change. The cynical, he argues, should look at America's past achievements to know that even this can be overcome. In the 1930s, pragmatic Americans channelled their popular anger in positive directions, avoiding the authoritarian and fascist route. Today, the rich need to be persuaded that they will do even better if the economy does better, and that can only be possible with greater equality and a large and stable middle class to generate economic activity.

Both documentaries end with Reich professing his faith in students and young people in general who, he believes, show dedication to make the system work and will form the pool from which future leaders can emerge. *Inequality for All* ends back in the lecture hall, on the last day of Reich's course at Berkeley. He receives a standing ovation when he asserts his belief that some of his students will change the community, society and perhaps the world. *Saving Capitalism* ends with a call to young people to organize and use their strength in numbers to hold politicians accountable. And only then can the rules of capitalism be changed. His advice is to

> . . . be tenacious and patient. Talk to people who disagree with you, get out of the bubble. Have some fun.

And to show what he means by fun, Reich dances joyfully out of the movie just before the end-credits, his on-screen showmanship negating any 'frumpy' and 'pedantic' image he might have presented in real life (Gelles, 2017).

Unhealthy Capitalism

Since the dawn of this new era of neoliberal injustice, when poverty and inequality have reached new heights, we have seen the production of several documentaries dealing very directly with the perverse impact of unbridled capitalism on health and wellness, focusing on fast-food, tobacco, healthcare and social media.

Super Size Me (2004) and its sequel *Super Size Me 2: Holy Chicken!* (2017) are highly performative documentaries made by Morgan Spurlock, who is also the protagonist in both. Some reviewers, according to film and cultural studies scholar James Lyons (2019), have described him as the

> . . . agit-doc successor to Michael Moore.

In *Super Size Me*, Spurlock takes on the challenge of eating three meals from McDonald's and nothing else for thirty days continuously. The rule is that he would be obliged to accept whenever he was asked during that period if he wanted to 'supersize' his meal. The aim is to measure the effects of subjecting his own body to a seemingly extreme diet that is in some ways not so different from what many fast-food-eating Americans are used to. The US, it seems, has become 'the fattest nation in the world' and fast-food a major contributor to a national crisis of obesity, which is fast overtaking smoking as the leading cause of death. Lyons (2019) noted how the movie makes obese bodies hyper-visibly resonant with the notion that all things are just bigger in the US. Through something akin to fat-shaming, the frequent employment of over-sized body imagery in the movie creates a 'biopedagogical' opportunity to engage a neoliberal discourse of personal responsibility, risk and danger to individual and public health. Almost all the nutritionists Spurlock consults in the documentary advise against eating any fast-food if people can help it.

Among the numerous fast-food restaurants in the US, McDonald's is by far the most popular. Its food tastes good. The cheerful experience of consuming it feels good. But then, customers very quickly after consuming their meals feel hungry again. Over the years, the serving portions have grown, first upsized, then supersized and priced in such a way as to make the biggest sizes seem like the best value for money. In 2002, two teenage girls tried to sue McDonald's, claiming that it was responsible for their obesity. The case was dismissed on the basis that consumers should make better choices if the consequences of their actions are known. The claim that fast-food was addictive, like tobacco, was also dismissed (Helliker and Leung, 2003). This sparked the idea for Spurlock's documentary. He finds that in many of the McDonald's outlets he visits, nutritional information is not easily available, making it difficult to expect patrons to exercise personal responsibility. The documentary also challenges the claim that McDonald's food is not addictive. The combination of cheese, soda, caffeine and other ingredients, Spurlock asserts, is calculated to play on customers' cravings. McDonald's even categorizes their customers into 'heavy users' who eat there at least once a week and 'super heavy users' who do so at least three times a week. During this segment of the documentary, Curtis Mayfield's 'Pusherman' plays in the background, underscoring how much fast-food is like a drug and McDonald's a drug-pusher.

Spurlock observes how McDonald's seems to be targeting children, through its choice of a clown named Ronald McDonald as its main mascot, the 'Happy Meal' packaging that comes with a small toy and the organizing of birthday parties. Its advertisements also seem to be directed at children. To amplify the point, Spurlock interviews the members of a family who are visiting the White House: none of them can recite the Pledge of Allegiance without faltering; but they have no problem singing McDonald's Big Mac advertising campaign jingle:

> Two all-beef patties, special sauce, lettuce, cheese, pickles, onions, on a sesame seed bun.

This recalls the opening scene of the movie, featuring a group of children chanting with gusto a popular camping song,

> Pizza Hut, a Pizza Hut, Kentucky Fried Chicken and a Pizza Hut . . .
> McDonalds, McDonalds, Kentucky Fried Chicken and a Pizza Hut . . .
> I like food, I like food, Kentucky Fried Chicken and a Pizza Hut,
> You like food, you like food, Kentucky Fried Chicken and a Pizza Hut . . .

Lyons (2019) closely analysed this opening scene as an example of how the risk of diet-related weight gain is performed by employing the bodies of children—including two obviously obese bodies—in the collective act of vocalizing both their innocence as well as their vulnerability.

This, the documentary seems to suggest, is part of a larger problem of food-based corporations profiteering at the expense of children's nutritional needs. Examples discussed in the documentary include canteens in many American schools that serve up ready-made food that appeal to children, even though they have low nutritional quality, because they can be supplied by centralized kitchens offering the lowest bids. Many soft drink companies are powerful enough to ensure their products are widely available in schools, where young people can become addicted to sugary drinks for life. Many corporations in the food industry and their powerful associations have lobbied the government effectively to prevent legislators from passing healthier laws and regulations, which will reduce their profits by encouraging people to eat less and balance their diet (Nestle, 2013). Meanwhile, children and the adults they eventually become are also the targets of the beauty, fashion and fitness industries that use idealized body imagery to play on their sense of insecurity, essentially to body shame them into consuming their products and the fantasies they peddle. It is a vicious cycle of feel-good consumption, addiction, health and body-image problems and more feel-good consumption to numb the pain of eternal deficiency.

Featured in the documentary is a progressive school that has successfully been able to turn around at-risk and out-of-control students, mainly by providing them with healthy natural food. The cost of doing so is no different from providing unhealthy food at other regular schools. And yet, these positive outcomes cannot be extended to schools nationwide because of political constraints imposed by corporate power.

Spurlock uses his own body perversely to experiment, make a graphic point, but also reinforce a biopedagogical message of health risk, personal responsibility and techniques of care. His thirty-day experiment is monitored by a medical professional, a dietitian and an exercise physiologist. At various points during the month, Spurlock reports of stomach-aches, flatulence, throwing up, pain in the genitals, chest pains, tiredness, breathlessness, heating up, heavy sweating, heart palpitations, weight-gain and depression. Among the many melodramatic flourishes that make this documentary particularly performative is the way Spurlock's doctor and dietitian keep urging him to stop the experiment as it can, they say, become life threatening. His girlfriend, a vegan and organic food advocate, also shows much concern for his deteriorating condition. With what looks like nearly fatal results from eating too much fast-food, Spurlock attempts to contact McDonald's to get an official reaction. Like the basic premise of Michael Moore's *Roger & Me* (1989), which records Moore's unsuccessful attempts to confront the CEO of General Motors, Spurlock is unable to get a proper response from the corporate spokesperson. The point, perhaps, in both movies is to stage a spectacular demonstration of a lack of care and responsiveness from these corporations when it comes to taking responsibility for the well-being of the customers from whom they profit.

Ross Singer (2011), a communications scholar, described Spurlock's activist tactic as 'spectacular self-subjugation', by which he gives his body temporarily to an exploitative system—the fast-food industry—so that it may be used to stage resistance against a system that is materially and rhetorically grotesque for a mainstream audience. This kind of anti-corporate resistance deploys carnivalesque humour that invites audiences to reidentify themselves with the food they eat and reconsider that relationship. However, this assumes that people have real choices that they can make about what they eat, that they have the money and the time to eat more healthily according to Spurlock's biopedagogy. But this, perhaps, is a privilege that not quite as many Americans enjoy (Lyons, 2019).

Twelve years later, Spurlock returns to the fast-food theme in his sequel *Super Size Me 2* (2017). By this time, the fast-food industry has a new narrative: that it has become healthier and more sustainable. There are now salads on the menu. When it comes to food containers, cardboard replaces Styrofoam. The choice of hand-lettered fonts, farm imagery, wood-grain finishing and artificial grill marks on the food all signal 'artisanal'. Through this narrative, McDonald's and other fast-food restaurant chains attempt to absolve themselves of the kind of unholy criticism Spurlock and others have levelled at them, sanctifying themselves with a new 'health halo' made up of terms like 'artisanal', 'fresh', 'natural', 'handcrafted', 'homemade' and 'made from scratch'. It turns out the perception of what is healthful matters a great deal more than what people are really eating. The same fried foods are now described as 'crispy' or 'fried grilled'. Ultimately, the industry still wants to serve food with high craveability.

Spurlock wants to expose the chain of profiteering, exploitation and manipulation involved in chicken-based fast-food restaurants. Free-range chickens, signified by the liberal use of imagery depicting idyllic farms, are in practice not much different from industrial meat chicken farming, since the US Department of Agriculture's specifications for the use of the 'free range' label are loose and the definition not legally enforceable. Like most other examples of the health halo, 'free range', the documentary argues, is simply a marketing ruse, behind which are some of the worst excesses of the chicken farming industry, dominated by five companies that make up 'big chicken'. In their farms, broiler chickens, raised purely for meat production, have been bred for rapid early growth in such a way that many suffer from heart attacks, obesity and brittle bones. But these sick chickens are safe enough to eat. The documentary also shows how big chicken exploits their farmers who rent farm space from them. By subjecting these farmers to a rigged 'tournament system', a fake meritocracy, they force them to compete with one another on unfair terms. One farmer who is interviewed explains that big chicken has every incentive to keep their farmers in debt, compliant and like 'indentured servants'. Their lobby group makes sure the public knows nothing of this.

Spurlock seeks to expose the dishonesty and hypocrisy of a fast-food industry whose exploitative practices at all levels of production are disguised by a health halo. True to his performative documentary style, he conducts his investigation under the pretext of wanting to set up his own restaurant serving healthy and sustainable food. He names this restaurant Holy Chicken! He rents farm space from big chicken and calls it Morganic Fresh Farm. In the process of learning how to open his own restaurant, he interviews consultants, farmers, restaurant workers and others in the business. Some of them seem to know who he is from *Super Size Me*, but almost all of them appear to believe that he is seriously looking to establish a healthy alternative to fast-food chains like McDonald's. And when he finally opens his restaurant, his customers are treated not only to his food but to informational signs all over the restaurant exposing the real story behind an exploitative and unsustainable industry, whose practice of deceiving customers, abusing chickens and exploiting farmers has been hidden behind a carefully re-constructed public image. This, Spurlock proclaims, is the

> . . . most honest, most transparent, most authentic restaurant you've ever been to.

While Spurlock's documentaries highlight the addictiveness of fast-food as a national cause of concern, another American documentary *Merchants of Doubt* (2014), directed by Robert Kenner, focuses on the addictiveness of tobacco and the dangers of smoking that the industry hid from the public for an unconscionable period of time. This expository documentary analyses similarities and differences in public beliefs about cigarette smoking and climate change, through the complex web of relationships involving science, ideology, corporate interests, public relations, media and government regulation.

If only science could produce pure answers straightforwardly, then policymakers would have an easier and more confident job of knowing what outcomes to pursue and which policy options to choose.

Science may be the most rigorous means of knowing the truth based on the best knowledge that we have, but this knowledge is never complete and could prove to be false when new evidence and information emerge in the future. Very often though, scientists themselves, even as they aspire to the heights of objectivity, are subjected to ideological framing that privileges one set of perspectives and values over others. In some cases, scientists may deliberately skew their work towards outcomes that are beneficial to the influential, the wealthy and the powerful, in the expectation that they will be rewarded for it. This, of course, is corruption. And even science is not immune to it.

Merchants of Doubt highlights how claims in the past and present about asbestos being harmless, or about cigarettes not being a cause of lung cancer, or about global warming being a hoax are political statements rather than scientific ones. The documentary would probably have included in this list, without discomfort, the fast-food industry's claims about the harmlessness and non-addictive nature of its products, as critiqued in Spurlock's *Super Size Me*. These are all claims that some corporations, which *Merchants of Doubt* describes as 'rich, politically powerful and mean', would want to advance as the truth so that they can continue profiteering from the misery of those who consume their products. These corporations mostly conduct good scientific work internally, but they are manipulative and deceptive when presenting the findings to the public. It took the courage of whistle-blowers to expose how tobacco companies knew as early as the 1950s that smoking causes cancer, and later, that it causes heart disease and that nicotine is addictive.

But *Merchants of Doubt* argues that even the scientific community are ideologically divided. Many of today's scientists who are sceptical of various aspects of the climate crisis, for instance, were associated with the tobacco industry at one time. Some were Cold War scientists who harboured deep misgivings about socialism and communism, viewing any sort of increase in government regulation as a slippery slope from freedom to tyranny. They viewed environmental movements as 'watermelons', green on the outside, but red on the inside. By the 1990s, they viewed the global warming movement, scornfully, as 'a kind of secular apocalypse, a millenarianism for liberals'. The documentary depicts 'experts' who were climate change sceptics, a minority in the scientific community, as data cherry-pickers. These sceptical experts mimicked the format and style of reports and presentations produced by mainstream scientists who believe in the validity of climate change claims, to refute them with as much of an appearance of legitimacy as possible.

Is freedom from authoritarianism the real reason for opposing scientists who advocate for greater pro-climate regulation? Or is the denigration of pro-climate scientists as part of an oppressive elite in fact a populist smokescreen, to conceal the corrupt motivations of those scientists who have sold their soul to the fossil-fuel industry?

Merchants of Doubt discusses the case of fire retardants that were developed to fire-proof furniture. These were found to cause health problems, particularly among children, and they did not really work. And yet, fire retardants are continually being pushed as the solution for preventing fires in homes, offices and other buildings. It turns out that cigarettes are often the real cause of these fires. People fall asleep on couches without putting out their cigarettes, for example. But the tobacco companies do not want to be more tightly regulated or to have to commit funding for developing self-extinguishing cigarettes. Instead, they buy expert witnesses to testify in their favour.

Profiteering corporations often co-opt scientists to legitimize their public relations efforts to deny or at least confuse the public about the harm their products can cause. Public-relations professionals are a key part of this process. A small group of people with skills that a lot of industries demand, they are the 'merchants of doubt' that the documentary focuses on. Included in their playbook are the following:

1. Manufacture doubt
2. Question the science
3. Find friendly scientists
4. Attack the messenger
5. Shift the blame
6. Create controversy
7. Use 'freedom' to justify
8. Delay regulation

Like magicians, their 'expertise is in deception'. They misdirect by using small lies to tell a bigger lie. They draw attention to something specific that engages the public in a way that makes them lose sight of everything else in the frame. Turning government regulations against products that science has deemed hazardous into a matter of authoritarian restrictions on freedom is a common example of this.

Meanwhile, highly partisan think tanks, funded by corporate interests, participate in the shaping of policy debates around questions to which they already have answers based not on science but on the ideological positions they occupy and the political allegiances to which they are committed. Some members of think tanks are themselves registered lobbyists. They have their dedicated media outlets. And even non-partisan media will include their voices in the interest of 'balance', having all sides of the argument represented. The idea of think tanks as independent centres of public-interested thinking has become a farce.

Another area where poorly regulated corporations have made life unhealthier for ordinary people is in medical care, where innovations in medical technology are increasingly being rolled out and then entrenched without adequate scientific testing and government regulation. This is the focus of *The Bleeding Edge* (2018), a Netflix Original documentary directed by Kirby Dick, which offered a combination of reasons for this. First, people are quite simply attracted to new and innovative products, regardless of whether they have been sufficiently proven to work. Such unproven products are often hyped up by advertising and celebrity endorsement. And doctors themselves seem to take an anecdotal approach to recommending new devices, sometimes aggressively.

Second, there are huge profits to be made by everyone in the chain, and often corruptly. For example, many doctors are confronted with perverse incentives to prescribe drugs and medical devices based on what they get in return from the companies that make them.

And third, the powerful medical device lobby exerts strong influence on the state. Although there are regulatory frameworks for medical devices, such things turn out to be far too technically complicated for the average legislator and policymaker to understand. For so many technological developments, legislation and regulations lag far behind. The medical device industry has made enormous investments in their capacity to lobby the government. The neoliberal message to weaken industry regulation on which lobbyists and politicians converge comfortably is that when governments get out of the way of the corporate sector, jobs can be created, innovation unleashed and prosperity achieved. The medical device industry makes significant political campaign contributions. The revolving door system means that when former regulators become lobbyists or employees of medical device companies, they have expert inside knowledge of how to get around the regulators, regulations and the regulatory process. The documentary pointed out many serious loopholes in the US federal regulatory system—the combined result of technical incompetence, irresponsibility, political interests and profiteering on the part of many stakeholders.

But it is ordinary Americans who pay the price for this. The human cost, as the documentary highlights, is tremendous. *The Bleeding Edge* features harrowing stories of people who suffered pain and even death after being encouraged to use new medical devices for birth control, hip replacement, pelvic floor treatment, remote surgery and CT scans. These are stories of profiteering, inadequate industry regulation, dishonest marketing, insufficient training, negligence, physical pain and emotional trauma. But *The Bleeding Edge* maintains an optimistic view that civic action—including old-fashioned on-site demonstrations, activist groups on social media, support groups for victims and scientist-led advocacy—can change things for the better.

By thoroughly manipulating how we relate to nutrition, recreational habits and medical care, corporate power—so weakly regulated in 21st-century neoliberal globalization—has had a seriously unhealthy influence on our lives. The specific problems of social media, so ubiquitous in our lives that most of us would not be able to imagine what it would be like without it, are the subject of the expository documentary *The Social Dilemma* (2020), directed by Jeff Orlowski. Social media works on persuasive technology that modifies behaviour through positive intermittent reinforcement, something that most users are not even aware of. It is, therefore, difficult to argue that social media is simply a tool, like any other technology, that can be put to good or bad use depending on whose hands it falls into. Social media, according to the documentary, has its own goals and actively controls the means of manipulating users to achieve them.

The Social Dilemma points to the dangers of living in a world that is effectively being run by artificial intelligence (AI), by a web of algorithms that keep learning and getting more and more intelligent. Most humans have already lost control of their world to these algorithms. Movies like *The Matrix* (1999) painted a dystopian world where an intelligent system of machines farmed humans for energy, while keeping them sedated, distracted and unconscious of this reality through a diet of simulated experiences.

The Social Dilemma shows how Facebook knows almost everything about you; but you know next to nothing about what happens inside Facebook. Facebook customizes social media experiences for you as you express your preferences in the simplest of choices and gestures. It surrounds you with those who agree with you and with experiences that you already know and like, thus reinforcing preferences and beliefs while eliminating the range of diverse perspectives and values that are necessary for the health and sustainability of a democratic public sphere, as discussed at the start of this book. This creates epistemic tribes and, where oppositional positions are already established, intensifies polarization and erodes the fabric of society. This can lead to conflict, violence and through the manipulation of voting behaviour the degradation of democracy itself.

As in the case of fast-food and tobacco, social media also uses sophisticated approaches to make the experience addictive for the user. Thus, social media is also like a drug. For many, it is the first thing they turn to when they get up and the last thing they hang on to before they go to sleep. So much of the day is spent at least glancing at devices on which social media is available. Even those who are fully aware of the addictive power of social media find themselves susceptible. Social media also plays on users' sense of self-worth, giving them false feelings of approval, affirmation and popularity through the sensation created through likes and shares. By presenting images of perfection and happiness curated by other users, social media generates customized demand for commercial products that promise to bring similar perfection and happiness. Users often end up feeling vacant and empty, in the worst cases self-destructive and suicidal. Young people are especially vulnerable.

Although *The Social Dilemma* suggests that our lives are now controlled by algorithmic systems that are mostly unsupervised by humans, it also points—rather contradictorily—to corporations and their unconstrained commercial incentives as a major source of the problem. Noting how the business of selling users and their data to advertisers lies at the heart of social media, the documentary gives the obvious warning that

> . . . if you are not paying for the product, then you are the product.

Given the vast profits to be made, social media companies cannot be expected to regulate themselves adequately. Governments must do so. However, governments are themselves complicit with the interests of the neoliberal corporate elite. And that is where the problem lies.

The Social Dilemma urges people to come together and put public pressure on the government and social media companies to reform the technology industry before it destroys the world. Just as these technologies were celebrated at the beginning for their potential to open new frontiers of freedom and creativity, that optimism can be reclaimed today for the development of humane technology following ethical design principles. The technology companies have the responsibility to rebuild according to these principles, but they are not incentivized or forced by the government to do so. Therefore, popular pressure will be necessary.

A second approach is 'user resistance'. The documentary urges users to make active choices and not just blindly accept recommendations made to them online. For instance, users should be vigilant and not fall for click bait. Users should try to make friends outside of the echo chambers formed in social media. All devices should be kept out of the bedroom. Children should not have access to social media until they reach sixteen years of age, after which screen time needs to be jointly budgeted in the family.

In 21st-century neoliberal globalization, corporate power has so vastly exceeded institutions of democratic governance, negatively affecting so many aspects of something as fundamental as health, that people must themselves resist at the individual and collective level to protect themselves and put enough pressure on the system for change.

School's Out

Income and wealth inequality would not be so unacceptable if there were sufficient opportunities and common resources in society for anyone, regardless of the circumstances of their birth, to do well. Those at the bottom, or their children, need to be able to rise through hard work, natural talent, cultivated skill and earned qualifications. Social mobility, which also implies the displacement of those who do not deserve to be ensconced at the top, is necessary for securing a belief in the fairness of the system, and thus its broader legitimacy and stability. From a capitalist point of view, social mobility and the rewards that come with success can also serve as incentives for people to do their best. Social mobility means that society can benefit from a wider pool of talent, including talented people who would otherwise be excluded from the system (Tan, 2008).

In 21st-century neoliberal globalization, the inequality gap has become so wide that those at the bottom find it virtually impossible to move upwards, while those at the top have all the opportunities and resources to ensure they, their children, and their allies stay there. The poor and the elite are both self-reproducing classes at both ends of the spectrum.

Education is often identified as a powerful social leveller, a means by which inequalities may be reduced, social mobility dynamized and poverty escaped. The Hamilton Project at the Brookings Institution, whose goal is to 'advance America's promise of opportunity, prosperity, and growth', published a report arguing that,

> . . . In a time of rising inequality and low social mobility, improving the quality of and access to education has the potential to increase equality of opportunity for all Americans. (Greenstone et al, 2013)

The report also found that rising inequality meant that wealthier families invest considerably more in their children's education compared to lower-income families. Tests have revealed that children of various socio-economic backgrounds begin life with broadly similar cognitive abilities, but they start to diverge very significantly between high- and low-income students as they go through the school system. College graduation rates, too, reflect this divergence. And the situation is getting worse.

We will look at three documentaries addressing the pathologies of the US education system, how neoliberal globalization has prevented it from reducing poverty and inequality, and what some people have been doing to challenge the system. *Waiting For 'Superman'* (2010) focuses on the school system, *Ivory Tower* (2014) on higher education and *Operation Varsity Blues: The College Admissions Scandal* (2021) on how elite universities have been complicit in corruption involving neoliberal elite circles.

In Davis Guggenheim's *Waiting For 'Superman'*, we are confronted by inequality in the form of a huge gulf separating private and public schools in the US. The public school system in many parts of the country has become a 'failure factory'. Dropout rates are high, with many students being pushed through the system without achieving the necessary levels of proficiency. School dropouts end up with neither formal qualifications nor employable skills. The worst performing schools, unsurprisingly, are in the most depressed neighbourhoods, reinforcing each other in a cycle of despair. We are told that 68 per cent of inmates in the Pennsylvania prison system are high-school dropouts and, at US$33,000 per inmate, it costs more to maintain a prisoner, who neither does salaried work nor contributes taxes, than to pay for them to attend private schools.

We are told also that in the high-technology industry, companies cannot find enough US graduates to hire and so must look for foreigners, many willing to accept lower pay. Surveys have shown US students falling behind those of other countries, and yet demonstrating overconfidence in their abilities. The idea of the US as 'the greatest nation in the world' continues, as the documentary laments, to prevail in the popular imagination. This, perhaps, will lead to its failure in the global economy. Clearly, the system is, in so many ways, broken.

Politicians often say they want to fix this system. *Waiting For 'Superman'* notes how so many US presidents have said they wanted to be the 'education president'. Many have thrown money at the problem, without necessarily leading to improved scores, especially in math and reading. To illustrate just how complicated the problems are, *Waiting For 'Superman'* shines a spotlight on the efforts of Michelle Rhee, Chancellor of District of Columbia Public Schools, to radically transform the failing system. As a former teacher herself, and not a career superintendent, Rhee can implement tough measures without worrying about the personal consequences of stepping on too many toes. She fires under-performing teachers and principals, and shuts down failing schools. Although these measures succeed in raising students' test scores, she is unable to push for extending school hours, subject teachers to regular evaluation, or alter the terms of their tenure. Standing in her way is a morass of red-tape, conflicting agendas and the lack of accountability that weighs down school governance. Her proposal to let individual teachers choose whether to keep their tenure and continue to receive a modest pay or give up tenure and get a substantial raise—a means of rewarding the most effective teachers—is met with strong resistance from the teachers' unions. In an interview, an obviously frustrated Rhee explains how this is all about adults protecting themselves, instead of looking out for the children.

Rhee's policies target the quality of teachers and their teaching. We are shown data to suggest that students with a good teacher can progress three times faster than those with a bad teacher. Good teachers can cover 150 per cent of required curriculum, while bad teachers can only cover 50 per cent. The problem, the documentary argues, is two-fold. First, the tenure system almost automatically gives teachers a guaranteed job for life after two probationary years. And second, the ideologically dogmatic and powerful teachers' unions refuse to allow the system to make distinctions among teachers. So, it costs a school the same to hire a good and a bad teacher, but good teachers cannot be rewarded for their performance and bad teachers, who cannot be fired, are simply passed around from school to school in what has been called a 'dance of the lemons'. We are told that 600 teachers accused of misconduct are being paid full salaries, often for years of doing nothing, while they wait in the New York City Department of Education's 'reassignment centres' for their cases to be resolved. This costs the government US$100 million a year.

Waiting For 'Superman' puts most of the blame for this on the teachers' unions. Originally a vital institution for protecting and advancing the interests of very poorly paid teachers who had been taken advantage of and disempowered in their classrooms, the unions have now become a powerful barrier to educational reform, we are told. Among the biggest campaign contributors, mainly to Democrats, the teachers' unions wield tremendous influence over legislators. It is interesting to see how institutions usually associated with the progressive left can be criticized in almost identical terms as the corporations of neoliberal globalization for their paralyzing influence over politicians.

But, according to *Waiting For 'Superman'*, all is not lost. In the education system are also alternative schools, particularly charter schools that are publicly funded and independently run. These schools can afford to increase classroom hours and provide more individualized attention to students who are falling behind. They seek to close the achievement gap and create viable pathways to college. They are pedagogically effective and innovative. But many of these schools have succeeded because of the creativity, idealism and determination of a few charismatic teachers and school leaders. In a few celebrated cases, their efforts and methods have been replicated throughout the country.

Waiting For 'Superman' gives us an intimate glimpse into the lives of children and their families, mostly from humble backgrounds, hoping to escape the public school system and make better lives for themselves. To gain access to charter schools, they are willing to travel far. But there are just not enough scholarships to help them afford the fees. There are also not enough places. Many must undergo the emotionally gruelling experience of a public lottery for admission. One of the most poignant scenes in the documentary shows the children and their parents sitting in large halls around the country, where lotteries are conducted to determine who gets a highly sought-after place in these schools. Failure to do so seems devastating.

The documentary ends with a scene from *The Adventures of Superman*, the first Superman show on black-and-white television in the

1950s. The all-American superhero flies in to save a group of children in a school bus that has gone out of control. He declares resonantly,

> The children are alright Miss Lane. Just a little shaken up . . . See for yourself. Someone destroyed his [the bus driver's] ability to think.

To uplifting music by John Legend ('Shine', 'Wake Up Everybody'), the documentary concludes with the message that people should take matters into their own hands rather than wait fruitlessly for a superhero to come and save the day. And this is what they are encouraged to do:

> Our system is broken. And it feels impossible to fix. But we can't wait . . . Great schools come from great people. In every town, people are doing it everyday. People like you. There are steps you can take to create great schools, to create your school, to create any school, to create every school. We know what works: quality teachers, more classroom time, world class standards, high expectations, real accountability. The problem is complex, but the steps are simple. It starts with teachers becoming the very best, leaders removing the barriers to change, neighbors committed to their schools, you willing to act . . . Great schools won't come from winning the lottery. They won't come from 'Superman'. They will come from you.

Most of the documentaries we have discussed so far have provided a thoroughgoing critique of neoliberal globalization. *Waiting For 'Superman'* is a little different in this regard. It argues that educational reforms based on market principles can help improve the quality of schools, teachers and teaching. In moderation, market principles can set the right incentives for good performance, making the system more responsive, transparent, performance driven and just, at least where the interests of children are at stake. As Robert Reich argues in his documentaries, capitalism is not in itself evil and beyond redemption. *Waiting For 'Superman'* shows how, in moderation, it can improve the education system by unshackling it from some of its more regressive legacies, and then making these improvements available to greater numbers of children, bettering their prospects for social mobility and perhaps stemming the tide of 21st-century inequality.

Ivory Tower (2004), on the other hand, takes a more critical view of capitalism, focusing on how neoliberalism has led to a crisis of higher education in the US. Near the beginning of this documentary directed by Andrew Rossi, we are given a potted history of American universities, starting from the establishment of Harvard University, which provides the DNA for the expansion of other American institutions of higher learning.

Fundamental policy changes in the 1970s are once again pivotal to understanding the decline. The Reagan administration cut spending on education and aimed to privatize higher education. It even wanted to disband the Department of Education. The effect of this was to reduce access of the poor to higher education. Others who were determined to get a college degree often had to take hefty tuition-fee loans and were in debt for many years after graduation.

But how did tuition fees get so high? This is one of the central questions that the documentary tackles.

Partly, it is to make up for cuts in government funding. But, as the documentary explains, it also has to do with competition for prestige, prompted by university-ranking exercises. The higher a university's rank, the bigger potentially its pool of student applicants and the more it can charge in fees. To justify its fee increases, it has to offer more programmes and more campus facilities. This starts to look like an 'arms race', forcing up tuition fees to unsustainable levels.

Universities have become large businesses, in fact mini-cities, with a construction boom on many campuses. University administrations have bloated. University leaders' salaries have skyrocketed. Students are treated like customers, and they behave like customers too. Universities trying to attract out-of-state students, who pay double the fees compared to in-state students, seem as interested in advertising their reputations for partying and drinking, as they are in demonstrating high academic standards.

With all the distractions of university life, students spend little time studying and hardly write papers, we are told. More than two-thirds fail to graduate in public universities. Professors, pressured by the requirements of promotion and tenure in universities that increasingly value and reward research, publications and grantsmanship over teaching, allocate their efforts accordingly. Where teaching is concerned, so much depends on course evaluations, which increasingly resemble consumer satisfaction surveys. Professors are thus incentivized not to be rigorous in their teaching, but to lower their expectations of learning and be lenient with grades. In many universities, full-time faculty are being replaced by part-time adjunct lecturers, the so-called 'adjunctariat', who are more easily exploitable.

In all of this, there is a conformity of mindset that makes many Americans think they need to get into the right colleges to secure the right future for themselves, even if they will be saddled with a lifetime of debt for an exorbitant yet low-quality educational product that does not come with any guarantees of employment. Banks capitalize on this irrational mindset, making loans so widely available that parents become insensitive to the actual price that they are paying for their children's higher education.

Are there viable alternatives to this dysfunctional system? *Ivory Tower* highlights a few. First, there is Deep Springs College, an institution of higher learning located in California, that admits about fifteen students each year on full scholarships. The intensely demanding programme, which consists of academics, student self-government and manual labour, is designed to graduate alumni who will dedicate their lives to the service of humanity. Students take charge of their learning, deciding on professors to engage and courses to be offered. According to the documentary, college classrooms are treated as spaces to rehearse for democracy, civility, self-respect and open-mindedness.

A second example is UnCollege (now rebranded as Year On), which was founded by 'elementary school dropout' Dale J. Stephens for young people to develop learning, work and life skills through programmes that include volunteer service in a foreign country, internships and personal projects. Stephens was among the inaugural batch of Thiel Fellows, a two-year programme founded by Peter Thiel in 2011, for young people who want to skip or get out of college so that they can build new things. Through this fellowship, Stephens was able to set up UnCollege.

MOOCs, or massive open online courses, are a third example. Through online platforms such as Udacity, Coursera and EdX, some of the best courses taught by the best professors at leading universities are made publicly available and often for free. Potentially, MOOCs can give everyone in the world, including some of the poorest people, access to high quality education, supported by videos and assignments graded through artificial intelligence. However, evidence has shown that there are low retention and pass rates for online courses. Students often need in-person help and end up frustrated by the experience. If cash-strapped or profit-seeking universities adopt the online approach more fully but without properly addressing its pedagogical shortcomings, students who can afford an elite education will continue to enjoy face time with their teachers, while those who cannot afford it will end up with sub-standard education that they may not be able to even complete.

A fourth example is Cooper Union, whose sizeable endowment aims to ensure perpetually free university education for its students. *Ivory Tower* shows how this arrangement is threatened by a new college president who wants to end free education, arguing that it is not sustainable to provide for small class sizes and individualized attention without charging a fee like other universities. We are told that the problem is not to do with the costs of running a high-quality education, but with the bad investments that the university leadership made in buildings and hedge funds, exacerbated by the Global Financial Crisis of 2007–2008. The leadership now needs to be bailed out through financial austerity, for which students would have to pay the price.

In response, the students organize themselves, protest the decision and forcefully occupy the administration building. They argue that Cooper Union can be part of a vision for the future of higher education, a viable alternative to the dysfunctional treatment of universities as businesses. 'We need a leap', they assert, 'not a gamble'. After sixty-five days of occupation and protest, the students negotiate an agreement to work on alternatives to charging tuition fees. The documentary ends on an optimistic note, that change is possible, even in the face of strong neoliberal pressures, when people care enough, are driven by shared ideals and can work together democratically. As one student says,

> Every time someone says you can't do that, a little trigger goes off in my head and I'm like but you can.

As mentioned previously, *Waiting For 'Superman'* highlights the challenges of the public school system and prospects for social mobility in an unequal society. *Ivory Tower* focuses on the escalation of tuition fees and student-loan debts resulting from an irrational demand for elite higher education in neoliberal universities in the US. *Operation Varsity Blues* exposes corruption in the inner workings of the neoliberal higher education system, where the rich and powerful seem to be able to buy their way into elite universities and onward to even greater success in life. Corruption of this kind makes universities reproducers and exacerbators of inequality, rather than levellers.

Directed by Chris Smith for Netflix, *Operation Varsity Blues* relies on extended re-enactments by actors to re-create wire-tapped dialogue. It explains that there are three ways to gain admission to top universities. Most come through the 'front door', after being favourably assessed in comparison with other similar candidates based on the strength of their applications, standardized test results and interviews. Some come through the 'back door', when their applications are singled out because of large donations that their families make, but without guarantee of offer. And then there is the 'side door', which is the focus of the documentary. The way it works is brazenly simple, we are told. Rich and powerful parents make sizeable donations to the charitable foundation arm of an independent college counsellor's company. The counsellor's job is not to coach the privileged candidates on doing well in standardized tests and admissions essays and obtaining great references. Instead, they use their admissions experience, expertise and networks to cheat the process, creating false application profiles, with photoshopped pictures, that wildly inflate their achievements. They arrange for proctors, whose job is to invigilate examinations, to fraudulently take the standardized tests for their clients. They work with college insiders, including corrupt admissions and athletic directors, to secure places for their clients. And they even try to prevent the candidates from knowing that their parents have paid enormous sums of money to make sure they get admitted to the elite colleges of their choice. In other words, the service includes sheltering the privileged elite from the knowledge that their success is the result of dishonesty, thus strengthening the sense of superiority and entitlement that already pervades the elite circles.

As Claire McNear (2021), writer for *The Ringer*, put it, the movie was about

> . . . mega-rich muckety-mucks gobbling up name-brand prestige on behalf of their good-for-nothing teens, already ensconced in leafy private high schools with sky-high tuition fees.

Operation Varsity Blues reveals how the entitled neoliberal elite have treated an Ivy League education as a commodity, a product to signal status and purchased for bragging rights. Some of these wealthy parents who had not themselves gone to elite colleges experience the prestige of doing so vicariously in the achievements of their children, even if they are fake. But this prestige is a mere illusion, often having little to do with educational quality. And yet, this illusion is so powerful that it makes so many young people put themselves through the agony of applying to Ivy League colleges, knowing that the acceptance rates are incredibly low.

The documentary has a happy ending. The Federal Bureau of Investigation (FBI) investigates the case and arrests the counsellor, who then cooperates to expose the many elite Americans who have availed themselves of these obviously corrupt services. They are well-aware that their actions are wrong. But they are only worried about getting caught. In the end, a whole string of them gets charged in court. Their sentences are notably very light: many are charged with just a few months in prison, for some a mere couple of weeks. Ironically, instead of deterring others from attempting this again or helping people see through the illusion of Ivy League prestige, these sentences make admission to these colleges seem even more valuable and desirable, in a meritocracy that neoliberal globalization has debased but that people still cling on to as their American dream.

Crime and Punishment

In contrast to the light slap on the wrist that elite Americans, mostly White, endure for their crimes, the Netflix documentary *13th* (2016) shows how and explains why poorer Black Americans are severely over-represented in the prison system. The opening lines of this documentary, directed by Ava DuVernay, states that the US—the so-called 'land of the free'—is home to 5 per cent of the world's population, but its prisons are filled with 25 per cent of the world's prisoners. We learn later than 40.2 per cent of the US prison population are Black men and that one in every three Black men is expected to go to jail.

For this movie, DuVernay draws on an impressive range of archival footage and riveting 'talking-head'-style commentary by luminaries such as Newt Gingrich, Angela Davis and Henry Louis Gates Jr. Informed by critical race theory, *13th* points to America's long history of slavery that officially ended with the passage of the Thirteenth Amendment of the US Constitution, hence the movie's title. As slavery became an integral part of the largely agrarian economies of the South that needed to be rebuilt after the end of the Civil War, there was strong incentive to 're-enslave' through an exception in the Thirteenth Amendment that states,

> Neither slavery nor involuntary servitude, except as a punishment for crime whereof the party shall have been duly convicted, shall exist . . .

Freed slaves were thus re-enslaved for the most minor crimes and, to support this, the ideology of Black criminality was disseminated through popular culture. By 1915, this ideology reached a high point in D.W. Griffith's monumental movie *The Birth of a Nation* (1915), which presented and further normalized deeply negative stereotypes of the Black man as animalistic, hypersexual, menacing and deserving of the most violent punishment.

Slavery transitioned into racial segregation, a period when Blacks were treated as second-class citizens and not allowed access to the same housing, education, medical care, transportation, restaurants and other public facilities as Whites. The civil rights movement in the 1950s and 1960s struggled to give Blacks equal rights under the law. However, as racial integration was still seen as a threat to the American way of life, the media portrayed civil rights activists and leaders—including Martin Luther King Jr.—as criminals. The movement was linked spuriously with rising crime rates.

By the 1970s, Republican President Richard Nixon took a tough stand on law and order, and waged war on drug addiction and dependency. We are told that he was hoping to gain the support of Southern voters by sending a coded message to them that he intended to come down hard on anti-war hippies who used marijuana and Blacks who used heroin. By the 1980s, Republican President Ronald Reagan launched a full-blown attack on drugs, in tandem with his neoliberal policies of cutting government spending and privatizing services, which increased poverty and worsened its effects, particularly on the Black community. Through the war on drugs, long prison sentences were imposed on dealers and users of crack cocaine, who were usually Blacks, Latinos and other people of colour. Users of cocaine, who were mostly Whites, were given far shorter sentences. Racial inequality seemed embedded in Reagan's neoliberalism. We are told that successive Presidents George Herbert Walker Bush (Republican) and Bill Clinton (Democrat) toughened their stand on crime as a populist issue for electoral gain. Under Clinton, the prison system expanded massively and became even more biased against people of colour. Many poor and innocent people have ended up in prison, where their human rights are often violated in conditions that are dehumanizing and not conducive to rehabilitation.

13th exposes the role of the neoliberal elite in the mass incarceration of Blacks, pivotal to which has been the American Legislative Exchange Council (ALEC), a non-profit organization formed in 1973, whose membership consists of representatives of corporate interests and mostly Republican state legislators. ALEC provides politicians with model bills that they can use in state legislatures. This gives corporate interests disproportionate political influence. The documentary notes that every ALEC bill has benefitted its members, a company that owns and manages private prisons and detention centres, another that produces GPS-monitoring and ankle-bracelet technology to incarcerate people in their communities and homes, another that supplies telephone services to prison inmates, another that provides catered food to prisons and a prison healthcare contractor. Prison inmates are also made to do forced labour for very low wages, if any. This is the prison-industrial complex, a system of mass incarceration and companies that profit from it. And with multi-million-dollar profits at stake, it is in the interest of the neoliberal elite to keep their prisons filled. Prison reform, therefore, is unlikely in neoliberal times.

While the neoliberal elite gains political legitimacy and profits from mass incarceration, which disproportionately affects Blacks and communities of colour, *13th* shows how the heightened racism and xenophobia of Trump's authoritarian populism provided even more impetus for criminalizing, arresting and imprisoning Blacks. We are shown footage of violence against Blacks in Jim Crow America juxtaposed with Trump's inflammatory words, inciting his base to act brutally against his opponents as 'Americans' used to do 'in the good old days'.

The documentary also argues that mass incarceration and heightened racism have instigated, even authorized, police mistreatment and brutality towards Blacks. In their review of the movie, public health scholars Vanessa Lopez-Littleton and Arto Woodley (2018) explained the African-American male experience with the criminal justice system in terms of 'administrative evil', which is the

> . . . institutionalization of practices whose resulting actions knowingly cause individual harm while divorcing those actions from their moral context, which in turn removes a sense of personal responsibility.

In this way, people may be dehumanized in the delivery of public service. This notion dovetails with Hannah Arendt's work on the 'banality of evil' discussed at the start of this book. Observing a senior Nazi official talk about his role and duty in executing a major part of the holocaust, Arendt concluded that evil was the result of unremarkable people simply conforming, following orders, avoiding responsibility and doing whatever was needed to get ahead in their careers. But this lack of thinking and judgement, rather than some monstrous evil, made them complicit in some of the most awful acts in modern human history. Will officials of the US criminal justice system, indeed the broader public sector, be judged in a similar way in future?

13th discusses racism and the disproportionate incarceration of Black Americans in terms of the unresolved history of slavery in the US, profit-making through neoliberal exploitation and White supremacy stoked by authoritarian populism. But *13th* does not merely present Black Americans as helpless victims. It is also a movie about resistance.

It recommends the use of social media to shock people with the visuality of racial injustice and police violence. An effective example is the video that went viral showing Eric Garner being arrested by a policeman and trapped in a prohibited chokehold, repeating the words, 'I can't breathe' eleven times. *13th* ends with an account of the Black Lives Matter movement and how it relates to the complexities of mass incarceration in the US, having the liberatory potential to rehumanize a society that seems not to have reconciled with its history of Black slavery.

On Wall Street, Greed is Good

Compared to the mass incarceration of Black Americans, a very different story of crime and punishment is told when it comes to the elite world of global finance.

Wall Street is a physical place in New York City where the New York Stock Exchange and many of the largest brokerage and investment banks are located. But it is also symbolic of the whole of the American financial system and certainly one of the most important nodes in the complex networks of global finance. In *Saving Capitalism*, Reich observes how, by the 2000s,

> … Wall Street went amuck, completely crazy, gambling with people's deposits, gambling with the entire economy. These are not aberrations. These are not accidents.

Crises such as the GFC of 2007–2008 should not be all that surprising as capitalism is driven by productive and consumptive desires that can easily turn destructive if left unrestrained. Ever-loosening government regulations since the 1980s enabled Wall Street in the 2000s to produce and sell credit derivatives and other complex financial instruments to middle-class people who did not fully understand what they were buying. This manipulation grew out of control as corporations found more and more ingenious ways of drawing profit from what they must have recognized as an untenable system, a ticking time bomb. And when it did explode, tens of millions of ordinary people lost their savings, jobs and homes, while the banks and financial institutions were rescued, in large part with taxpayers' money, and CEOs rewarded themselves with million-dollar bonuses.

In the 1980s, Susan Strange (1986), perhaps the most influential international political economist, compared the financial system of the West to a 'vast casino', in which players gambled and speculated unstoppably, beyond the control of governments. Two decades later, the world was struck by the GFC. Here was casino capitalism, gambling with the entire economy, not just of the US, but of the world. Knowing that Wall Street was too big to be allowed to fail, its inhabitants acted in ever more reckless and self-serving ways as if they would not have to pay the price of losing. This confidence is buttressed every time the banks and other financial institutions are bailed out in a crisis. And so, it is hardly surprising that we are locked in what seem like eternal cycles of crisis.

There are several movies that deal with this theme. Among them are two documentaries: *Inside Job* (2010) and *Park Avenue: Money, Power and the American Dream* (2012). Directed by Charles Ferguson, *Inside Job* aims to expose corruption in Wall Street, the role it played in the GFC and the ways in which neoliberal government had become so complicit in it. The documentary explains the shocking extent of large-scale criminal activity that US financial companies have been involved in, successfully brushing them aside as mere 'mistakes' whenever they are caught doing it. As the financial sector became increasingly de-regulated following Reagan's neoliberal policies in the 1980s, the committers of this criminal activity have not only managed to get away with it, but also prospered because of it. Against this background, it is much easier to understand how the GFC could have happened.

Exempted by law from regulation, derivatives and other related financial instruments were highly innovative and technically complex financial products that few could even understand. The positive spin at the time was that these products distributed risk and helped to stabilize the economy. *Inside Job* demystifies some of this through careful, clear and diagrammatic explanations that a layperson can intuitively understand. Collateralized Debt Obligations (CDOs), for instance, were designed to make lenders less worried about whether borrowers could pay back. Thus, there was greater incentive to maximize profits by making more and more loans. The riskiest among these, and therefore the most potentially profitable, were subprime mortgage loans that carried higher interest rates. Home loans and housing prices increased rapidly, inflating a housing and credit bubble to dangerous proportions.

The system was designed to allow players on Wall Street to take huge cash bonuses on short-term profits, imposing no penalties for later losses. Thus, there were strong incentives to take risks that may destroy their own firms or the entire financial system. *Inside Job* paints a vivid profile of the Wall Street elite. They are Type A personalities who enjoy lavish lifestyles and own mansions, private jets and other ostentatious possessions. Nothing is ever enough as they compare what they have with others of their kind in a sort of 'pissing contest'. They hire prostitutes and use drugs rampantly. They are impulsive risk-takers, who seem not to have a care for anyone other than themselves, and certainly not the millions of middle-class Americans whose homes went into foreclosure. When they were found to have done wrong, they claimed that these were just mistakes that could not have been foreseen. In the aftermath of the crisis, after being bailed out, they paid themselves huge bonuses. Hardly anyone was criminally prosecuted, and some continued to be in power, still fiercely opposing regulatory reform, masking their own self-interest with the pieties of neoliberal ideology that they had inherited from Reagan's America.

Inside Job also shows how the pathological Wall Street elite could not on their own have created such economic and social wreckage without the complicity of the neoliberal political elite in Washington, DC as well as the academic experts whose efforts have prevented regulations from being adequately strengthened. Those who blocked financial regulation were then rewarded with money and appointments. The more progressive leaders in government, as capable as they no doubt were, seemed nevertheless helpless to hold the CEOs accountable for their wrongdoing in senate investigation hearings, even though the CEOs could offer no satisfactory answers. Even President Barack Obama, who promised reform, ended up appointing the Wall Street elite to government positions, many of them responsible for creating the problems in the first place.

The documentary ends on a hopeful and inspirational note, even as it re-states what any serious attempt at regulatory reform would be up against. Hollywood actor Matt Damon, the narrator who did an admirable job of interviewing numerous members of the elite for this documentary, added his considerable star power to the final image, an aerial shot of the Statue of Liberty, as he asserted,

> Some things are still worth fighting for.

While *Inside Job* focuses on the GFC as a case study of casino capitalism, Alex Gibney's *Park Avenue* presents a broader discussion of the concentration of wealth and power through the institutions of Wall Street and the Washington establishment, and the gradual impoverishment of America's middle class. *Park Avenue* plays on the stark contrast between the wealthy and powerful who live on the North-East Side of New York City and poorer people who live in South Bronx. We are given a glimpse into the extravagant and flamboyant lives of an exclusive group within the elite, portrayed as ridiculous, tight-fisted, entitled people who complain about those who demonize success and accuse lower-income people of not paying their taxes. The ultra-rich are, in the movie, described as detestable people.

The documentary, however, aims not to simply showcase their eccentricities and character flaws, but to explain how they have used their wealth to influence the rules of the game so that they and their families can continue to occupy the upper echelons of society. They have done this, we are told, by making sizeable financial contributions to politicians at all levels, especially for their election campaigns. US politicians, regardless of party, spend a great deal of time soliciting donations and so, unsurprisingly, major donors are likely to have a hugely disproportionate influence on laws and regulations. This would explain why billionaires in the US get away with paying incredibly low taxes.

These billionaires have also funded political advocacy groups, think tanks and universities that are willing to promote neoliberal ideologies and policies that benefit them. Ayn Rand's laissez-faire views have been particularly useful for providing ideological support for cutting taxes and regulations. Neoliberalism's pretence of economic freedom for all obfuscates the reality that economic freedom is only really enjoyed by the wealthy elite through the free market, lower taxes and deregulation, as well as the clever accounting that they can afford for finding loopholes and tax breaks. Trickle-down economics, the ideology that all including the worst off in society will benefit in some way if the rich are taken care of, remains unproven.

America, the documentary notes, celebrates equal opportunities and the dream of social mobility. Education, especially a college education, is crucial for getting the kind of jobs that can lift one out of poverty. However, as tuition fees have become so high, college is increasingly out of reach for so many. The economy itself finds a severe shortage of skilled labour. Given the large income and wealth gap, America is no longer a middle-class society. In South Bronx, where there is severe lack of opportunity and mobility, some of the poorest people struggle to make a living. The unions that represent them have been drastically curtailed, even destroyed, largely through the sustained efforts of corporate interests. They are poorly represented in government, where politicians are more responsive to their wealthy donors. Without adequate democracy, in a country where money can buy almost everything, the nation's wealth naturally floats to the top. And when the corporate elite, who have disparaged the people as scroungers, gamble with and destroy their own companies as well as the national and global economy out of pathological greed, it is ordinary people who must bear the cost of bailing them out and, most egregiously, of paying the hefty bonuses that the elite continue to award themselves.

The US and Global Inequality

Inside Job discusses the catastrophic impact of Wall Street's greed, not only on American society and economy, but also on other parts of our highly interconnected world. For instance, the prospects for migrant workers in China were severely affected by closures of American manufacturing companies such as General Motors and Ford. This should alert us to the historic role that the US and the West continue to play in determining the prospects of the rest of the world in this era of neoliberal globalization. This is, in fact, the theme of Philippe Diaz's documentary *The End of Poverty?* (2008).

The documentary opens with the question,

> In a world where there is so much wealth, with modern cities and plentiful resources, how can we still have so much poverty?

The US, we are told, makes up only 5 per cent of the world's population, accounts for 25 per cent of its wealth, but contributes 30 per cent of the world's major pollution.

Just as *13th* traces incarceration and racial inequality in contemporary America to its history of Black slavery, *The End of Poverty?* traces contemporary global poverty and inequality to the historic colonial system, in which global capitalist expansion relied heavily on the free labour of slavery and the slave trade. Colonizing countries, we are told, imported raw materials and agricultural products from colonies, and exported manufactured goods back to them, keeping them in a position of dependency. The colonizer also effectively weakened the economies of their colonies by imposing monocultures. Colonial ideologies of race, underlined by Christianity, supported a kind of apartheid. Many of these practices persisted and morphed into other forms long after the colonies gained independence, so that patterns of individual ownership and consumerism in the advanced countries of the West and dispossession in the developing world also continue in various forms today.

We are given the example of how the International Monetary Fund (IMF) and the World Bank have dictated policies to independent post-colonies through loans for development. By creating Third World debt in this way, the West and their corporations can reclaim the sovereignty of post-colonies. The money from these loans flows (back) to Western corporations often to build big infrastructure projects in the post-colonies, without necessarily benefitting them. The details of the relationships and the players themselves may not be the same, but this exploitative arrangement is neo-colonial.

Neoliberal globalization is the religion that this new colonialism imposes on the post-colonies. Through the triumvirate of the US Treasury, the IMF and the World Bank, forming the Washington Consensus, developing countries are pressured to let the market govern everything, in accordance with the dogmas of the Reagan-Thatcher pantheon. Developing countries are pressured to liberalize trade and capital, reduce taxes and sell off state assets in the belief that this will enable them to achieve economic growth. Instead, we are told in the documentary, poor people in the developing countries lose their homes, their lands and access to healthcare and education, which—in some cases—lead to social and political instability.

Where loans and aid have not been sufficient to pressure developing countries to neoliberalize in ways that benefit the West, more violent means have been employed, we are told. The US has intervened to instal governments, including brutally authoritarian ones, that would align with its interests. The documentary offers several examples of how democratically elected leaders were deposed or assassinated. They include Mohammad Mossadegh of Iran in 1953, Jacobo Árbenz of Guatemala in 1954 and Salvador Allende of Chile in 1973. This is a kind of 'military neoliberalism' akin to the classic 'gunboat diplomacy' to force open markets in colonial times.

The global economic system, since colonial times, has been financed by the poor. And since trickle-down mechanisms have not worked, *The End of Poverty?* concludes with an exhortation for the global poor to insist on justice from the advanced countries of the West and not their charity. The documentary calls for taxes to be focused on property ownership and not wages, agrarian reform and an end to the privatization of natural resources, so that the commons may be restored and the overconsumption of the planet stemmed before it is too late.

Chapter Four

Destroying Our Planet

Michael Moore's *Fahrenheit 9/11* (2004) begins with the accusation that George W. Bush stole the presidential elections from his Democratic rival Al Gore, who lost by only the slimmest of margins. Gore had been vice president during the Clinton administration. His policy interests during those years centred on environmental issues. He played an important role in putting together the 1997 Kyoto Protocol, an intergovernmental strategy to reduce greenhouse gas emissions globally, though, to his great disappointment, the US has never ratified it. Gore's interest in climate change began during his student days at Harvard University. Over the years since then, he had regularly made presentations on the topic based on his 'slide show' that developed into the basis of a movie directed by Davis Guggenheim—who would later make *Waiting For 'Superman'* (2010)—titled *An Inconvenient Truth* (2006). It went on to win an Oscar for best documentary feature in 2006. It is still one of the highest grossing documentaries of all time. Gore's efforts to warn the world about the climate crisis were recognized with a Nobel Peace Prize awarded in 2007.

An Inconvenient Truth is an expository documentary with a strong central thesis to defend. It is the movie version of Gore's impressively well-researched lecture-presentation, expanded with visually stunning illustrations and evidence for the claims he makes about the danger and urgency of human-caused climate change or 'global warming' as it was more popularly called at the time. Gore addresses his audience in a voiceover that is friendly (even folksy at times), persuasive and without condescension. At points when he gets more emotional, you can often hear his voice lowered in volume and cracking at the end of sentences. Gore reveals the motivations behind his pursuit of the often-frustrating life of an environmental activist in a powerful country that, at the time, was the highest emitter of greenhouse gases and whose politicians, captured by corporate interests, predictably take the most conservative positions on the environment. He reveals how his personal mission has been shaped by several episodes in his own life, including his six-year-old son's road accident, which prompted him to ask,

> How should I spend my time on this Earth?

He explains how his sister's death from lung cancer made him reconsider his political support for the tobacco industry, recalling how as a child he had enjoyed working on his own family's tobacco fields. And he admits how losing the presidential elections in 2000 reignited his determination to make a change

> . . . city by city, person by person, and family by family.

The performative elements in Gore's voiceover narration and his larger-than-life 'rock star' presence make this one of the most arresting documentaries on climate change. As film scholar James Lyons (2019) observed,

> While Gore may have been at pains to stress the 'power of reason and logical debate', his performance in the film was shaped to a significant extent to coax the audience to 'feel the risk'.

An Inconvenient Truth vividly highlights the consequences of ignoring climate change, without allowing the arguments, especially the more technical ones, to become too abstract, theoretical and distant. The documentary features spectacular footage of natural disasters such as hurricanes, including the Category 5 Hurricane Katrina that took thousands of lives and caused billions of dollars in damage in 2005, just a year before the documentary's release. It features dramatic footage of floods, drought, collapsing glaciers and ice shelves, drowning polar bears, the bleaching of coral reefs, rising sea levels, new diseases and climate refugees, joining all the dots for its audience, to make sure that man-made climate change is firmly at the centre of it all. To hammer home the point for American audiences especially, the movie includes a simulation to demonstrate how major sections of New York City, including the site of the bombed twin towers of the World Trade Centre, will be submerged with rising sea levels. The question left on audiences' minds is,

> Shouldn't Americans be as concerned about climate as they are about terrorism?

A similar documentary was released just a year after. *The 11th Hour* (2007), directed by Nadia Conners and Leila Conners, has a much more linear structure that begins by establishing the problems and their causes, identifying the constraints that stand in the way of necessary changes, asserting the human capacity for self-awareness and ingenuity, and then ending with hopeful examples of how humankind is already acting imaginatively and creatively to save the world even in its eleventh hour.

The bulk of the documentary involves 'talking-head' interviews with more than fifty experts from numerous fields, including renowned scientist Stephen Hawking and former Soviet President Mikhail Gorbachev. By interweaving the views of these experts, Hollywood actor Leonardo DiCaprio—the narrator, creator, producer and writer of this documentary—can drive home the message that Earth's human occupants, even more than the planet itself, are in serious trouble. Nature will survive, but we will have made it uninhabitable for ourselves. The problem lies in the way we separate ourselves from the rest of nature, consider ourselves superior to it and then dominate it to survive and prosper. With what seems like natural abundance comes the dangerous idea of progress defined in terms of limitless growth and expansion. We take much more than we need from nature, leaving insufficient resources for the rest of the planet, in a culture of over-production, excessive consumption, possessiveness and waste.

Instead of appreciating how the economy needs the biosphere fundamentally, we invert this relationship so that the health of the economy is paramount, even at the expense of a healthy biosphere. We lose sight of the basic fact that we are part of nature, not set apart from it. The mass media's constant depiction of natural disasters as isolated events has further weakened our understanding of how fundamentally interdependent we are in this planetary ecosystem. DiCaprio's documentary attempts to show how everything is related and dependent upon one another in a thoroughly human-centred story about the only home that we have and are at great risk of losing.

The documentary also explains the key factors blocking coordinated action for positive change. Corporations, especially in the fossil-fuel industry, are at the heart of the problem, treating nature exploitatively as mere 'property', since human laws have not given it any fundamental rights. Politicians, who should attempt to protect the human habitat for everyone they represent, are instead more responsive to corporate interests and their financial contributions. What emerges out of this is a chasm between a public that wants more eco-friendly policies and a government that is in many respects beholden to fossil-fuel corporations. The system—and its vital democratic basis—is broken. Meanwhile, the good life becomes defined by consumerism, and liberal values are transformed into the kind of choices that only consumerism offers. The mass media greatly exacerbates this culture, in which people experience psychic numbness, manifested in the loss of their sense of the world's beauty, for which they compensate by wanting to possess even more of it.

In what seems like an effort to re-sensitize its audiences through the affective powers of the Earth's visual beauty, *The 11th Hour* floods the screen with breath-taking images of the diversity of nature across the globe. These images, stunning as they are, could not but inspire a deep sense of awe and respect for Earth's majesty and a sense of regret for what we have already done to destroy it. As far as documentaries go, this one is thoroughly straightforward in its structure and modality. In fact, if not for the beautiful views of the planet that serve as welcome cadences in the relentless flow of information, this very wordy documentary might be rather difficult to watch given the sheer quantity of facts, figures, analyses and perspectives that are packed into it and conveyed by one talking head after another in rapid succession.

An Inconvenient Truth also relies on the affective power of the image. At one point in his lecture, Gore displays some of the earliest colour photographs of Planet Earth taken in the 1960s by astronauts from outer space, acknowledging their importance for inspiring the early environmental movements. He also shows the 'Pale Blue Dot' picture of Planet Earth taken in 1990 from six billion kilometres away, evoking a humbling self-awareness of how insignificant we all are in the great scheme of things and the fragility of life that so desperately needs to be protected.

The Great Warming (2006) is another eco-documentary released in the same year as *An Inconvenient Truth*. For this movie, writer and director Michael Taylor shoots beautifully evocative footage around the world and seems not to want to scare the audience with disaster shots. Narrated by singer-songwriter Alanis Morissette and Hollywood actor Keanu Reeves, *The Great Warming* highlights the social-justice angle of climate change by focusing not just on its impact on Americans, but also on individuals from many different parts of the world. The impact of climate change is not the same for everyone and this is an inequality that needs to be considered. It is a moral issue, as Al Gore argues in *An Inconvenient Truth*.

The Great Warming is supported by the American Evangelical Christian community, whose leaders had at the time just launched the Evangelical Climate Initiative to lobby for legislation to reduce carbon dioxide emissions. Given the traditionally strong political alignment between the Evangelical Church and the Republican Party in the US, and the latter's strong tendency to downplay or even deny the human causes of climate change, having a segment of the church support the environmental cause in this way is not a trivial matter. And it did, at the time, cause some tension within the traditional conservative constellation in the US.

All three documentaries end with specific ideas for what needs to be done. *An Inconvenient Truth* warns against being that proverbial frog in the pot of slowly boiling water that does nothing. Gore argues that Americans already know all they need to know to deal with the problem. History has shown them to be capable of rising above every ordeal to become the great nation that they consider themselves to be. What they lack in these current times is political will. Gore urges his audience to consider that future generations will ask why their parents and grandparents did not do anything when they could. In the end credits, the movie presents numerous ideas for what individuals can do, including reducing carbon emission; buying energy-efficient appliances; changing thermostats; weatherizing homes; recycling; driving hybrid cars, walking or taking public transport; and so on.

The 11th Hour, like *An Inconvenient Truth*, also notes the importance of good leadership and politics, so that courageous policies such as taxes on fossil fuel can raise funds to promote more progressive industries. *The 11th Hour* also presents some interesting technical solutions involving not only the turn to solar power, but also the implementation of sustainable design principles. The documentary highlights the benefits of mimicking nature, for instance producing materials that resemble a spider's web or mushroom mycelium or building a house that is like a tree. Ultimately, cultural change will be necessary, a slow process to move away from dependence on consumerism to achieve self-actualization.

The Great Warming (2006) offers an even more diverse set of examples of what is being done all over the world: solar panels in Mongolian yurts, aquaculture fish cages in Bangladesh, a student competition to design low-emission private vehicles in Arizona and a performance of an ecology-themed musical in New Hampshire.

Science, Credibility and Conspiracy

In all these eco-documentaries, the credibility and strength of the argument about climate change depended fundamentally and above all else on the scientific basis of their claims. Movie critics often turned on the factual correctness and scientific accuracy of the claims made in these documentaries. That is likely why it was so important for Al Gore to talk about the scientific research that he had been fortunate enough to learn as a student at Harvard and that propelled him to pursue the life of an eco-activist. That is why it was important for Gore to talk about how the meta-analysis of a large sample of published research showed convergence on the proposition that climate change was real and caused by human choices and actions. That is why it was important for DiCaprio to put on display the talking heads of more than fifty experts who not only demonstrated consensus but also legitimized the claims in the strongest possible way. It was vital for these documentaries to present their collective credentials and a unified voice to establish the scientific truth and their claim to it.

Just as important was their ability to communicate complicated scientific knowledge to a lay public. This was not an easy task given the general decline in the quality of science and technology education in the public school system, not just in the US but in many other parts of the world as well (Moore, 1990; Potvin and Hasni, 2014). Gore's lecture slides made very effective use of data visualization tools, which—when energized by his own dynamic and sometimes theatrical style of presenting—managed to hold his audience's attention and made a wealth of statistics and information much more accessible. These eco-documentaries were able to popularize science in much more effective and far-reaching ways than any formal academic scholarship or publication could ever hope to do. In *Everything's Cool* (2007), another eco-documentary released in 2007 and directed by Daniel B. Gold and Judith Helfand, the voiceover narration is clearly scripted to be easily understood, without being too condescending and therefore off-putting. It is conversational and non-threatening in style. Pared-down animation brings clarity to complicated ideas without reducing their significance.

Beyond the science, *Everything's Cool* also explains how a gap has formed between scientists and the public when it comes to climate change. Both *Everything's Cool* and *An Inconvenient Truth* tell the story of how a high-ranking government official who had no scientific expertise at all brazenly edited a scientific report in such a way as to make climate change sound more like a 'theory' than a 'fact'. This had the effect of casting doubt among the public. When this was revealed, the official resigned and went on to work for an international oil and gas company that had everything to gain from public doubt over the climate crisis and the industry's culpability for it. *Everything's Cool* describes this as scientific fraud.

We should not, however, imagine that science is infallible. Scientists can make mistakes and their claims can be wrong or found to be wrong when more evidence comes to light or better analytical methods are developed that weaken or disprove earlier conclusions. Scientists, after all, do disagree among themselves and there certainly are several competing paradigms and unresolved debates in different scientific fields. This is all part of the scientific method's rigour and dynamism. But it does make it difficult for a layperson to know what to believe, in the most practical sense, when there seem to be fundamental differences and evolving truths within the scientific community itself.

A bit of critical thinking should also reveal that scientists—who are themselves all too human—are susceptible like everyone else to human desire for career advancement, reputation, influence, funding and personal wealth. Some scientists may unwittingly, perhaps even deliberately, offer their expertise and credentials to the highest bidder, providing opinions and research results that support claims made by and in the interest of the powerful and wealthy. Science, like any other thing, can be politicized too. And how this happens may not be so apparent to members of the public, who just want to know what the right thing to do is.

The Great Global Warming Swindle (2007) is a British television documentary, directed by Martin Durkin, which features about twenty experts including academics, activists and former politicians who challenge the consensus surrounding human-made or 'anthropogenic' climate change. They point out technical inconsistencies in the arguments and propose alternative theories. But they also criticize what they identify as the ideological, political and even financial interests behind a 'global warming activist industry' that ostracizes, disadvantages and silences dissenting voices from within the scientific community to create the strong impression that science is unanimous about the human causes of climate change. The documentary also puts forth a global social-justice argument trenchantly criticizing climate-change activism for withholding fossil fuels from African countries, where some of the poorest people live. Renewable energy such as wind and solar power, which many African countries are forced to adopt, are found to be expensive, unreliable and inadequate for achieving their development goals. The affluent world, we are told, is in fact killing the 'African dream'.

The Great Global Warming Swindle received many heavyweight criticisms from the journalistic and scientific communities, including two of the documentary's featured experts who claimed their views and research were misrepresented. Revisions were consequently made for subsequent broadcasts and releases. The British broadcasting regulator pointed out several deficiencies in the documentary, though it did not conclude that it misled the audience to cause harm and offence. The UK's Channel 4, which premiered the documentary, believed that it was important to show all sides of the debate, including the views of a minority within the scientific community. Does broadcasting a controversial documentary like this, which received so much criticism from respected sources, rebalance a mainstream bias in the global media and thus help to enrich the plurality of ideas necessary for deliberation in the public sphere? Is broadcasting a documentary criticized for numerous errors an irresponsible decision that causes unnecessary confusion or even mischief in an already complicated and yet urgent debate? Or is commercial benefit the real motivation for broadcasting a documentary that can generate public controversy, improve television ratings and increase advertising revenue?

British politician David Miliband (2007) and Australian journalist John Quiggin (2007) were among the many who described *The Great Global Warming Swindle* as engaging in conspiracy theory. Movies that do so tend to attract a lot of public interest. This movie was criticized not only for being mistaken in its science, but also for deliberately propagating explanations for a majorly distressing phenomenon like climate change that involved plots by a powerful network of elite people and organizations with sinister intentions and destructively exploitative goals. This is what conspiracy theory looks like. Its explanations are known to a small and privileged group of conspiracy theorists who wish to disseminate this knowledge that is well-hidden from a public that they believe has been kept ignorant and misinformed by a conspiratorial elite. Conspiracy theories may seem outlandish, especially when there are simpler, more direct, more obvious and more widely shared explanations along with supporting evidence available to everyone. Conspiracy theories are also thought to be constructed out of unsubstantiated or selectively substantiated conjectures, in contrast with mainstream explanations consensually upheld by recognized experts. They are often designed to be unverifiable and therefore insulated from refutation. To achieve this, conspiracy theorists claim that the elite guard their secrets very carefully, hide evidence to support conspiracy theories and even tactically produce misinformation to falsify the explanations and accusations that conspiracy theorists try to advance. Thus, conspiracy theorists make it very nearly impossible to refute their claims about the elite.

While these categorical distinctions between legitimately rational critical thinking and conspiracy theories seem easy to understand and appreciate in theory, things are rather less clear-cut in practice. Take the three *Zeitgeist* internet movies by director/producer Peter Joseph, for instance, that are perhaps among the best examples of 'conspiracy theory' movies.

The first, *Zeitgeist: The Movie* (2007), makes three interlocking sets of claims. The first is that Christianity and its central figure of Jesus are derived from pre-Christian myths and traditions. It denies the historical authenticity of Jesus and argues that the Christianity and the Jesus that we know today were both shaped by political opportunism. The second claim argues that the US government was not innocent when it came to the 9/11 attacks, allowing it to happen—maybe even secretly participating in its implementation—to legitimize its subsequent attacks on Afghanistan and Iraq, and the authoritarian restrictions placed domestically on civil liberties, as well as to conceal the material benefits that the establishment stood to gain. And the third claim argues that the US central banking system—known as 'The Fed'—is controlled by a secret group of international bankers who engineer conflicts around the world to enrich themselves through the raising of government loans. The Fed, we are told, is also an instrument of achieving totalitarian world government, technologically equipped to exercise control over every individual.

The second movie in the series is *Zeitgeist: Addendum* (2008), released a year after the first. Its first claim is that the modern monetary system promotes individual debt to create a system of economic slavery.

Its second claim describes the US as a corporatocracy, its government and multinational corporations acting covertly to subvert foreign governments and economies to further their own interests. And then the movie proposes a change from the profit-making capitalist paradigm to a 'resource-based economy', centred on sustainability, ecology and abundance, where technology and not politics will provide the solutions to our many problems. It invites support for a new 'Zeitgeist Movement' and a rejection of powerful capitalist institutions such as the political system, banks, news networks, defence industries and energy corporations.

The third movie is *Zeitgeist: Moving Forward* (2011), released three years after. Rather less engaged in telling elaborate conspiracy theories compared to the previous movies in the series, this one focuses on presenting a critique of capitalism not so dissimilar to Marxian critiques. Showing how the world is rapidly regressing into disaster, the documentary calls for a revolution that can urgently restart human civilization so that a resource-based economy—also advocated in the previous movie—can properly manage the balance among human demands, resources and the environment.

The first of these *Zeitgeist* movies is more immediately recognizable as a conspiracy theory movie. The accusations and the claims upon which they are built seem rather outlandish. They are highly speculative, pointing to gaps and weaknesses in mainstream explanations, but ultimately unable to offer solid evidence to support their alternative positions. Often, the movie has to resort to highly suggestive editorial tricks to make a point where the right evidence is unavailable. Not surprisingly, reviews of the movie were almost entirely negative. Davin O'Dwyer (2007) of the *Irish Times*, for example, slammed the documentary when he wrote:

> One really wishes Zeitgeist was a masterful pastiche of 21st-century paranoia, a hilarious mockumentary to rival Spinal Tap. But it's just deluded, disingenuous and manipulative nonsense.

However, as we move on to the second and the third in the series, the conspiratorial element seems to be increasingly downplayed and a more conventional—a kind of watered-down Marxian—critique starts to take over and prepare the audience for a revolution that does not really sound all that outlandish when compared to familiar discourses on sustainability and care for the environment. Taken as a series, how different are the three *Zeitgeist* movies from Michael Moore's documentaries, which are usually not described as built on conspiracy theories, even though they have been criticized heavily for taking liberties with the facts? Is this just a difference of degree? Could it be argued that both, after all, deploy exaggeration, spectacle and performativity to reveal a 'higher' truth, attract interest and spur people to action? So, in both cases, the means justify the ends.

It could be argued that there is positive value in conspiracy theories in the way they use exaggeration and half-truths to draw wider attention to corruption and abuse that would otherwise go unnoticed in society. They can raise awareness, provoke righteous indignation and motivate popular action for change, where apathy and learned helplessness would otherwise prevail. From this perspective, it follows, we might think of 'conspiracy theory' as a weaponized label wielded by the wealthy, the powerful and their army of experts to discredit criticism that could undermine a system of hidden exploitation and oppression. The accusation of conspiracy theory suppresses critical thinking and revolutionary action.

On the other hand, it could also be argued that conspiracy theories may not actually draw attention to the right problems, serving (perhaps unwittingly) to distract from and thus to undermine legitimate questions in a more serious agenda for change. Moore's documentaries, even when they employ half-truths, present explanations that can be supported with factual evidence and are thus much less speculative than the *Zeitgeist* movies. Moore's movies are focused on concrete problems that do not require fanciful decoding before they become apparent. His solutions are concrete and demonstrable. The *Zeitgeist* movies, on the other hand, excite audiences because of the hidden puzzles that they unravel, much like the revelation of a magician's secrets. The connections between the conspiratorial secrets, the real problems facing our world and the prescribed solutions are less convincing. One might also argue that heightening sensitivity to conspiracies everywhere can lead to numbing paranoia, manifested in widespread alienation, mistrust and antisocial behaviour. These would certainly not be the best conditions for personal efficacy, collective action and revolutionary change (Douglas, Sutton and Cichocka, 2017).

Authoritarian Populism and Moral Panic

'What is the Truth?' is such a difficult question to resolve. In our diverse and cosmopolitan societies today, where there are so many different and yet legitimate perspectives that people hold on to, it seems more reasonable to talk about truths in the plural and with a small 't', and how we can work towards making them compatible in a continuous process of open deliberation with maximum and equal access to information.

Thus, we should perhaps be less concerned about the factual truth of a movie—which, as an art form, obeys aesthetic rules as well as scientific ones—and focus instead on whether the manipulation of ideas expressed through them can cause clear, immediate and substantial harm, especially to the vulnerable in all our societies. In times of crisis, for example, movies that incite violence or self-endangering behaviour need to be addressed decisively, openly and with as much information as possible. This should be done not only by the traditional elite, who are often the object of suspicion, but also with the help of other influential people and organizations in society. Harvard legal scholars Cass Sunstein and Adrian Vermeule (2009) recommended that governments try to weaken the hold of extremist groups, which supply conspiracy theories, by enlisting the help of allies in society to destabilize these theories by openly or anonymously planting doubts and introducing a variety of different points of view. The perspectives gained from actively thinking through many points of view is a more sustainable solution than futile efforts to outlaw dangerous ideas, since they will usually just flow into darker spaces where they will have a greater hold over suspicious minds.

One way in which conspiracy theories can be especially harmful is when they scapegoat disadvantaged groups such as migrants, ethnic minorities and the LGBTQIA+ community. Journalists Chip Berlet and Matthew Lyons (2000) explained how historically repressive right-wing populist movements in the US have been successful at channelling popular anger towards sections of the elite or towards other groups that they wrongly described as the elite. Most of this anger, however, was directed at marginalized and oppressed social groups, demonized as enemies of the common good and part of a secret plot by the elite against the common folk. Populists often view the neoliberal elite as having liberal, globalist and cosmopolitan values, which uphold pluralism, diversity and inclusivity. Populist conspiracy theorists portray the neoliberal elite as the masterminds behind policies to privilege foreigners and minorities at the expense of 'the people'. Thinking this way deflects popular discontent from effecting progressive social change. Academic psychologist Rob Brotherton (2015) explained how conspiracy theorists are not psychologically disturbed people on the fringes of society. All of us, in fact, are attracted to

> . . . implausible, unproven and unproveable conspiracy theories . . .

because of the way our brains are naturally wired. Therefore, if most people can come to believe in a theory that victimizes a minority, disadvantaged and oppressed group, then the dangers are very real.

Many episodes of moral panic, as discussed at the start of this book, are phenomena that occur within the dialectical space between neoliberal globalization and authoritarian populism. Media, including some movies, have played a significant role in disproportionately amplifying a consensual hostility towards folk devils. Moral panics are sparked more easily when the aggrieved masses have come to embrace or are susceptible to believing conspiracy theories. Fuelled by misinformation and disinformation, conspiracy theories can circulate rapidly through social media and electronic messaging networks, especially in uncertain times. In this environment, scientific claims are doubted, not in a healthily sceptical way, but in a conspiratorial way, shaped often by extreme right-wing ideologies. Such ideologies often appear xenophobic, racist, homophobic and sexist. They are attractive to the increasing numbers of those whom neoliberal globalization has left behind, believing that they have been exploited by the progressive policies of an arrogant, condescending and self-serving liberal and globalist elite.

The root and branch denial of climate change by powerful quarters in the US today has found very fertile ground in the rise of authoritarian populism, a combination of anti-elite feelings, hyper-patriotic nativism, victimhood and magical thinking, stirred up by charismatic and manipulative leaders. Populist politics of this kind has led to US withdrawal from global efforts that are necessary to confront the problem. Under the Trump administration, the US pulled out of the Paris Accord, a climate agreement in 2015 that nearly every country on Earth has signed up to with the aim of keeping the rise in global temperatures below 1.5°C and, within the 21st century, under 2°C.

In its landmark 2021 assessment report, the Intergovernmental Panel on Climate Change (IPCC) (2021) concluded that all the considered emissions scenarios pointed to a continual increase in global surface temperatures by between 1.5°C and 2°C, until at least 2050. Evidence of human influence on climate extremes such as heatwaves, heavy precipitation, droughts and tropical cyclones has strengthened. And unless we see deep reductions in the emission of carbon dioxide and other greenhouse gases within the coming decades, global surface temperatures will increase beyond 2°C during the 21st century. The UN Secretary-General described this as a 'code red for humanity' (McGrath, 2021).

As we saw in *Merchants of Doubt*, corporate interests that stand to lose profits from more substantive climate action will likely turn up the dial on their spin machinery to confound public understanding, bait public anger against 'elite' scientists and policymakers, and heighten patriotic sentiments around climate-change activism as an attack on the American way of life. The neoliberalism of Reagan's America—the ideology of small government, free markets and individual freedom—will be activated again to delay substantive regulatory actions for as long as possible. As asserted in *Merchants of Doubt*, it took fifty years to acknowledge that the tobacco industry had 'deliberately deceived the American public' about the danger and addictive quality of cigarette smoking. But fifty years is too long to wait in the case of the climate crisis since we are 'running out of time to prevent a train wreck'.

So, what can the scientific community do?

It is still important to strengthen protocols of reasoning, community standards enforced by peer review systems and high standards of scientific training and preparation. These will continue to produce the most reliable source of knowledge for public access. The scientific community must continue to bring greater clarity to the problem by providing the highest quality data and analysis of the situation. But optics are also important. Scientists should try to show that their analysis is politically disinterested and neutral by demonstrating in an open and comprehensible way their scientific method and protocol. They should deliberately form scientific research communities that cross national boundaries and therefore implied loyalties. Results of research by a visibly more diverse and cosmopolitan community of scientists can appear more compelling in the eyes of the world's public. Scientists should collaborate more creatively with the younger generation, who are already predisposed to climate action. Harnessing youthful energies to generate wider public interest in science can improve science literacy.

There should be more public-facing scientists who pay more attention to messaging, the medium and style. Movies are an excellent resource for doing this. They can be turned into public-pedagogical opportunities to raise awareness of the issues and to provoke popular discussion about good and bad science, to hone more rigorous scientific thinking. Alongside the documentaries discussed here, there have been numerous documentaries produced after the UN launched its Sustainable Development Goals in 2015. *How to Change the World* (2015) tells the complex and inspiring story of Greenpeace, the global network of organizations that campaign for environmental solutions using peaceful protest and creative educational methods. *A Plastic Ocean* (2016) shows how plastic waste that enters the oceans, and therefore the food chain, attract toxins that end up in the food that we eat. *Before the Flood* (2016), another documentary boosted by the star power of Leonardo DiCaprio, showcases the impact of climate change in different parts of the world, highlighting the political reasons for climate denial in the US and the benefits of a carbon tax. *Time to Choose* (2016) similarly surveys the impact of climate change in the world but focuses attention on the rapid growth and development of alternative clean-energy technology such as solar and wind power. And there is also a sequel to *An Inconvenient*

Truth, titled *An Inconvenient Sequel: Truth to Power* (2017), which provides a response to Al Gore's detractors and documents his efforts to get the US to sign the Paris Agreement in 2016.

Audiences must be exposed to rigorous and accessible scientific reasoning before we can build a shared public understanding and appreciation of the seriousness of climate change. Otherwise, it will be difficult for all of us around the world to agree to do something about it and to put enough pressure on the politicians, corporations and media organizations that profit from widespread confusion and ignorance. Several of the documentaries discussed in this chapter have succeeded in presenting scientific reasoning in vivid and sometimes compelling ways. But documentaries should also try to appeal more strongly to the senses. This is vital. As psychologist Jonathan Haidt (2012) argued, moral reasoning is often a post-hoc justification—even fabrication—of our deeper moral intuitions and emotions, which make us automatically more receptive to certain moral foundations over others. Therefore, even more important than appealing to the intellect perhaps is a movie's ability to connect with the innate or 'gut' feelings about right and wrong.

Feature movies—with their fictional narratives and characters, imaginary worlds, symbolism and wide range of audio-visual possibilities—can connect especially well to our moral intuitions. Blockbuster movies such as *Twister* (1996), *The Day After Tomorrow* (2004) and *Don't Look Up* (2021) are powerful ways of drawing audiences into fictional situations that resonate very strongly with real life and the dangers that confront us as our habitat deteriorates. For instance, the star-studded *Don't Look Up*, directed by Adam McKay and to date the second-most-watched Netflix Original movie (in terms of hours watched in the first twenty-eight days), satirizes our helplessness to save ourselves in the face of planetary destruction. In particular, the government, media and tech corporations—well-equipped to save our planet from the devastating impact of a fast-approaching comet—come under acute criticism for focusing instead on popularity in the polls, audience ratings and profit. In the next part of the book, we will focus on feature movies like these.

Part Two

Feature Movies

Chapter Five

Narrating Poverty, Inequality and Revolution

Can movies influence our understanding of the world and provoke us to try and change it for the better? In the first chapter of this book, we discussed how the problems of poverty, inequality and ecological degradation continue to confront us at all levels, even as we see overall progress in so many other ways. These problems have been exacerbated by the proliferating dynamics of neoliberal globalization since the 1980s, which have in turn provoked a rise of authoritarian populism in the 2010s. In Chapters Two, Three, and Four, we discussed how documentaries have attempted to explain, interpret and critique various aspects of these conditions, often proposing practical ways to bring change, even revolution. These documentaries, from the most expository to the highly performative, have been directly and indirectly didactic, aiming in their own ways to teach audiences the 'truth' of their world by joining the dots for them. These documentaries connect seemingly disparate people, organizations and events for the audience, giving them the big picture, its significance for the future of humanity and its implications for how we choose to act.

In Chapters Five and Six, we will discuss feature movies, which tell a fictional or fictionalized story. These movies are usually longer than an hour and produced with both commercial and artistic motivations. In Chapter Six, we will discuss movies that feature monstrous figures such as the psychopath and the zombie, with a view to considering how useful these figures are as metaphors for making sense of how human life has evolved within that tense space between neoliberal globalization and authoritarian populism in the contemporary world. In this chapter, we will closely discuss four feature movies that tell stories about poverty and inequality in different parts of the world, where a crisis of capitalism has become so thoroughly pervasive. These four movies—*Downton Abbey* in the UK, *Joker* in the US, *Parasite* in South Korea and *The Platform* in Spain—were produced in 2019, the year before the COVID-19 pandemic began.

All four movies enjoyed international success, in both commercial as well as critical terms. Part of their appeal surely has to do with the effective ways that these themes of poverty and inequality have been dramatically developed to resonate with contemporary socio-political concerns among not only national audiences but also worldwide ones experiencing some aspect or effect of neoliberal globalization and authoritarian populism in their everyday lives. *Parasite* won four Academy Awards, including Best Picture, the first non-English language movie to do so. *Joker* won two. *Downton Abbey* and *The Platform*, like *Parasite* and *Joker*, have received mostly positive critical and audience reviews, as tallied by aggregators such as Rotten Tomatoes. Just a month into its theatrical release, *Joker* passed the US$1 billion box-office mark. *Parasite* and *Downton Abbey* grossed US$266.9 million and US$96.9 million, respectively. And having received a worldwide streaming deal from Netflix, *The Platform* was immediately listed among its top ten most sampled titles upon its release in the US (Kelley, 2020).

Since the 1970s, parties and politicians on the left as much as the right have embraced neoliberalism as orthodoxy in countries all around the world. This is true in the US, the UK and—to a more moderate extent—Spain (Denzau and Roy, 2004; Ban, 2016). Following the Asian Financial Crisis of 1997, South Korea's developmental state also adopted neoliberal reforms and, in doing so, assumed even greater powers, which it justified as necessary for resolving new economic and social problems (Hundt, 2015).

However, the world has witnessed a rise of populism in the 21st century, a reaction against the excesses of unbridled capitalism on a global scale. In more authoritarian 'right-wing' varieties of populism, demagogues use anti-establishment, anti-pluralist, nativist, xenophobic and racist language to galvanize the collective feelings of victimhood, betrayal and anger among those who perceive themselves as the losers of neoliberal globalization. These aggressive energies are channelled towards the neoliberal establishment, comprising a technocratic elite, a corporate elite, and even intellectuals and experts who may not be in direct support of neoliberalism. These aggressive energies are also channelled towards marginalized groups, including immigrants and racial minorities.

The UK's Brexit vote (Crewe, 2020; Bartle, Sanders and Twyman, 2020; Marsh, 2020) and Donald Trump's election as US President (Whiteley, Clarke and Stewart, 2020; Kellner, 2016), both occurring in 2016, are often explained in terms of authoritarian populism, highlighting a nativist aversion to immigrants and 'white' working-class fears of being left behind. For countries such as the US, UK and Spain, the populist surge was especially strong in the decade following the Global Financial Crisis of 2007–2008 (Wolf, 2017), when Spain, in particular, witnessed populist struggles against massive unemployment and government austerity plans (Mann, 2012). Populist currents—not necessarily right-wing—also reached Korea in 2016, when protestors, in the hundreds of thousands, demanded the impeachment of their president for corruption and cronyism. Populist criticism was also more broadly targeted at the economic dominance of elite families, widening income inequality, youth unemployment and economic hardship (Kim, 2016).

These recent socio-political developments around the world resonate strongly with the four movies' central themes of inequality, poverty and revolution. *Downton Abbey* is a period movie that depicts life in the 1920s in and around the stately home of an aristocratic family in the north of England. It portrays British social hierarchy in its most rigid and unchanging form, with members of different classes defining and accepting their purpose and role in terms of duties and responsibilities associated with their station in life, even as they compete within their classes for prestige and benefit. The movie's nostalgic appeal is found in the melodramatic means by which forces of modernity are minimized, co-opted and managed to preserve a pristine, romanticized and ultimately fragile image of hegemonic Englishness and a utopianized social order fundamentally based on inequality. *Joker*, in stark contrast, is a dystopian account of the American underclass's urban nightmare lived every day in the most powerful nation on Earth. *Parasite* similarly features an immiserated Korean underclass living in basement apartments in a country celebrated in the 1980s and 1990s as one of the four high-growth Asian Tiger economies. Both the American and Korean underclasses are living through a crisis of neoliberal globalization, which affects the different classes in each society in vastly different ways. Members of the underclass in both countries are exploited, humiliated, neglected, alienated and set against one another, essentially helpless until their tolerance levels reach the tipping point of a revolution. *The Platform* dramatizes these socio-political conditions in the most abstract and philosophical way, exploring the practical limitations of idealism, realism, rationalism, social mobility, collective action, democratic socialism and armed communist revolution.

Contemporary movies such as these are not only a narrativized reflection of socio-political realities, but can also be engaged usefully in social-scientific inquiry into the nuances of sociological and political phenomena (Sutherland and Feltey, 2012).

The commercial and critical success of all four movies may be explained in terms of their appeal to audiences negotiating meanings and pleasures within the dynamic contradictions between neoliberal globalization and authoritarian populism.

Nostalgia and Populist Pleasures: *Downton Abbey*

Riding on the highly popular six-season television series that preceded it, *Downton Abbey*, as mentioned above, is a period movie, directed by Michael Engler, which depicts life in the 1920s in and around the stately home of an aristocratic family in the north of England. Its central theme is the fragility and continuity of a romanticized feudal order, whose basic structure consists of the monarchy, aristocracy and 'peasants'. This social order is threatened by modern 20th-century sensibilities, those of egalitarianism, individual autonomy, scientific scepticism and nationalist independence. They have crept into and sometimes collided with a mostly cloistered world of certainty, tradition, hierarchy and empire.

The movie induces a nostalgic yearning for the 'old days', an authoritarian-populist fantasy of all-White Englishness. By doing so, it performs the ideological work of rejecting the intrusive otherness and disruptive forces admitted by modernity and globalization a century later. This nostalgia also predisposes audiences to accept their station in life, the duties to which they must attend and the dignity of serving one's superiors in a harmonious social hierarchy. In these conservative ways, the movie may appeal to and draw out the authoritarian personality that forms the socio-psychological basis of a broader nationalist and right-leaning populism that congeals around the politics of Brexit. According to Theodore Adorno and his colleagues (1950), who researched this concept to help explain such phenomena as fascism and anti-Semitism, people with an authoritarian personality type submit themselves readily and even blindly to authority, in the form of uncompromisingly strong leaders as well as conventional beliefs about morality expressed in starkly black-and-white terms. They behave aggressively towards those who are different, creative or have unconventional ways of thinking. They project their own inadequacies on to minority groups as scapegoats, just as folk devils are evoked in moral panic.

The Monarchy

There is a pronounced verticality in the social structure depicted in *Downton Abbey*. The household is literally organized according to the classic 'upstairs, downstairs' motif. As one of the servants explains,

> . . . grace and serenity above, demented kicking down below.

This is especially so when King George V and Queen Mary decide to visit Downton Abbey. The village grocer, overcome by the excitement of supplying food for the royal table, exclaims in pure delight,

> This is the peak of my career, the peak of my life.

Molesley, a servant, exclaims excitedly,

> . . . that we should deserve such an honour! . . . Will you let me wait on my King and Queen?

Carson, the butler, proudly declares,

> . . . I must go where my King needs me.

The lower classes are portrayed as rule-abiding, selfless and deferential, defined solely by the quality of service they are privileged to render to the superior classes, at the pinnacle of which is the monarchy. Cora Crawley, the Countess of Grantham and an American, appreciates how the monarchy's role is to

> . . . brighten the lives of the nation with stateliness and glamour.

Her eldest daughter, Lady Mary, hearkens back to the divine right of kings, when she declares on the sunlit morning of the royal visit,

> Well, the day has dawned, and the weather proves conclusively that God is a monarchist.

Carson responds,

> Who could doubt it, milady?

Downstairs, one or two younger servants are rather less enthusiastic about the monarchy. Their mutedly expressed scepticism is aberrant and very quickly corrected by the more obsequious senior staff. One, for instance, asserts,

> Not everyone's like Robespierre. Let's hear it for the King and Queen.

Actual opposition to the monarchy does, in fact, come in the form of a failed assassination attempt by Major Chetwode, a sympathizer with Irish republicanism, pretending to be a royal detective. Aiming to free Ireland from a

> . . . bloody crown around its neck . . .

Chetwode mistakenly thinks he has an ally in Tom Branson, the Granthams' Irish son-in-law, a socialist, republican and former chauffeur. Branson's republican convictions are expressed in very little more than a lack of enthusiasm for the royal visit. It is, in fact, he who scuppers Chetwode's assassination attempt, saving the life of the King. Thus, the most 'revolutionary' moment in the movie serves instead to re-establish and strengthen, through a loyal Irishman's intervention, the hegemony of English monarchism over Irish independence. Branson brushes off his co-optation and trivializes the contradictions when, in good humour, he says,

> This is what you lot did to me ... You can love people you disagree with.

He reduces deep political conflict to a trite observation of how his noble relatives can be

> . . . silly too and snobbish at times.

Similarly, in answer to the King's brief interest in a recent general strike, the Dowager Countess replies that her maid, a communist, was quite expectedly curt towards her. The movie thus trivializes class conflict as well.

While continuously asserting the supreme power and authority of the monarchy, the movie also manages to humanize the monarchs as basically kind and gracious people, rather than symbols of dominance and exploitation. In one particularly memorable scene, Molesley forgets himself during a royal banquet and speaks directly to the King. The whole room goes silent. Molesley quivers in terror. The Queen, however, lightens the moment with grace and humour.

The Aristocracy

The aristocrats live a beautiful life. They are portrayed as being deeply concerned about appearances, their true feelings and intentions repressed by stiff etiquette and formal speech, sometimes dexterously enlivened by aphorisms and witticisms. They also appear self-pitying. Mary laments the burdens that her aristocratic class must shoulder,

> I want everything to stop being such a struggle.

In the movie, these struggles include being delivered the wrong ball dress, having to entertain dinner guests whom they find uninteresting, having to move furniture in the rain in preparation for the royal parade and scheming over inheritance claims. Such is their privilege.

But the real aristocratic struggle, of course, is what is clearly the impending decline of their class. Reflecting on the fate of other minor aristocratic families like her own, Mary contemplates selling Downton Abbey. Her servant immediately disavows her of this idea, assuring her that the family are

> . . . making a centre for the people who work here, for this village, for the county.

The servant describes Downton as

> . . . the heart of this community, and you're keeping it beating.

In the closing moments of the movie, Carson asserts,

> A hundred years from now, Downton will still be standing and the Crawleys will still be here. And that is a promise.

The Servants

Downstairs is a fleshlier place, where sexual attractions, tensions, seductions and jealousies play out. Working-class bodies express youthful virility. Their conversation contains sexual innuendo and bawdy humour. In contrast with the nobles upstairs, the people downstairs are less restrained and repressed. One of the subplots on a homosexual relationship that develops between two staff members, however, culminates in a police raid on an illegal same-sex establishment, which they narrowly escape. While the pair long for a time when male homosexuality would not be so heavily policed, they nevertheless accept the social order that they are a part of.

Downstairs is also where Miss Lawton, the Queen's dresser who arrives as part of the royal entourage, is discovered stealing ornaments from the Downton household. Anna, the Downton maid who discovers this, blackmails her into making urgent dress alterations to fit Lady Edith for a ball the next day. Lawton succumbs but protests,

> Doesn't it ever worry you that on each table in this house is an ornament that you couldn't buy with a year's wages . . . why can't I have them? . . . they won't miss what I take.

Outraged by this, Anna replies,

> But they are not yours . . . and they never will be . . . What if people were to think Her Majesty was light fingered?

Brushing aside the deep inequality of this society, Anna is more interested in preserving the reputation of their superiors.

Anna's moralistic remarks, even as she blackmails a fellow servant, points to an important aspect of this social hierarchy—not the subordinating relations between unequal classes, but the competitiveness within them. Servants manipulatively compete with and scheme against one another for recognition, prestige and promotion. When the royal servants arrive at Downton, they immediately take charge, treating the Downton staff with arrogance and disrespect. Carson, who tries to reclaim the dignity of his staff, is told,

> You are a retired servant in a minor provincial house, serving an undistinguished family.

Courbet, the royal chef and a Frenchman, refers to the Downton servants as 'barbarians'. To defend Downton's honour, the servants formulate and successfully execute a plan to incapacitate and then replace the royal staff. They joke about being punished for 'disloyalty', 'treason' or a 'revolution', which is ironic since it is precisely this intra-class competition that disunifies the subordinate classes and prevents them from collectively challenging their exploiters. Doubly ironic is the fact that both servant groups are competing for the honour and privilege of serving their oppressors.

The feudalistic social order in the world of Downton Abbey is rigidly demarcated by unequal classes, within which there is much competition, but between which there is little mobility. There are two exceptions to this in the movie. One is Branson, a working-class Irishman who marries into the aristocratic family. When asked if it has been easy to fit in, he answers,

> Very hard, between my old world and my new one, sometimes I didn't really know who I was.

A second exception is Lucy Smith, the secret illegitimate daughter of Lady Bagshaw, the Queen's lady-in-waiting. Bagshaw names Lucy her heir, even as she disguises her as her maid, an act that draws much disapproval from relatives:

> To treat your maid as a blood relation is to unpick every fibre of the English way of life.

Lucy and Branson are attracted to each other. But, as signalled by their having to quietly slip out of the ballroom to dance on the balcony, away from the judgmental eyes of royals, aristocrats and servants, the couple will always be on the fringe, marginalized even as they break through the usually impenetrable class ceiling.

Joker and the Revolt of the Ignored

In stark contrast with the basic orderliness of inter-war rural life in Downton Abbey, *Joker*, directed by Todd Phillips, is set in Gotham City, a fictionalized version of a crumbling New York City in the late 1970s. Wrecked by urban degeneration, social disintegration and a crisis of governance, the dysfunctional city is infested by 'super-rats', its garbage piling up as collectors constantly go on strike. In such an environment, it is the working class that suffers the most, their lives increasingly precarious. Social dissatisfaction is mounting and social unrest—even revolutionary change—seems probable.

In this dystopian nightmare, Arthur Fleck lives with his immobile mother, Penny, in a run-down apartment. He works as a part-time clown, is savagely attacked by a group of teenagers and then gets his salary docked. Later, while performing at a children's hospital, he drops his gun in full view of the children. He loses his job and learns that he has been framed by a co-worker who sold him the gun in the first place. In Gotham, the working class are not only disempowered, but also atomized, competing against one another for limited opportunities in a fragmented, disconnected and harshly alienating society.

Arthur believes—or perhaps makes believe—that he is afflicted with a neurological condition that makes him laugh uncontrollably during uncomfortable situations. He carries around a card to alert the public of his condition, but this is met with indifference, intolerance and even hostility and violence. To manage his mental illness, Arthur relies heavily on medication, which he obtains through regular counselling from the public health service. With across-the-board cuts in public spending, typical of the social disinvestment agendas of neoliberal governments, this support comes to an end. Without public assistance, he cannot afford the medication he believes he needs. His counsellor tells him,

> They don't give a shit about people like you, Arthur. And they don't give a shit about people like me either.

The crisis of Gotham's healthcare system is powerfully expressed in a short elevator scene in Arkam State Hospital, where a man strapped in a stretcher struggles and screams, but his voice cannot be heard over the doleful soundtrack. Arthur's screaming is also silenced and his struggles repressed. But they build up to an explosive rage, as he reveals,

> I haven't been happy one minute of my fucking life.

In Gotham, the prospect of moving up the social ladder and out of poverty is utterly bleak for the working class. Arthur wishes to pursue a career in comedy, believing—as Penny tells him—that he is

> . . . put here to spread joy and laughter.

In the day, he takes on stagnant, soul-crushing work as a part-time clown. In the evenings, he learns to do stand-up comedy by listening to other comedians, taking copious notes and writing his own material. When he is given a chance to perform, he does a terrible job on stage, partly because of bad material but also because he cannot control his own laughter. He works hard, but his efforts are betrayed by the limits of his own talent.

Fantasy and Repression

Arthur retreats into a world of fantasy. While he is bombing on stage, he floats into a delusion of success. His jokes are met by peals of appreciative laughter from the audience. And in that audience is Sophie, his neighbour and new love interest. She turns out to also be part of this fantasy, their relationship merely a figment of his imagination.

Also in Arthur's fantasy are two father figures. The first is billionaire Thomas Wayne, who is campaigning to be mayor of Gotham. Penny, who used to work as a servant in the Wayne household, regularly writes him letters and waits every day for replies that never come. Arthur intercepts one of her letters and learns that Thomas is his father. Eager to reunite, he goes unannounced to the Wayne mansion, meets Thomas' son, Bruce (whom the audience recognizes as the future Batman), and is chased away by the butler. Undaunted, Arthur sneaks into a benefit event at Wayne Hall to meet Thomas, who angrily denies that he is his father. He explains that Arthur was adopted by Penny when she worked for him and that she was mentally unwell. Arthur is insistent and starts laughing uncontrollably. Thomas punches him in the face and threatens,

> Touch my fucking son again, and I'll kill you.

The powerful but absent father he fantasizes about violently rejects him in real life.

Arthur later obtains hospital records that indicate Penny is not his birth mother, and that she failed to nourish, protect and nurture him in his childhood, exposing him instead to the violence of her boyfriend. He was found tied to a radiator in a filthy apartment, malnourished, severely bruised and suffering from head trauma. Penny was diagnosed with delusional psychosis and narcissistic personality disorder. The movie, however, does suggest that this record of her mental illness and abusive behaviour was fabricated by the Wayne family, who wanted to get rid of Penny and her illegitimate child to protect their elite reputation.

Endowed with wealth and power, the Wayne family was able to make the police and public health systems do their bidding.

Arthur goes home and murders Penny, the maternal monstrosity in his life, who transgresses all boundaries between mother and son. As psychoanalytical feminist philosopher Julia Kristeva theorized, we must cast away or 'abject' the maternal, the object that created us, so that we can construct our identity. Arthur's violent disavowal of his insane mother and, with her, the fantasy of a powerful father who will one day return, opens the way for him to emerge as an individualized adult. Arthur now turns to the second father figure in his fantasy: television talk-show host Murray Franklin. Near the beginning of the movie, Arthur watches Murray's show with his dozing mother and drifts into a fantasy in which Murray invites Arthur on to the stage and, like an encouraging father, says there is

> . . . something special about you Arthur.

The audience cheers and there is love all around. Later in the movie, while watching another episode of the show, Arthur sees that he has become the butt of Murray's jokes, directed mean-spiritedly at a video clip of his failed stand-up routine. He accepts an invitation to be a guest on the show, even though it is obvious Murray is setting him up for further humiliation, a second paternal betrayal. On the show, Arthur confesses to shooting three executives from Wayne Investments, a high-profile crime reminiscent of the real-life public uproar in 1984 surrounding the New York trial of 'subway vigilante' Bernard Goetz. Arthur exclaims,

> Everyone is awful these days. It's enough to make you crazy . . . nobody's civil anymore . . . you [Murray] just wanted to make fun of me.

He then shoots Murray on the show: at one level, an act of vengeance for the humiliation he had to endure; at a deeper level, this is symbolic patricide, the total renunciation of structure, law and order, a decisive point in Arthur's descent into madness, obsession and violent criminality.

Meritocracy's Winners and Losers

While campaigning to be mayor, Thomas Wayne—presented as a Donald Trump-like figure—offers his neoliberal, right-wing interpretation of the subway murders. He celebrates the individuals

> . . . who make something of themselves . . .

in a meritocratic society. And he condemns its losers as envious and cowardly people who hide behind masks to commit acts of violence against the successful. Thomas calls the losers 'clowns' and asserts that there is something fundamentally wrong with them. The neoliberal elite celebrate their achievements, while obfuscating their hidden privilege as well as the structural and systemic barriers to social mobility that prevent the disadvantaged from advancing in life. Thomas seeks political power to match his corporate wealth, projecting himself as a saviour, promising to lift everyone out of poverty if he is elected mayor. In the opulent Wayne Hall, where Thomas violently rejects Arthur, the Gotham elite, dressed in black tie, congregate to watch the movie *Modern Times* (1936). They laugh in enjoyment at the comedic antics of another clown, Charlie Chaplin, performing in a movie about exploitation, alienation and hardship in industrial society during the 1930s' Great Depression.

As the elite continue blissfully to enjoy their gilded lives, working-class immiseration reaches an unbearable point. The response to Arthur's subway murders exposes deep problems of social injustice, inspiring social unrest. His clown costume and Thomas' reference to the poor as clowns inspire a new populist movement, dubbed 'Kill the Rich', in which rioters take to the streets wearing clown masks. By the end of the movie, there is rioting, looting and burning in Gotham. Bullied and ignored, Arthur and the underclass can no longer conceal their rage, which explodes into violence and brutality. Amidst the chaos, Bruce witnesses the murder of both his parents in a dark alley, a traumatic episode that drives the future Bruce to fight crime as his alter-ego, Batman. Arthur says,

> I'm not political, I'm just trying to make people laugh . . .

Yet, he emerges out of the chaos and despair as a deviant 'revolutionary' populist hero, foreshadowing Batman's later emergence as his 'reactionary' neoliberal-elite nemesis.

The critical relevance of *Joker* to contemporary life in the US is clear. Craig Mazin (2019) explains,

> The Joker doesn't exist because someone made him that way. The Joker exists because no one bothered to help.

In a review, Owen Gleiberman (2019) argues,

> What it's expressing is the inner tenor of a certain moment in time—in America, and maybe the world—when hate has begun to take over. The culprits seem obvious enough. A U.S. president who revels in any destruction he can cause, flaunting his lack of empathy, demonizing those who aren't 'normal' Americans. The followers who support and mimic whatever he does, as if they were part of a cult of white rage.

And Michael Moore (2019) observes,

> This movie is not about Trump. It's about the America that gave us Trump—the America which feels no need to help the outcast, the destitute. The America where the filthy rich just get richer and filthier. Except in this story a discomfiting question is posed: What if one day the dispossessed decide to fight back?

Parasite, Crisis and Ghosts from the Basement

Like *Joker*, the genre-ambiguous and tone-shifting movie *Parasite*, directed by Bong Joon-ho, portrays parts of the Korean working class as an exploited underclass of impoverished and ignored people, banished to the city's underbelly. But unlike the underclass in *Joker*, they are depicted as grifters, cunning enough to outsmart, and at times even confidently dominate, their social superiors in a world painted in the most cynical colours. Quite unlike virtuous East Asian models of meritocracy (Bell and Li, 2013), where talent and hard work are conscientiously identified and rewarded with upward mobility, prestige and leadership positions, the world of *Parasite* is based on a realist view that winning can only really be the result of successful scheming, cheating and manipulation in a world that is patently unfair, where the rich get richer and the poor more distant from anything even remotely like an equal opportunity. This is economic Darwinism at its most grotesque. The line between exploited and exploiter, between victim and villain, is unclear. Everyone turns out to be monstrous, each one a parasite that feeds selfishly and greedily on others in this socially interdependent ecosystem, in which tragedy emerges in the most unexpected and spectacular ways, with nobody really winning in the end.

Upstairs, Downstairs

Parasite plays on the parallels between social and spatial verticality in ostensibly similar ways to *Downton Abbey*. The Kim family are part of an underclass that literally inhabits bug-infested basement apartments beneath upper-class homes. With no means of their own, the underclass lives parasitically off the well-to-do families upstairs. Unable to pay their telephone bills, for instance, the Kims mooch off their upstairs neighbour's Wi-Fi. They leave their windows open when there is outdoor fumigation, enduring the severe discomfort of breathing in the poisonous fumes, to kill the pests in their home without paying for the service.

As a metaphor for the underclass, pests are a dominant motif in the movie, repugnant and yet difficult to be rid of, like Gotham's super-rats. So internalized is this metaphor that Chung-sook, mother of the Kim family, teases her husband Ki-taek in front of their children, calling him a cockroach that scurries away whenever his superiors enter the room. The joke quickly turns into a quarrel and then a physical fight. The couple then reveals that they are only playfully pretending to fight. But the deep-seated resentment, beneath the quality of resilience that cockroaches represent, is obvious.

While *Joker* provides only a brief caricature of upper-class life, splendidly cocooned for the most part from the horrors of urban poverty, *Parasite* presents the upper-class world in a fully elaborated form, in fact the primary site of class struggle. The wealthy and successful Park family live in a large modern home, designed by a famous architect.

In stark contrast to the Kim basement home, which is subterranean, cramped, messy and smelly, the Park home sits high walled and elevated on a hill, bathed in sunlight and surrounded by a beautiful garden. The many staircases and open spaces of the sophisticated interior evoke the feel of rising, reflecting the upward mobility and elevated status of the successful in Korean society. In this gracefully designed interior, people move elegantly and are moved by the spirit of creativity, all upper-middle-class affectations that obscure the injuries inflicted by neoliberal globalization that have made all this beauty possible. Everywhere, there are ostentatious markers of success and wealth, from the family portraiture to the insignia of achievement. Nathan, the young and virile patriarch of the Park family, is an award-winning innovator in the world of augmented reality and high-tech gaming. The industry is an example of a larger trend known as the Fourth Industrial Revolution, where—just as we discussed before—data, artificial intelligence, automation and the internet of things have started to disrupt the traditional economy. These disruptions have made many jobs obsolete and put many people—including those from the middle class—out of work.

Reputation and public image are of great importance to the Parks, fuelling their vanity and sense of entitlement. They go glamping to celebrate their little son's birthday. Their three dogs enjoy meticulously individualized menus. They drink Voss water, signifying the ability and willingness to pay an exorbitant price for basic items. The West is a powerful signifier of high-class status. The Parks' elitism is derived from a stylized idea of rugged, affluent and liberal America in the Korean social imaginary, shaped by a complex historical and geopolitical relationship that has evolved since the Korean War in the 1950s. More interested in the brand provenance than the products themselves, Yeon-gyo buys her young son Da-song a bow-and-arrow toy set and a 'tee-pee'-style tent from the US. She sends him to join the cub scouts to learn focus and moderation.

> American Indian is the very spirit of the cub scouts,

she is told. The Native American motif is interesting in the parallels that can be found between European settlers who brutally took possession of lands belonging to the first nations in America, and the ways in which economic development and neoliberal globalization have transformed traditional and indigenous Korean culture and community, sometimes brutally. Quite ironically, the privileged Park family can afford to appropriate the stereotyped imagery of a subjugated indigenous people, victimized and debased by a foreign power so admired by the Korean elite. The Native American reference here also foreshadows the violent 'revolutionary' ending of the movie, when conquered and immiserated people attempt to rise forcefully and reclaim their dignity but end up with more deaths on their side.

The movie makes clear that the elite and the working class live parasitically off each other in essentially interdependent ways. Elite families like the Parks need the services of working-class people to make their lives functional and comfortable, but they are disdainful towards this class. Several times in the movie, Nathan and Yeon-gyo make casual reference to the offensive odour of working-class people. They try to describe it to each other as the smell of a basement, an old radish, a boiled rag or the 'special smell' of people who ride the subway. Later, while riding in their car and unable to tolerate the body odour of Ki-taek, who by this time has connived to become the family driver, Yeon-gyo covers her nose and rolls down the window in disgust. Throughout the scene, the details of Ki-taek's facial expression reveal years of humiliation and pent-up anger over both small and large indignities with which the lower classes have had to put up for all their lives.

Moving Up

While much of the movie is about how the upper class looks down on the impoverished working class, living parasitically in their metaphorical and sometimes literal 'basements', the movie also offers a bleak perspective on the prospects for social mobility and meritocracy, which is commonly held up as an organizing principle of East Asian societies (Bell and Li, 2013), among which Korea is considered the most Confucianist.

At the start of the movie, the Kims are shown making a living by folding pizza boxes, which they fail to do satisfactorily, almost losing some of their already meagre earnings, if not for some quick-witted actions. In fact, the Kims are a family of quick-witted people, who find themselves at the bottom of the social ladder after losing employment in an economic downturn. Ki-taek says,

> . . . an opening for a security guard [position] attracts 500 university graduates.

So, in a country that prioritizes education, even a university degree is no guarantee of success.

Nevertheless, it is a university degree that must first be achieved before there is even a chance of progressing up the social ladder. This is something Ki-woo and Ki-jung, the son and daughter of the Kim family, lack. So, at his friend's recommendation, Ki-woo takes a job as an English-language tutor to the daughter of the Park family, Da-hye. He forges a diploma from the prestigious Yonsei University and manages to impress the Parks, who decide to call him 'Kevin'. Thus, the Kims begin their vigorous ascent into the upper-class world through a series of confidence tricks that play on the dependency that the wealthy have developed on lower-class labour. Next, Ki-jung pretends to be a US-trained art teacher and therapist, adopts 'Jessica' as her Western name and is also hired by the Park family to tutor their hyperactive son Da-song, who she soon learns was traumatized when he thought he saw a ghost in the house. All the street-smart 'Jessica' has to do to prepare for the job interview and impress the Parks is to google 'art therapy' and ad-lib the rest. This reflects the innate intelligence and cunning of the underclass, and the ignorance and naivete of the upper class.

Servants, in this upper-class world, are portrayed as a more privileged segment of the working class. Housekeepers and drivers—like the ones in *Downton Abbey*—get to work and live in a luxurious environment and to draw on the exalted status of their employers to behave arrogantly towards their working-class inferiors. Eyeing these servant positions in the Park household, 'Jessica' frames their driver for sexual indiscretion and persuades the Parks to hire Ki-taek (who they do not know is her father) as his replacement. They go on to trick the Parks into thinking that their long-serving housekeeper Moon-gwang has tuberculosis, convincing them to hire Chung-sook (who they also do not know is the mother) as her replacement.

Disempowered by a deeply unequal society, the Kims possess only what James C. Scott (1985) called the 'weapons of the weak', the little acts of resistance that, in this case, include seduction, flattery, adaptability, strategic thinking, deceptiveness and superior acting skills. These weapons seem, at first, adequate to gradually move them out of poverty by winning the trust of the gullible elite. In a moment of great irony, Yeon-gyo remarks,

> Jessica, you're too young and innocent! You have a lot to learn about people.

Drunken banter between Ki-taek and Chung-sook reveal their almost contemptuous regard for the elite:

> . . . this family is so gullible, right? The madame especially . . . She's so naïve and nice. She's rich, but still nice. / Not rich but still nice. Nice because she's rich . . . Hell, if I had all this money. I'd be nice too! Even nicer / Rich people are naïve. No resentments. No creases on them. / It all gets ironed out. Money is an iron.

But the Kims' upward mobility is not without limits. Nathan pays much attention to a line he draws that the lower classes must never cross.

While some social mobility may be achieved through guile and dishonesty, exploiting a basic dependency that the elite have on the working class, it also highlights how the Kims show no compunction about stepping on other members of the working class to rise. As in the case of *Downton Abbey*'s servant class and *Joker*'s underclass, moral solidarity and collective action against exploitation are difficult to achieve among workers who compete with one another just to survive. When Ki-taek feels guilty and expresses concern for the driver who was unfairly dismissed, 'Jessica' snaps at him,

> Fucking hell! We're the ones who need help. Worry about us, okay?

Here is the economic Darwinism that prevents the exploited from working together as a class to overcome their exploiters. Instead, the exploited are themselves exploiters.

Crisis and the Return of the Repressed

The storm is one of the most symbolically important moments in the movie. To the Parks, the storm is little more than an inconvenience that puts an end to their extravagant glamping trip to celebrate the birthday of their youngest son. In fact, from the comfort of their living room, they can sit back and enjoy watching through their glass walls the cleansing and therapeutic effect of rain. For the Kims and other poor families in their neighbourhood, the torrential rains flood their basement apartments with sewage, destroying most of what little they possess. The struggle to bail out the water from their home is futile. In one of the most poignant scenes, sewage shoots out of their toilet bowl as 'Jessica' helplessly and calmly sits on the cover, smoking her last cigarette. In the aftermath, the poor families gather in a community shelter, their homes and possessions severely damaged. In contrast, the Parks decide to make 'lemons into lemonade' and organize an impromptu garden party after the storm. 'Kevin' and 'Jessica' are invited to the party and their parents are summoned to the Park residence to prepare for the elaborate event. As Chung-sook single-handedly labours to set up the garden furniture, Nathan tells her to do it quietly as his little boy is still asleep. Whether it is the Asian Financial Crisis of 1997, or the GFC in 2007–2008, or the COVID-19 pandemic that broke out shortly after the movie's release, crisis affects the different classes in profoundly different ways.

The climax of the movie occurs during the party, which is organized to celebrate Da-song's birthday. It is also designed to help him recover from his trauma of seeing a 'ghost' in the house. They ask 'Jessica' to bring in the birthday cake and then have Nathan and Ki-taek, dressed as 'bad' Native Americans, jump out of the bushes and pretend to attack her. This will create an opportunity for Da-song—who is dressed as a 'good' Native American—to rescue her, save the day and advance through a rite of passage into normal life.

However, the plan is completely disrupted by the emergence of Geun-sae, a man who has been hiding for about four years in the Parks' secret bunker below the basement, unbeknownst to anyone other than his wife, Moon-gwang, the replaced housekeeper. Geun-sae knocks

'Kevin' unconscious, kills 'Jessica' just as she is bringing in the cake and then attempts to kill Chung-sook, who narrowly escapes death by stabbing Geun-sae with a meat skewer. In his dying moments, he salutes Nathan, exclaiming, 'Respect!' But Nathan simply pushes him aside to retrieve his car keys trapped under his dying body. Ki-taek is triggered when he notices Nathan covering his nose in disgust at Geun-sae's smell and stabs him to death, escaping into the secret basement where he remains hidden from everyone.

Geun-sae is a very important figure in the movie. He was a failed businessman who fell into deep indebtedness and did not qualify for the national pension. The movie's political-economic context often refers to the Korean government's austerity and neoliberal propensity for social disinvestment, even in a time of national crisis. Unable to repay loan-sharks, he needed to hide to save his life. In the womb-like safety of the hidden basement, he is infantilized and behaves like a child, in fact like a prisoner with great respect and affection for his jailor. Geun-sae operates the 'automatic' lighting in the house by banging his head against the switches. He also uses this same mechanism to send Nathan signals of praise and gratitude in Morse code. At the end of each message, Geun-sae ritually salutes the family and exclaims, 'Respect!' The Parks are completely unaware of any of this and think that the lights come on due to electronic motion sensors. The ideology of respecting superiors and their sense of entitlement, akin to the code that the *Downton Abbey* servants abide by, becomes so ingrained in the material world of the upper class that they hardly notice the extent of labour that goes into making their comfortable lives possible. This is what feminist scholar Peggy McIntosh (1988), referring to American society, called 'privilege', a hidden structure of advantage that the elite enjoy, often without having earned it or even being conscious of it.

Hiding for so many years in the deepest basement, unknown to almost everyone, Geun-sae is the horrifically primal object of exploitation. He was a contributor to Korean society's meteoric rise from post-war abject poverty to sterling economic success as an Asian 'tiger economy'. Once also a beneficiary of this success, in neoliberal times, he has become its victim. Losers in meritocratic society are sometimes put on display to magnify the success of the winners and to serve as a warning to others against indolence and complacency. But losers whose visible presence assaults the legitimacy of meritocracy by showing up its injustice and inhumanity are instead repressed, hidden away in the 'unconscious' parts of society so that it can get on with neoliberal life, pretending to others and to themselves that nothing is wrong.

Austrian founder of psychoanalysis Sigmund Freud (1915) famously introduced the modern concept of the 'unconscious' mind, where unpleasant or unacceptable thoughts, feelings, desires and memories are repressed and thus eliminated from consciousness. But what has been repressed in these 'sub-basements' of the mind remain influential, always threatening to return. The 'ghost' that Da-song—the spoilt child who represents the future of neoliberal elitism—encounters in his moment of trauma is, in fact, Geun-sae, who emerged momentarily from hiding in the middle of the night. The casualties and cruelty of neoliberalism, repressed into the unconscious of the wealthy, successful and powerful elite, continue to haunt their affluent and comfortable world. And at some tipping point, they might return, violently. And so, Geun-sae, who stands for an exploitative society's unconscionable yet forgotten guilt and shame, emerges violently from the hidden basements of society's consciousness and takes revenge of the most gruesome kind.

Thus, the superstition—the soothing neoliberal ideology—that the Parks tell themselves,

> They say a ghost in the house brings wealth . . .

is shattered. And yet, the movie ends with Ki-woo dreaming about achieving wealth and success in his society, buying the Parks' house and releasing his father from the secret basement where he continues to hide. The fantasy of neoliberalism—that all that matters is that one should do whatever it takes to become rich in and through the system—is still powerful and ultimately unshatterable.

The Dialectic of Revolution in *The Platform*

Of the four movies, the Spanish-language *The Platform*, directed by Galder Gaztelu-Urrutia, is the most conceptual, highlighting aspects of the 'dark side of capitalism' (Kelley, 2020) such as inequality, poverty and violence, while exploring the prospects of social mobility, collective action and revolution.

The movie centres on a fictional social system known as The Pit, or formally a 'Vertical Self-Management Centre'. There is no background on how this system came about or how it relates to other social and political institutions. Individuals join The Pit for a fixed period, voluntarily or involuntarily, to gain some benefit or to serve out a punishment. Everyone is allowed to take with them one item from the outside world. There is a basic tower-like architecture, at the top of which is a kitchen where chefs produce gourmet cuisine every day, plating each dish beautifully under watchful supervision. Below the kitchen are more than 300 levels of square windowless cells. In the middle of each cell on each level is a square opening through which a table of food prepared by the kitchen descends every day, stopping on each level for a fixed period to allow occupants of each room to eat whatever is on it. But they are not allowed to keep any food once the table moves. Two individuals are allocated to each level. At the end of every month, they are moved to a different level, in a seemingly random fashion.

This sets up an interesting dynamic. Those occupying the higher levels, closer to the kitchen, can enjoy the most amount of food, of greater variety and in better condition. Those many levels down will have to contend with the leftovers, which by that time may be already inedible or simply non-existent. As it turns out, those at the top not only eat more than they need, but they also mischievously destroy the food that they do not eat. Those occupying the next levels have food to eat, but it is in an unpalatable and unhygienic condition. And they too spit on the food for those below, since those above them, they believe, have done the same. Those at the bottom levels have almost nothing left, and so they either starve or—as we learn later—resort to cannibalism. The bottom levels are brutal. To do well in this system, one needs to have during the bad months the capacity and genetic predisposition for survival, as well as the ingenuity to protect oneself from harm and to identify and pursue opportunities to survive and flourish. But ultimately, luck determines the floor on which one finds oneself every month. This is what social mobility looks like in this system.

Idealism vs Realism

The protagonist of the movie is Goreng, who volunteers to spend six months in The Pit in exchange for an accredited degree. The item he chooses to bring with him is a copy of Cervantes' *Don Quixote*. Much like the book's title character, Goreng begins as an idealist who wishes to improve the world and revive chivalry but does this in the most impractical and unrealistic manner. He begins on level forty-eight, sharing the room with Trimagasi who, as a staunch realist, is Goreng's antithesis. Trimagasi is in The Pit to serve out a punishment for intentionally killing someone whom he describes as an 'illegal immigrant'. He brings with him a self-sharpening knife. While he makes friends with Goreng, who reads to him from *Don Quixote*, Trimagasi tells him,

> I don't think you'll survive for long . . . you have a big heart.

Trimagasi believes that to survive in such a place, one must kill or be killed. He says,

> Hunger will drive you mad, and down here it's better to eat than be eaten.

From experience, he knows that friendships deteriorate into suspicion, which leads to violence. True to form, on the morning of the new month when they find themselves on level 171, where there is likely to be almost nothing left on the table, Trimagasi binds Goreng to his bed with the intention of slowly eating him alive. Goreng only manages to escape when Miharu, a young Asian mother who is said to kill her cellmate and descend the tower every month in search of her child, slays Trimagasi, releases Goreng and feeds him Trimagasi's flesh. Miharu plays a dialectical role in drawing Goreng to higher levels of synthesis, knowledge and truth. She is philosophy. Her incessant search for her child mirrors the teleological journey that Goreng takes from naïve idealism to the truth that he wishes to learn.

Rationality, Spontaneous Solidarity, Coercion

In the next month, Goreng finds himself on level thirty-three with Imoguiri, a bureaucrat who believes that, when rationality prevails, selfish individualism can give way to spontaneous formations of solidarity and collective action. She attempts technocratically to persuade the people occupying the level below them that there is enough food for everyone if they simply ate only what they needed. Day after day, she asks them to eat only the portions she sets aside for them, which she believes contain as many calories as they need, and to set aside similar portions for the people below them. She tries to convince them that those who find themselves on higher levels have a responsibility to help those at the bottom levels who may be dying.

Imoguiri believes that reason and persuasion are sufficient to create a just system of distribution so that no one need suffer. Her rationalist approach recalls the American moral and political philosopher John Rawls' celebrated attempt to answer the question, 'What terms of cooperation would free and equal citizens agree to under fair conditions?' The occupants of The Pit are in some key respects like participants in Rawls' thought-experimental 'original position', where they make fundamental decisions about the basic structure of society that they and those they represent will live in. They do this behind a 'veil of ignorance', deprived of knowing the specific individuating characteristics of the citizens they represent and their conceptions of the good (Rawls, 1971). Similarly, the random monthly assignment to different levels in The Pit is like a veil of ignorance. If one knew there was a random chance that they could be assigned to suffer on the lowest levels of society, they would—wherever they might be now—affirm more impartially those principles that benefit even the least advantaged.

And yet, the people below Imoguiri ignore her words entirely and her efforts completely fail, just as Goreng expects, his original idealism now tempered by Trimagasi's realism. Goreng intervenes by threatening to defecate all over the table if they do not do as Imoguiri says. Only then, when reason is enforced with coercion, do they comply. Imoguiri wonders aloud if Goreng's approach could also gain compliance from the people on levels above them. Goreng does not think so, explaining

> I can't shit upwards.

Discrimination, Democratic Socialism, Communist Armed Revolution

The following month, Goreng and Imoguiri are both assigned to level 202, a level so low that there is nothing to eat. Imoguiri, who we find out is dying of cancer, hangs herself, which Goreng understands to be an act of self-sacrifice. To stay alive, he eats the pages of his book, which signifies the end of his romanticized idealism and political naïveté. He then proceeds to eat Imoguiri's cancer-ridden body, which signifies the end of a diseased faith in reasonable human behaviour.

The next month, having survived level 202, Goreng now finds himself on level six, together with Baharat, a Black man who desperately wants to climb to the top using his rope. Baharat pleads with the White couple on the floor above them to help him climb up. Grotesquely, they make him profess Christianity as his religion before they agree and then, when he is about to reach the next level, they defecate on him. He falls back to his floor and loses his rope. This vividly reflects the fundamental inequality, injustice and cruelty of colonialism and its racist societal legacies. It also describes the obstacles and humiliation that minoritized people must overcome in a system that is so severely stacked against them.

Goreng and Baharat decide to use their higher-level status—on level six—to force change down below. They arm themselves with weapons, jump on to the table and descend the hole, level by level, only allowing people below level fifty to eat the food portions that they carefully ration out. For a brief spell, they try using reason, dialogue and education to request a day of fasting, instead of terror and brutality to demand it. But they quickly switch back from what sounds like the consensual redistribution of 'democratic socialism' to 'armed revolution' as the most effective way to redistribute resources, forcefully and violently, to create a communist society.

As they both descend to the lowest depths, Goreng sees Miharu being violently stabbed: philosophy is brutally killed before it reaches the truth. Exhausted and in despair, they descend to level 333 and find Miharu's child. Goreng realizes that he has been distracted by other 'messages' along the way and here, at last, he has reached his end goal and ultimate purpose as a human being, what Aristotle called 'telos'. If Goreng's journey is representative of the progress of History, then here is what Hegel called Spirit, as discussed at the beginning of this book. The movie's rather obscure ending deliberately leaves telos and Spirit unclear and unsubstantiated for the audience.

Chapter Six

Capitalist Psychos and Cinematic Zombies

In many of the documentaries discussed earlier, 21st-century Wall Street and American corporate interests, in general, have been portrayed as the root of our problems today. Wall Street is depicted as a site of depravity, its inhabitants as pathologically greedy, risk-loving and incapable of empathizing with others. Feature movies have sensationalized these characteristics even further, making American capitalists appear almost psychotic and zombie-like. While these movies give audiences voyeuristic pleasure and provoke outrage, their real critical power lies in their ability to make us see ourselves in these capitalist psychopaths. By pointing accusatory fingers at pathological capitalist caricatures, do we absolve ourselves of complicity in a system built on poverty, inequality and the long-term destruction of our habitat? Or do we see more clearly how irrational and depraved our own daily actions really are and take personal responsibility for the world that we are collectively destroying?

To answer this, we look at two sets of feature movies. The first includes movies about Wall Street, mainly in the years following the GFC of 2007–2008. The second includes zombie movies. While the use of the zombie as a critical metaphor for various aspects of modern society and politics is well-known, we will consider what it can also say about neoliberal globalization and authoritarian populism, particularly in the age of pandemics.

Psychotic / Psychopathic Capitalism

The National Institute of Mental Health in the US defines psychosis as

> . . . conditions that affect the mind, where there has been some loss of contact with reality . . . [when] a person's thoughts and perceptions are disturbed, and the individual may have difficulty understanding what is real and what is not.

Symptoms the institute lists include delusions (false beliefs), hallucinations (seeing or hearing things that others do not see or hear), incoherent or nonsense speech, and behaviour that is inappropriate for the situation. People in psychotic episodes may experience depression, anxiety, sleep problems, social withdrawal, lack of motivation and difficulty with overall functioning.

Psychopathy, unlike psychosis, is rather less well defined. Not officially sanctioned by professional psychiatric or psychological bodies for diagnosis, the concept appears more significant in the field of criminology, where an influential checklist exists for controlled experimental research but also as an assessment tool used in the criminal justice system (Spiegel, 2011). According to Encyclopaedia Britannica, psychopathy is

> . . . characterized by an abiding pattern of disregard for and violation of the rights of others, as manifested through three or more of the following habitual or continual behaviors: (1) serious violations of criminal laws; (2) deceitfulness for personal gain or pleasure, including lying, swindling, or trickery; (3) impulsiveness or failure to plan ahead; (4) irritability and aggressiveness often resulting in physical assaults; (5) reckless disregard for the safety of oneself or others; (6) failure to meet important adult responsibilities, including job- and family-related duties and financial obligations; and (7) lack of meaningful remorse or guilt—to the point of complete indifference—regarding the serious harm or distress one's actions cause other people. (Duignan, no date)

The protagonist in the movie *American Psycho* (2000), Patrick Bateman, is a Wall Street investment banker in the 1980s, with an

Ivy League business-school degree. In voiceover narration, Patrick reflects on himself as

> . . . some kind of an abstract idea, but there is no real me, only an entity, something illusory.

He says,

> I have all the characteristics of a human being, flesh, blood, skin, hair, but not a single clear identifiable emotion, except for greed and disgust. Something horrible is happening inside of me and I don't know why.

This illusory idea of himself is carefully cultivated, not least through a highly disciplined fitness and beauty regimen that he puts himself through at the start of each day. He does a thousand stomach crunches. He applies copious amounts of expensive products on his face and body. He picks out the right Valentino suit. His interactions with colleagues and acquaintances mainly involve admiring and envying one another's appearance, flaunting and complimenting recently acquired luxury items. In one scene, they all compare the design and quality of their business cards, like jocks in a locker room comparing penis sizes. Apart from a well-groomed appearance, Patrick is eloquent. While dining at a fancy restaurant, he talks glibly about the world's problems such as apartheid, the nuclear arms race, terrorism, hunger, shelter, racial discrimination, civil rights, women's rights, traditional moral values and—most ironic of all—materialism.

In Patrick's world, what matters most is the ability to get a reservation at the trendiest restaurants, membership of exclusive clubs and a fancy apartment with a good address. Drug use, pornography and prostitution are rampant. The culture is racist and antisemitic, sexist and misogynistic. Patrick tells his new secretary what to wear. He cheats on his fiancée, who is a source of irritation to him, and then breaks up with her. Conversations are full of lines like

> . . . the only girls with good personalities . . . are ugly chicks.

Shockingly, Patrick imagines

> . . . what her head would look like on a stick . . .

and keeps a sketchbook of violent drawings of how he would like to kill women. Before too long, we discover that Patrick leads the life of a serial killer. The movie already suggests this very strongly in its opening image of sliced duck served on a plate in a restaurant, the drops of a red sauce easily confused with drops and trails of human blood.

Patrick's murderous instincts get progressively more brutal. They begin as a voice in his head. To a female bartender, the voice says,

> You're a fucking ugly bitch. I want to stab you to death and then play around with your blood.

At a Chinese laundry, the voice tells the operators who are unable to remove his stains,

> If you don't shut your fucking mouth, I will kill you.

He stabs a homeless person in a dark alley, telling him,

> If you're so hungry, why don't you get a job? . . . You got to get your act together . . . Do you know what a fucking loser you are?

And then he kills his rival Paul Allen, who seems like a mirror image of himself, only better. Paul has the nicest business card in the group. He has a better apartment. He can get a reservation at the exclusive restaurant Dorsia. Patrick cannot. Paul calls Patrick 'Marcus Halberstrand' by mistake and then tells him that Patrick Bateman is a dork. With clinical precision, Patrick prepares his apartment to prevent it from being blood-stained, puts on a raincoat, and then—whilst commenting on 'Hip To Be Square' by Huey Lewis and the News in the style of a magazine review—he kills Paul with a shiny axe, disposes of the body in a Jean Paul Gaultier overnight bag and leaves a message on his answering machine to suggest that he is away on a business trip to London.

In the most gruesome scene in the movie, Patrick uses a chainsaw to kill a prostitute, whom he names 'Christie', in Paul Allen's now vacant apartment. This reminds us of an earlier scene when he does his morning stomach crunch exercises while the movie *The Texas Chainsaw Massacre* (1974) plays on his television in the background. As the prostitute tries to escape, she finds mutilated bodies stored away in the apartment. 'Christie' had been picked up by Patrick twice. The first time at his own apartment, Patrick introduced himself to her and to another prostitute he had ordered as 'Paul Allen' and added 'I work on Wall Street'. The three had sex in front of a video camera, but the narcissistic Patrick was clearly focusing on his own image in the mirror, posing and flexing his body.

Towards the end of the movie, Patrick goes on a shooting spree, ending up in his office where he leaves a message on his lawyer's telephone, confessing in detail to the murder of twenty to forty people, including Paul Allen. In the end, it turns out that no one has taken his confession seriously, suggesting that he might have imagined everything, a projection of his internal pain on to a fantasy of violence that he has inflicted upon others. 'This confession', he laments as he realizes that his actions were as hollow, illusory and insignificant as his identity, 'has meant nothing'. Freudian psychoanalytical theory would tell us that Patrick's serial-killer fantasy remains repressed in his unconscious. As much as he wants to liberate them through a therapeutic confession, Wall Street refuses to acknowledge this. Neoliberal capitalism, it seems, is not only quite indifferent to the psychopathic behaviour of its own, but also requires extreme repression for it to thrive.

Directed in 2000 by Mary Harron, *American Psycho* is a re-visioning of 1980s Wall Street in Reagan's America. Reagan appears on television lying about the Iran Contra scandal, while the group of bankers who see this wonder out loud if the neoliberal president is not himself a psycho.

While Patrick Bateman is a loathsome and narcissistic creature of a degenerate Wall Street, whose impact on the world is limited to an elaborate fantasy of physical brutality, Jordan Belfort—the protagonist of Martin Scorsese's *The Wolf of Wall Street* (2013)—is much less detestable. Audiences may even find him likeable, not because he shows moral virtues or even human decency, but because the world that he conquers through determination, ingenuity and guile is thoroughly glamorized in the blockbuster movie. This is also the Wall Street of the 1980s and 1990s, when Reagan's neoliberal deregulation of the financial system led to an intoxicated culture of big money, ostentatious lifestyles and unlimited greed. Jordan's voiceover narration tells us,

> We were making more money than we knew what to do with.

In the opening scene of the movie, we are straightaway introduced to the heady world of luxury living: sportscars, yachts, mansions, trophy wives, prostitutes, alcohol, drugs. The latter, no doubt, to numb the pain that comes with conquering the world.

In these successful Wall Street firms, there is misogyny, bullying, cursing and swearing, alongside hubris, fearlessness and extravagance. Jordan tells us,

> It was a madhouse, a greed fest, with equal parts cocaine, testosterone and body fluids.

He is told, at the beginning of his career, that none of this is real—the slang to describe all this irreparable fakeness is 'fugazi'. His boss, a swaggering stockbroker, tells him,

> We don't create shit. We don't build anything.

False value is generated through the manipulation of financial markets, symbolic movements partly driven by deception and fantasy that—it is suggested here—do not amount to any real value. Like the world of *American Psycho*, all is illusory—merely an idea, an image to live up to, a bubble. In *American Psycho*, the bubble refuses to burst, as fantasy provides a nihilistic escape route for repressed desires harmful to the neoliberal order. In *The Wolf of Wall Street*, it bursts, several times, but keeps re-inflating. Such is the resilience of greed, ingenuity and the adrenaline rush of neoliberalism.

The Wolf of Wall Street takes us on the same exhilarating ride as the protagonist. He addresses us directly in voiceover narration, regaling us with outrageous stories told with alpha-male bravado and charm. Here is a man who always seems to get away with wrongdoing. Even when he is caught, he gets off lightly, spending jail time playing tennis. We almost root for him, especially knowing that he started from the bottom and rose to the top, unlike

> . . . most of the Wall Street jackasses that . . . are to the manor born. Their fathers are douchebags, just like their fathers before them,

as a detective explains. Gordon Gekko was probably the original 'douchebag', the central figure in Oliver Stone's movie *Wall Street* (1987, for which Michael Douglas's portrayal won an Academy Award for Best Actor) and its sequel *Wall Street: Money Never Sleeps* (2010). In their study of psychopathy in cinema, psychiatrists Samuel J. Leistedt and Paul Linkowski (2014) identified Gekko (of the 1987 movie) as a 'successful psychopath', who is

> . . . one of the most interesting, manipulative, psychopathic fictional characters to date.

They noted that,

> Films and series presenting characters such as brokers, dishonest traders, vicious lawyers, and those engaged in corporate espionage are emerging (e.g., *Mad Men*, *The Wire*) and are generally related to the global economy and international business. Again, we see a strong parallelism between what happens in our society and what happens in film.

In *Wall Street*, Gekko is the villainous corporate raider, pitted against forces of good such as the honest veteran stockbroker Lou Mannheim and union leader Carl Fox, both seemingly relics of a more humane time. At the centre is the protagonist Bud Fox, a young, impressionable and ambitious stockbroker. Lou, Bud's earliest mentor, believes in taking time to build things up in the real economy. Carl, Bud's working-class father, worked his way up in the aviation industry to become a union leader for the maintenance workers. Lou is a sober, morally upright and patrician exception in the vulgar and cut-throat milieu of Wall Street, while Carl is the tough, uncompromising opposer of almost all that the unjust and effete Wall Street stands for. But Bud initially inveigles himself into Gekko's orbit, seeking his attention and mentorship. Naively impressed by Gekko's endless stream of cynical aphorisms affirming the acquisitive, possessive, manipulative and destructive get-rich-quick nihilism of Wall Street capitalism, Bud gets quickly drawn into criminal activities such as insider trading and securities fraud. The law catches up with him, even as his inner struggle moves him closer to the side of honesty and dignity, and he is at least partially redeemed when he cooperates with the investigating authorities to bring Gekko to justice.

The sequel, *Wall Street: Money Never Sleeps*, begins with Gekko's release from prison. He gives lectures on his new book questioning his most famous 'greed . . . is good' aphorism and sending out a warning about an impending economic downturn, which turns out to be the 2007–2008 GFC. In one of his lectures, he says,

> Greed got greedier, with a little bit of envy mixed in . . . No one is responsible, because everyone's drinking the same Kool-Aid . . . The mother of all evil is speculation . . . it's a bankrupt business model, it won't work . . . it's a disease. And we got to fight back.

Wall Street is portrayed as a decadent space of extravagance and excess, featuring big year-end bonuses, jewellery-store private rooms, trendy restaurants and clubs, US$10,000-a-seat fundraisers, private helicopters and thrill-seeking motorcycle racing in the forest. Against this background, a young and ambitious proprietary trader named Jake Moore wants to raise money for investments in clean-energy research. In this protagonist, the progressive seeds of redemption have already been planted right from the start. His fiancée Winnie, who is Gekko's estranged daughter, runs a liberal blog called 'Frozen News'.

Like Bud in the first *Wall Street*, Jake struggles internally to know the right thing to do. He is motivated by career ambition, revenge, romantic love and making the world better. Jake strikes a Mephistophelian deal with Gekko: he will help Gekko get back into his daughter's life, and in return, Gekko will help him exact revenge on his mentor's enemy. Later, Gekko tricks Jake into getting Winnie to sign over her US$100 million trust fund to Jake who, naively believing that this would be invested in the clean-energy project, transfers all the money to Gekko. True to form, Gekko absconds with the money and uses it to set up what becomes a highly successful investment company in London. And then, just as we think Gekko is irredeemable, he tells Jake that he has decided to deposit US$100 million anonymously into the research project. This abrupt turn of events leads to an even more jarring conclusion when we see the whole family united a year later, as Gekko joins Jake and Winnie to celebrate the first birthday party of their son.

Thus, one of the most interesting fictional Wall Street psychopaths turns—incredibly—into a good guy at the end. As a morality tale, what effect could a movie like this have on audiences? Perhaps, the lesson is that even the worst people can be saved, so don't give up on them. Or perhaps that if you play your game cunningly and pursue big money through whatever means, fair or foul, you'll still get to purchase a happy ending if you succeed. Or perhaps, as Satya Gabriel (2001), an economics professor, argued, the moral polarities of the movie could be reversed according to who's watching it. So, to young traders, the movie could be

> . . . turned into a parable of *how to get rich the Gekko way* while reducing the probability of getting caught by the evil [authorities] . . . For the hip-hop Wall Streeters, Gordon Gekko was the hero of the film and Bud Fox was his Judas, the ungrateful disciple. Gekko represented possibility (of rise from rags to riches, of using one's wits to overcome obstacles, of overcoming the banality of love and morality in favor of a neoclassical logic of naked and boundless self-interest). The wanna-be-Gekkos, the foot soldiers of money manipulation and deal-making could see themselves in his shoes, as Gekko the Great. They could not identify or sympathize with Carl Fox, the mechanic and labor leader, or the pathetic figure of Lou Mannheim.

Wall Street: Money Never Sleeps depicts Wall Street around the time of the GFC of 2007–2008. It adds human drama to the otherwise technical treatment of the crisis in many documentaries that seek to explain what is usually beyond the grasp of most people. Colourful dialogue using vivid metaphors helps us appreciate the thrust of what went wrong. Gekko describes money as

> . . . a bitch that never sleeps.

We learn that subprime is

> . . . crap . . ./ We like insurance . . ./ Easy selling crack to kids in a school playground.

A corporate chairman predicts that

> Money markets will dry up around the world by the end of the week. ATMs will stop spitting bills. Federal Deposit Insurance will collapse. Banks will close. Mobs, panic. It's going to be the end of the world.

There were quite a few other movies about the GFC that were driven by human drama and the complex psychological and moral struggles that exceeded the caricatures of greedy neoliberal capitalists and corrupt regulators, without necessarily exonerating them from culpability. *Too Big to Fail* (2011) narrates the events surrounding the GFC, focusing on the actions of Henry Paulson, the US treasury secretary, and Ben Bernanke, chairman of the US Federal Reserve System. *Margin Call* (2011) focuses on the employees of a fictional investment bank, whose survivalist goal during the onset of the GFC was to protect the firm and their individual prospects within it, without any care at all for the public good. Its dialogue is tense, but colourful, for example:

> The music is about to stop and we're going to be left holding the biggest bag of odorous excrement ever assembled in the history of capitalism.

The Big Short (2015) focuses on the fraudulent housing market as the source of the GFC. In cameo appearances, celebrity chef Anthony Bourdain, singer Selena Gomez, academic Richard Thaler and other well-known faces explain to us directly and in almost comically simplified yet thoroughly effective ways what the relevant financial concepts mean. The writing is vivid. One of the main characters makes an impassioned speech:

> We live in an era of fraud in America. Not just in banking, but in government, education, religion, food, even baseball . . . What bothers me isn't that fraud is not nice. Or that fraud is mean. For fifteen thousand years, fraud and short sighted thinking have never, ever worked. Not once. Eventually, you get caught, things go south. When the hell did we forget all that? . . . I just know that at the end of the day regular people are going to pay for all of this. Because they always, always do.

The narrator explains what happened in the most economical and yet provocative of terms:

> Banks took the money the American people gave them, and used it to pay themselves huge bonuses, and lobby the Congress to kill big reform. And then they blamed immigrants and poor people, and this time even teachers! And when all was said and done, only one single banker went to jail . . .

And at the end of the movie, we see history repeat itself yet again:

> When the dust settled from the collapse, 5 trillion dollars in pension money, real estate value, 401k, savings, and bonds had disappeared. 8 million people lost their jobs, 6 million lost their homes. And that was just in the USA . . . In 2015, several large banks began selling billions in something called a 'bespoke tranche opportunity', which, according to Bloomberg News, is just another name for a CDO.

Driven by adrenaline, greed and a deep sense of entitlement, the Wall Street perpetrators of crisis keep doing more of the same, crisis after crisis. By thinking through Hannah Arendt's depiction of evil as thoughtless, conformist, careerist and banal—as discussed in the first chapter—we might consider how Wall Street capitalists may be less like monstrously satanic psychopaths and more like zombies, moving mindlessly in throngs and seeking human flesh to consume and infect, dead on the inside and terrifyingly apocalyptic.

Cinematic Zombies

Philosopher Gilles Deleuze and psychoanalyst Félix Guattari (1987/1972: 335) wrote that the

. . . only modern myth is the myth of zombies.

Since the 1990s, along with the rise of neoliberal globalization, the figure of the zombie has emerged out of cult status to proliferate in cinema, television and merchandise. It has also become an increasingly serious object of interdisciplinary academic study around the world. This is remarkable given its very specific origins in Haitian folklore, the transatlantic slave trade and its historically specific appeal in American popular culture. Sarah Juliet Lauro (2017), editor of a large volume of essays that theorized the phenomenon of zombies, identified a renaissance in the late 1990s and then, in the 2010s, an explosion of interest in the study of this cinematic monster. She observed that the meaning of zombies has been numerous and diverse, and all the while evolving over time and historical circumstance, continuing to reveal so much that we still do not understand about the human condition.

21st century audiences have not tired of the never-ending throng of zombie movies. There seems to be much vitality left in the genre, including the capacity to refresh, reboot and reinvent itself, to spawn sequels and remakes that keep the undead very much alive in the popular culture of each successive generation. Zombies from the classic movies of the 1960s and 1970s—mainly slow-moving and inscrutable—may no longer provoke the same kind of terror, shock and disbelief for today's audience, who are more used to viciously gory zombies that move at a heart-thumping pace. The realistic and intensely thrilling scenes made possible by vast improvements in moviemaking technology have perhaps de-sensitized us to the creepiness, violence and special-effects gore of earlier movies. We may even find classic 'old-school' zombies amusing, campy and predictable, though we may still enjoy and appreciate their cult status. And yet, when it comes to producing new zombie movies, the industry continues to surpass itself and audience expectations, as box office takings and critical awards might indicate. New movies do not simply follow the rules of zombie moviemaking; they creatively bend and twist the rules and sometimes even break them, much to both the chagrin and the delight of aficionados. The range of zombie movies produced in the 21st century is wide. Some continue the traditional classic elements. Others intersect with and even transform into action, comedy and romantic comedy styles. Some of them self-consciously play on the genre and its rules, sometimes making fun of itself so the audience almost forgets about the zombies that the movies are supposed to be about. Zombie movies are being made in every inhabited continent, modulated to reflect the tastes, concerns and political contexts of each society and culture.

But there must be more than just the thrill and pleasure of watching zombie movies as they proliferate in all these many directions. What is also pleasurable is the feeling of being drawn into these apocalyptic worlds and the vicarious thrill of struggling to survive in them. Survival, adaptability and resilience, after all, are part of the dominant language of our time. We say we live in a dangerous world. Proponents of neoliberal globalization assure us that the only option we have to survive and prosper in such a world is to open economic borders, attend to the needs of wealthy capitalists and corporations, and restrain other people's freedoms that can threaten elite interests. Everyone needs to work hard and stop depending on others. And eventually, the benefits will trickle down to all. For many who find themselves helpless against this hegemonic shibboleth, daily struggles are symbolized, augmented and projected on to movie, television and personal device screens everywhere as fantasies that valorize the perseverance, ingenuity and can-do spirit of humanity and its hero-protagonists in times of adversity. Indulging in the pleasure of these fantasies helps them cope with the horrors of real life.

In the cinematic world of a zombie crisis, we see humanity at its worst and its best. Under severe stress and strain, there are characters who simply give up or turn against one another, whilst others offer help, cooperation, trustworthiness, leadership and self-sacrifice. In real life, we also see these behaviours in times of war, economic crisis and pandemics. Zombie movies can even seem to teach us practical lessons for survival in an apocalyptic future, offering us a manual for lasting as long as we can in times of crisis and moments of danger. We learn and rehearse in our heads how to endure, survive, resist and even thrive when danger strikes. We may even learn some science, including, of course, some wildly inaccurate science that comes with cinematic licence. We may become interested to know more science and be better equipped to discern the truth from among the masses of fake news. Have zombie movies and their theme of contagion taught us how to survive the COVID-19 attack?

Maybe not. But more important than the vicarious thrill of watching and the acquisition of survival skills are the alarm bells that zombie movies ring vigorously. Zombies violently taking over our world can serve as a very powerful cautionary tale. If we continue to do the harmful and dangerous things that we are doing today, our world can end up in disaster, and we will pay the ultimate price for it. Some zombie movies are quite explicit about the source of the outbreak: often an unintended consequence of scientific, industrial, commercial or military activity gone awry because of greed, mischief or an accident. Others are more suggestive, for instance, those movies that show in the opening credits a rapid sequence of images of unspecified violence, destruction and chaos around the world. In all cases, the message is loud and clear: a world overrun by infectious and deadly flesh-eating monsters, without any recognizable human capacity for thought, moral reasoning or empathy is the apocalyptic vision of a future that we are headed for if we all continue unthinkingly and selfishly to indulge our most debased human desires.

In the age of neoliberal globalization, these include crude materialism, mindless consumerism, rapacious environmental degradation and exploitative social relations that degrade human dignity. As radical philosopher Henry Giroux (2014) argued,

> The macabre double movement between 'the dead that walk' and those who are alive but are dying and suffering cannot be understood outside of the casino capitalism that now shapes every aspect of society in its own image. A casino capitalist zombie politics views competition as a form of social combat, celebrates war as an extension of politics, and legitimates a ruthless Social Darwinism in which particular individuals and groups are considered simply redundant, disposable—nothing more than human waste left to stew in their own misfortune—easy prey for the zombies who have a ravenous appetite for chaos and revel in apocalyptic visions filled with destruction, decay, abandoned houses, burned-out cars, gutted landscapes, and trashed gas stations.

In some sense, zombie movies are a kind of cinematic 'pre-mortem', an essentially tragic narrative leading spectacularly to a future demise of the human species. As the audience, we are drawn into this narrative and confronted directly and very vividly with the reasons and factors that could lead to our own mass extinction. We become acutely conscious of these reasons and factors. We also learn how systems, no matter how well-conceived and meticulously implemented, can never be perfect and perpetual. Nothing can be hermetically sealed. The zombie threat cannot be fully contained. Human subjectivity and unpredictability always threaten to unravel even the finest of systems. We come to accept this and the need to be vigilant, adaptive and resilient.

Cinema is powerful in its dual ability to draw us into strange worlds uncannily like our own and yet, in that strangeness, help us to recognize more acutely many familiar aspects of ourselves and our contemporary world that are easily obscured in the rapid flow of day-to-day experiences. The zombie is a powerful metaphor. Zombie movies have an allegorical quality, capable of producing insightful and critical commentary on contemporary society.

For example, in zombie movies, we might see a reflection of our collective anxieties. Looking at the zombie reminds us of how vulnerable our own bodies are, and how insecure we have become about their adequacy in the light of cultural and aesthetic expectations, monstrously shaped by a thriving and often exploitative health, wellness and beauty industry. We fear how susceptible our bodies are to injury, violence and disease. We become acutely aware of how porous the boundary between human and zombie really is. Some zombie movies deliberately highlight the visual and auditory resemblance between the two to play up this ambiguity, making the protagonist or the audience at least momentarily unclear whether they are seeing humans or zombies. Through this irony, we are meant to be provoked by the notion that in real life, our human actions may be as grotesque as the behaviour of zombies, perhaps even more so.

In *Super Size Me* (2004), discussed in Chapter Three, we are forced to look at the mindless and insatiable eating habits of the American throng, profitably lured to a ubiquitous fast-food industry designed to mass-produce cravings. The hypervisibility of over-weight bodies in the movie prepares us for Morgan Spurlock's own grotesque pedagogical experiment, a spectacle set up to horrify us so that experts can teach us to be personally responsible for our bodily health and aesthetic. In *The Social Dilemma* (2020), also discussed in Chapter Three, we see how we as humans have already lost control of ourselves and our world to the algorithms of social media, whose persuasive technology modifies our behaviour through positive intermittent reinforcement. Looking at both these movies through the lens of the zombie metaphor can make their critical message pop more vividly.

But we might also see in the zombie metaphor not ourselves but others very different from ourselves, who threaten who we think we are, what we think our way of life is and why we think that is valuable and under threat. In Trump's America, as discussed earlier, White working-class males have been described as feeling deeply threatened by a liberal elite who have, over the decades since the countercultural and civil rights movements of the 1960s, been de-centring a sometimes-nostalgic imagination of the American way of life, by insisting upon gender, sexual and racial equality, diversity and inclusiveness, as well as an internationalist and even cosmopolitan outlook associated with globalization. From their point of view, zombies may represent virulent racial contamination of what they perceive as the 'real America' and their place in it. They may identify zombies with the negative influence of foreign cultures, or competition from immigrants for their nation's limited resources, or the influx of undocumented immigrants bringing with them crime, violence and disease, or terrorists who threaten to destroy their civilization. The image of a throng of zombies reflects the source of fear and anxiety for a disadvantaged conservative audience confronted by a world becoming increasingly unfamiliar, alienating and dangerous. Their response, like the actions of the hero-protagonists of zombie movies (who turn out mostly to be White and male), is to fight back and to fight against the soft and cowardly approaches of their 'liberal' character rivals. They man up, equip themselves with guns and lead the charge against this new form of tyranny.

However, this same image may reflect something quite different for a liberal audience, who may see in the throng of zombies a conservative backlash of people mindlessly galvanized through a provocative language of fear and hate to storm the bastions of liberal democracy and pluralism. Scenes, endlessly replayed in the news, of Trump followers storming the Capitol building in defiance of his liberal rival Joe Biden's victory in the 2020 presidential elections resonate strongly with the mindless yet dangerous throngs of cinematic zombies in the streets. In this way, zombie movies are an allegory of authoritarian populism, where the manipulable masses of people who feel disenfranchised are the source of our liberal anxieties. The moral polarities of the zombie narrative can be easily reversed according to the audience.

Cutting across conservative and liberal interpretations of the zombie movie is a more fundamental critique of capitalism. *Dawn of the Dead* (1978), the second in George A. Romero's 'Dead' series of zombie movies, is mostly set in a shopping mall, which serves not only as a source of material sustenance during the crisis, but also as a highly symbolic background against which a critique of commercialism and consumerism may be advanced. Images of slow-moving zombies mindlessly haunting these caverns, corridors and bridges of consumerism are as obvious in their social criticism for audiences in the 1970s as they are for us today. Driven almost entirely by a machine-like appetite for flesh and an efficient system of reproduction, the cinematic zombie is the grossest and most direct expression of materialism. No intellect, ambition, morality, aesthetic, language or empathy gets in the way of that.

From a more basic critique of capitalism in the 1970s, zombie movies have taken on the more elaborate world of neoliberal globalization in the 21st century. The zombies, in this case, turn out to be the neoliberal elite, the rich and the powerful who feast on the helpless bodies of working-class people, who in turn become infected by the sickness that is neoliberal globalization. We all will eventually become dangerously numb in this self-destructive world. The regularity with which the media reports on school shootings in the US—as depicted in documentaries like Michael Moore's *Bowling for Columbine* (2002)—has numbed the audience into automatic expressions of grief in their litany of 'thoughts and prayers', articulated with little optimism that any real change will be possible. In his criticism of the Bush-Cheney administration in the US (2001–09), neo-Marxist scholar Douglas Kellner (2010) observed how

> . . . the proliferation of zombie films indeed provides allegories of deadened masses of people and irrational violence that has specific societal origins and references with the politics of the 2000s. While conservative catastrophe films show evil coming from sources external to the existing system or from more supernatural sources, a socially critical tradition exhibited in many of the 2000s catastrophe films discussed here, shows evil and monstrosity emerging from out-of-control aspects of the existing society.

Giroux (2014) sharply posed these rhetorical questions:

> What kind of society emerges when it is governed by the market-driven assumption that the only value that matters is exchange value, when the common good is denigrated to the status of a mall, and the larger social order is composed only of individuals free to pursue their own interests? What happens to democracy when a government inflicts on the American public narrow market-driven values, corporate relations of power, and policies that impose gross inequities on society, and condemns young people to a precarious, debt-ridden existence in which the future begins to resemble a society of zombies engaged in a remake of dystopian films . . .

Zombie Remakes and New Concepts

Romero's 1978 classic was 're-envisioned' in 2004 by Zack Snyder, his first feature movie, also titled *Dawn of the Dead.* A box office success that grossed more than US$100 million worldwide, the remake was also highly regarded by critics. The shopping mall, the main setting for both movies, presented opportunities for social commentary on consumerism. Zombies instinctively move towards the mall as a 'memory' of how their human lives were mostly spent, which we can assume involved wandering aimlessly in the air-conditioned spaces designed to induce needless purchases that kept them in a perpetual cycle of debt and meaningless work.

Snyder's remake introduced the zombie apocalypse in the quiet, middle-class suburbs, where affluence, contentment and the sedation of American life are ruptured by an outbreak of zombie violence. Romero's zombies, their faces painted grey, move slowly and menacingly towards their victims, while Snyder's zombies are shockingly fast and strong, making the 2004 version much more of a gory, high-tempo action movie. Scenes of vicious zombie attacks, dead humans re-animating into zombies and the birth of a zombie baby are gruesome, even for a 21st-century audience. Writing about Snyder's remake with great admiration, horror novelist Stephen King (2010) pointed to its strong resonance with the spectacle of 9/11 that had taken place just three years earlier and that occupied the public imagination not only in the US but also in the rest of the world.

> What haunted our nightmares was the idea of suicide bombers driven by an unforgiving (and unthinking, most of us believed) ideology and religious fervor. You could beat 'em up or burn 'em, but they'd just keep coming, the news reports assured us. They would keep on coming until either we were dead or they were. The only way to stop them was a bullet in the head. That's exactly what Snyder's zombies are, it seems to me: fast-moving terrorists who never quit. You can't debate with them, you can't parley with them, you can't even threaten their homes or families with reprisals.

The opening credits in Snyder's *Dawn of the Dead* begin with a brief image of Muslims bowing in prayer, followed by a rapid sequence of violent and destructive imagery around the world. In the Islamophobic climate that 9/11 generated, Muslims were easily the folk devils of moral panic. In one scene in the shopping mall, a televangelist can be heard appealing to Christian conservatism by pointing fingers at the sins of other folk devils associated with sex out of marriage, abortion, and homosexuality. He explains,

> When there's no more room in hell, the dead will walk the earth.

In the movie, we get to see the worst and the best of humanity, as we do in times of crisis such as the years following the terrorist attack. When a group of people try to take refuge in the shopping mall, the security guards there at first refuse to let them stay and then treat them like prisoners. One of the guards warns,

> I'll kill each and every one of you to stay alive. You hear me?

Eventually, they—especially the alpha-male rivals—start to work together, even making the ultimate self-sacrifice for the interests of others. While they can 'progress' socially in times of adversity, the moral aspects often degenerate. The question of whether to kill the infected before they turn dangerous is often resolved pragmatically. The monstrous dehumanization of the enemy makes it easier to numb the emotions and moral sentiments to kill rather than be killed. But reflected in the convenient dehumanization of zombies is also the dehumanization of people. In one scene, for instance, humans shoot at the zombies from the shopping mall rooftops seemingly just for the fun of it, gunning down zombies who resemble celebrities like Jay Leno and Rosie O'Donnell. This reflects the desensitization and mindlessness of gun violence, evoking the perverse yet normalized culture of school shootings in the US. Michael Moore's *Bowling for Columbine* (2002) actually draws connections between 9/11, the demonization of enemies, the weapons industry and gun violence, especially in schools.

Almost a decade after Synder's *Dawn of the Dead*, amid an explosion of zombie movies everywhere, *World War Z* (2013) was released. Directed by Marc Forster, it continues to be the highest-grossing zombie movie of all time, taking US$540 million to date. Forster's zombies can run at great speed, making this also more like an action movie. The infected turn into zombies within ten short seconds. Unusually, these zombies respond mainly to sound.

Like Snyder's movie, *World War Z* begins with a rapid sequence of scenes depicting a dysfunctional world, including carbon dioxide emissions, reality television, pandemics and so on. Throughout the movie, there are numerous scenes of chaos in the city and human-to-human violence.

World War Z's narrative is more strongly driven by a hero-protagonist. Gerry Lane, a brooding former UN investigator, is played by Hollywood A-list celebrity and humanitarian activist Brad Pitt. Depicted as a family man, Gerry must answer a higher national calling to draw upon his international skills and experience to save the world. These 'American' values embodied in a more traditional Hollywood leading man may help to explain the movie's commercial appeal and success.

The movie also gives more prominence to the role of science and scientific reasoning. Nature itself is described as a 'serial killer'. With his powers of observation and ingenuity, Gerry observes how the zombies avoid people who are sick. From that, it is conjectured that zombies look for healthy human hosts to infect and will generally ignore those with sickness. And from that, he comes up with a strategy to camouflage people from the zombies by infecting them with a deadly but curable pathogen. He is willing to test this hypothesis by courageously and self-sacrificially using his own body.

As a former UN agent who travels the world (most prominently to Israel) to find a solution and who collaborates with scientists at the World Health Organization, Gerry also represents 'multilateral' internationalism, a pro-Israeli position, as well as US global leadership. The second and third of these are particularly aligned with dominant American values. The movie ends with scenes of various countries—including the US's Cold-War enemy Russia—fighting the zombies in their own ways but empowered to do so by the American solution that Gerry has implemented. In voiceover narration at the end of the movie, Gerry urges,

> If you can fight, fight. Be prepared for anything. Our war has just begun.

This war is, in fact, a reactionary, rather than revolutionary, fight against the forces that threaten to destroy neoliberal globalization and, through that, US global leadership.

Zombies have also featured in 21st-century British cinema. In fact, it was probably the British movie *28 Days Later* (2002), directed by Danny Boyle, which did the most to revive this cinematic genre in the 21st century. From both a commercial and critical point of view, it continues to be one of the most successful zombie movies of all time. Boyle's were the first cinematic zombies to move quickly, enabling a more effective integration between the zombie movie and action movie genres.

In the movie are many haunting scenes of London as a desolate city, its monuments of former civilizational greatness left devoid of life and relevance. Great Britain, these images seem to suggest, is no longer great. Its status in the world has declined. And all that is left is anarchy, the complete breakdown of social order, marked by the absence or uselessness of government, police, army, church and money. The only way to survive is to move in small gangs.

This is Britain's zombie apocalypse, the deadly result of a failed attempt by animal rights activists to rescue chimpanzees from a laboratory. It is Britain that needs to be quarantined from the rest of the world. The impact is so severe that the recent past now seems so long ago, accessed only through nostalgia. In one scene, a family of horses runs free in the English countryside. In another, the protagonist—after finding his parents dead—watches videos of his happy childhood, only to have the memory fiercely interrupted by zombies attacking him in the middle of the night. The old world and Britain's place in it have ended.

And yet, there are desperate efforts to revive the old Britain, even as the world has changed. A group of military officers takes over a stately home, turning it into a safe house. However, their real intention is to trick female survivors into sexual slavery, using them to re-populate their country. The symbolism is utterly clear: A hierarchical hyper-masculine order mobilized for war and destruction uses deception to rape women as a means of preserving and extending itself into the new world. One military officer notes how people have been killing other people long before the zombie apocalypse: nothing has really changed. In these words, we are reminded of the movie's opening credits, where scenes of conflict, riots and war reinforce the significance of his words:

> People killing people, which to my mind, puts us in a state of normality right now.

28 Weeks Later (2007), the sequel, was directed by Juan Carlos Fresnadillo and revolves around the aftermath of the fictional 'Rage Virus' pandemic that ravaged Britain in the first movie. After taking control of Britain, NATO forces and the US military confidently declare Britain infection free, even though they have yet to fully understand the virus. They start to resettle people into safe zones, where they will be locked down. Like the first movie, the sequel projects an apocalyptic vision of Great Britain in decline and the US—the global leader of our time—exerting its immense power to occupy and reconstruct a collapsed nation. This reminds us of US and international efforts to 'reconstruct' Afghanistan and Iraq after the US-led retaliatory attack on them in the years following 9/11.

Another UK zombie movie, made almost a decade later, explores the line dividing the human and zombie conditions. Colm McCarthy's *The Girl with All the Gifts* (2016) features an England in which humans who have been infected by a fungal disease turn into dangerously fast zombies called 'hungries'. In this world, a new generation of children, who are human-zombie hybrids, can think, learn and behave like free-willed humans but, like hungries, they cannot control their ravenous appetite for human flesh. They come into the world by eating their way out of their mothers' bodies. The children are held—perhaps more accurately imprisoned—in an army base, guarded and administered by soldiers. They attend classes taught by a compassionate teacher. Scientists observe and experiment on them constantly.

The children are all heavily guarded all the time, their bodies physically restrained in wheelchairs, their heads strapped and mouths muzzled. Humans apply gels called 'blockers' on themselves to throw off the hungries. Humans regard hybrids as essentially dangerous. On this assumption rests their authoritarian treatment, an approach to first dehumanize in order to re-humanize through experimentation and education. The symbolism is clear: what can we say about the institutions of education, incarceration and science in a highly divided society, whose hierarchy is justified by notions of innate violence? The answers to these questions can tell us much about institutionalized racism. It can shed an interesting light on critical race theory that informs movies such as *13th* (2016), discussed in Chapter Three.

One of the children, Melanie, is particularly intelligent and bears many endearing human qualities. She escapes the army base together with her teacher and a couple of sympathetic soldiers, continuing to wear the restraints and finding nutrition in stray animals to keep her human companions safe. The group come across a massive tower of fungal growth sprouting out of zombie bodies, heaped against the BT Tower in London. The fungus sprouts seed pods everywhere, which—

if released—will bring so much destruction as to herald the end of humankind.

Eventually, Melanie realizes that she is not simply an object for scientific experimentation, but part of a hybrid generation in which lies the potential for a future world. In an act of revolution, she sets fire to the tower, releasing spores everywhere, to generate a new world of hungries and hybrids. While this marks the end of humans, one human—her teacher—survives in a sealed mobile laboratory and, from there, continues to educate the new generation. Here, we see the zombie antithesis colliding with humanity in a Hegelian dialectic to create a new synthesis, the subject of the post-revolutionary post-human age, a potentially superior age, which nevertheless continues to carry with it the best parts of human civilization.

We also find the dominant theme of authoritarian control and revolutionary change in the Irish zombie movie *The Cured* (2017), directed by David Freyne. The 'Maze Virus' had ravaged all of Europe and Ireland, in particular, until they were able to cure 75 per cent of the infected and imprison the rest. 'The Cured'—as the 75 per cent are called—can remember in gruesome detail the things they did when they were infected. Many of them experience post-traumatic stress disorder. The Cured are also immune to the virus, and 'the Infected' do not seem to attack them.

In this society, people who have never been infected continue to be fearful of the Cured, doubting the possibility that they can be humanely rehabilitated and reintegrated into the mainstream. The never-infected people suspect the Cured of secretly desiring a new outbreak when they would have an advantage and become socially and politically superior. The Cured are treated with harshness and contempt by the rehabilitation authorities. They are given menial jobs when they re-enter society, treated almost like 'lepers' and 'animals'. Some of them form an underground movement called the Cured Alliance, which campaign for their civil liberties.

The government, clearly capitalizing on populist fears, decides to euthanize the approximately 5,000 who remain infected, even though scientists have been informing the public about a superior vaccine that they are about to produce. This provokes the Cured Alliance to become more militant, performing acts of terror and then freeing the Infected from their imprisonment to create chaos in the streets. Once the government can restore order, imprisoning most of the Infected (including the newly infected), they return to discussions about executing them.

While the historically specific resonances with the troubles in Northern Ireland and the Irish Republican Army are clear, the broader themes of terrorism, fear, discrimination, inequality, apartheid, trust, integration and social cohesion are relatable in many other parts of the world. Like *The Girl with All the Gifts*, *The Cured* can also be watched profitably with *13th*, to understand contemporary racism and incarceration in the US.

The Australian zombie movie *Cargo* (2017), directed by Ben Howling and Yolanda Ramke, features some very strong acting that brings emotional depth and intensity to this non-Anglo-American treatment of the zombie theme that resonates powerfully with the aboriginal landscape and culture. In this world, people infected by a virus turn into violent, fast-moving zombies within forty-eight hours. They wear wrist devices to monitor how much more time they have before turning. And they also possess devices to effect suicide. Others opt to bury their heads in the ground to prevent turning.

The aboriginal people in this movie represent an original civilization in harmony with nature, which was displaced and corrupted by the civilization of the 'gupper' (White man) who settled on this land. One of the aboriginal elders observes how,

> They're poisoning this land, you know? This country, changing. It's sick. We all get sick. You get sick too.

The virus, presumably, was introduced into this ancient land through the White man's culture. Indeed, we see how a White man captures and puts into cages an aboriginal girl and her father as bait for zombies. This is his way of accumulating things in preparation for a return to normal times when commodities will be in demand again.

Here are opportunism and exploitative capitalism extending themselves in the most grotesque way into an apocalyptic time.

When the zombie apocalypse started, many young aboriginals discarded their modern trappings and went back to the 'old ways'. The movie ends with young aboriginal 'warriors' slaying zombies and then adopting a White man's child, after he turns. On the child's stomach, her father wrote 'thank you', perhaps expressing a new hope for the future of modernity, less about greed and destruction and more aligned with the natural principles of our world.

Another non-US/UK zombie movie was released in the same year, this time in the French language and set in rural areas of Quebec in Canada. Directed by Robin Aubert, *Ravenous* (2017) has a quirky and philosophical arthouse feel to it. Throughout the movie, there are scenes depicting zombies behaving in ways that are not very distinguishable from what humans do every day. A girl, who jealously attacks another for flirting with a race-car driver, turns out to be a zombie. The kids terrorizing people in a forest also turn out to be zombies.

Eventually, we learn that the zombies are moving towards an invasion. It turns out they are all converging at a field and ritualistically creating an ever-growing pile of objects, including chairs. At one level, a populist reading might connect the zombies to foreign people and their unfamiliar cultures—including Islamic practices—intruding into the liberal-conservative axis that defines Canadian public culture. At another level, a conservative reading might take these zombies to signify a return to a purer, more communitarian rural order, replacing the dominant corrupting modernity of the city. At yet another level, a progressive reading might see in the actions of these zombies the replacement of capitalism's individualistic and competitive accumulation, possessiveness and materialism with the more collective sensibility and shared responsibility of a new and more egalitarian socialist order.

Zombie Comedies

Some of these successful zombie movies, though dark in tone and pessimistic about the future, nevertheless have hopeful endings. Some present comic elements to diffuse the tension. Sometimes, it is to heighten the terror through contrast. But they all are basically tragic in nature. They point to the violent end of humanity, a self-destructive future brought on by the same qualities, values and logics that had made humanity great in the first place.

However, also popular in the 21st century have been zombie movies that are more like comedies than tragedies, featuring jokes, irony, parody and a self-consciously iconoclastic attitude towards the genre and its conventions. These comedies do not end in obvious tragedy. Instead, they lead to a social arrangement where humans can learn how to live not against zombies, but with them, accepting them for what they are. Although this arrangement might seem fragile, it is the most practical means of securing the continuity of humans.

The British zombie comedy *Shaun of the Dead* (2004), directed by Edgar Wright, was released in the same year as Zack Snyder's *Dawn of the Dead* remake. Shaun, the protagonist in the former, is a 'loser' with no purpose in life, minimal job prospects working at a supermarket and a girlfriend who breaks up with him for another man. His friends keep telling him,

> . . . sort out your fucking life, man!

The quintessential anti-hero, Shaun wakes up every morning looking and sounding like a zombie.

In fact, the movie very deliberately makes people in this north London neighbourhood behave like zombies in their everyday life activities: for instance, shoppers and cashiers going about their routines at a supermarket, drunkards stumbling down streets filled with litter the morning after and so on. It takes Shaun a long time, one fine morning, before he realizes that he is surrounded by zombies and in the middle of an apocalypse.

There is a clear British style of self-deprecating and understated humour here. Members of the survivor group goof around even as they make their way under very dangerous circumstances to the Winchester Pub, where—strangely—they hope to find safety. When Shaun's mother is about to die and reanimate as a zombie, she observes,

It's been a funny sort of day, hasn't it?

The movie ends with a scene showing the aftermath of the apocalypse, in which humans and zombies live together, with the latter appropriately restrained. They celebrate Z-Day to mark the end of the zombie apocalypse. They organize a charity fundraiser called ZombAid. Zombies work in supermarkets, participate in television game shows and appear in talk shows. And Shaun gets to play video games with his now zombified—and suitably restrained—friend Ed. This is the new normal, when humans accept zombies in their world, make practical adjustments and live as well as they can in the new circumstances.

Zombie comedies have also been popular and successful in the US. *Zombieland* (2009) and its sequel *Zombieland: Double Tap* (2019), both directed by Ruben Fleischer, are stylish movies with a quirky sense of humour. The fast-moving zombies are infected by 'mad zombie disease', which morphed from 'mad person disease', which in turn had morphed from 'mad cow disease'. The characters take their city of origin as their nicknames to keep their human relations as impersonal as possible. This is a way of coping with a new world in which people you grow attached to may suddenly be killed and turn into your attacker.

Like Shaun, the protagonist of *Zombieland*, Columbus, is something of an anti-hero. He is a lonely, video-game-playing college student, with numerous phobias and irritable bowel syndrome. The movie is as much about his efforts to get the girl who has commitment issues as it is about escaping zombies.

Zombieland takes a playful view of survivalism, the basic Darwinian theme at the ideological heart of most zombie movies. From his own experience, Columbus comes up with at least thirty-three rules of survival. Constantly referred to during the movie, the rules include:

Rule #1: Cardio
Rule #2: Double Tap
Rule #3: Beware of bathrooms
Rule #4: Seatbelts
Rule #17: Don't be a hero

Rule #31: Check the back seat
Rule #32: Enjoy the little things

During the journey, Columbus eventually gets the girl and becomes close to his fellow travellers. At the ending, Columbus says,

> . . . we had hope. We had each other. And without other people, well you might as well be a zombie.

In the sequel, Columbus and his team become even more expert in their knowledge of the zombie world, classifying zombies into slow-witted Homers, intelligent Hawkings, stealthy Ninjas and super-surviving T-800s. There are long scenes set in the White House, a shopping mall and Elvis's Graceland, all abandoned by this time to show zombification of politics, consumerism and entertainment, perhaps a criticism from the left. However, the movies can seem to justify the importance of guns as vital to individual freedom and even glorify violence, which helps a right-wing ideological agenda.

Another US zombie comedy movie released in 2019 was *The Dead Don't Die* (2019), directed by Jim Jarmusch. Much more arthouse in style than the *Zombieland* movies, Jarmusch's movie is strong on wit and ensemble acting.

The movie is intriguingly fragmented and difficult to piece together, which keeps the audience constantly trying to figure out what indeed is going on. Characters in the movie make numerous references to horror movie genres. One of the characters reveals that the director Jarmusch himself let him read the script of the movie they are in, so he knows how the movie and their lives are going to end. At that point, a spaceship suddenly appears, even though it is not in this script.

While the overall narrative can be rather puzzling, especially towards the end, there are some clear ideas developed. For instance, the zombie apocalypse (and the idea of total planetary destruction) is linked to polar fracking, which has moved Earth off its axis, changed the hours of the day and affected the behaviour of animals. The government and energy interests vehemently deny this, as one would expect in neoliberal globalization.

The movie concludes with the lead characters, Cliff and Ronnie, confronting their fate and slaying the zombies. A forest hermit, unencumbered by the material trappings of capitalist modernity, watches from afar and provides commentary:

> Cliff and little Ronnie. Warriors. Among the dead. Zombies. Remnants of the materialist people . . . I guess they've been zombies all along. Ghosts . . . 'Nameless miseries of the numberless mortals.' . . . Ashes to ashes. Dust to dust . . . The dead just don't want to die today. Reanimated and all jacked up, just like those ants. The end of the world. I guess all them ghost people plumb lost their goddamn souls. Must have traded 'em away or sold 'em for gold or whatnot. New trucks, kitchen appliances, new trousers, Nintendo Game Boys, shit like that. Just hungry for more stuff. Oh, down they go. The sad end of Cliff and Ronnie. What a fucked-up world.

A third zombie comedy movie released in 2019 was *Little Monsters* (2019), an Australian movie directed by Abe Forsythe. The heroine of the movie is kindergarten teacher Miss Caroline, who manages to shepherd the children in her class safely out of a zombie apocalypse on a country farm. In this, she is assisted by the uncle of one of the children, a screw-up who transforms into a responsible human being and finds his calling working with children.

The infection starts when a zombie escapes from a US military facility in Australia, where presumably they are conducting tests. The symbolism of a foreign power—especially the military-industrial complex of the US—introducing danger into an innocent Australian community is not difficult to miss. And although it is the US military that kills the zombies in the end, they almost shoot at the whole group of children by mistake as they are leaving the farm. If we think of the US as symbolizing global (but really Western and White) power and wealth, then we can more easily understand the Australian ambivalence towards nativist anxieties about foreign interference on the one hand and the attraction and prospects of embracing (Western and White) neoliberal globalization on the other. From 1901 to as recent as the mid-1970s, after all, a 'White Australia' immigration policy aimed to restrict non-White population growth on the continent. And yet, to *Little Monsters*' credit, the part of the heroine Miss Caroline, who saves the children and the bumbling White Australian man, is outstandingly performed by Lupita Nyong'o, a Kenyan and Mexican actress. In different parts of the world, the space between neoliberal globalization and authoritarian populism is nearly always ambivalent, dynamic and complex.

Asian Zombies

From the US to parts of Europe, and even to Australia, the cinematic zombie has travelled to nearly all parts of the world, including Asia. Although Asia has its own very rich and diverse folklore that features ghosts and monsters of various kinds, its moviemakers have appropriated the Western cinematic zombie almost wholesale. Many of these movies treat the zombies and the humans who must deal with them in a cartoonish way. Others use the zombie as a metaphor for social commentary. Some of these are directly critical of capitalism and the bureaucratic and corrupt governments that support and profit from it.

The Malaysian zombie comedy movie, *KL Zombie* (2013), was directed by Woo Ming Jin. The 'KL' in the title refers to Kuala Lumpur, the Malaysian capital city. This is a fun movie, clearly drawing inspiration from *Shaun of the Dead* (2004), but it does not really aim to bring anything new to the zombie genre other than a very local Southeast Asian context. The protagonist is a motorcycle-riding, pizza-delivering, hockey-playing slacker, who mans up to the challenge of leading a group to safety during a zombie apocalypse, slaying many zombies along the way. In the end, they discover that a beauty cream product, sold through a get-rich-quick multi-level marketing scheme, can serve as an antidote to the zombie infection. The movie ends with a montage of how the product is further commercialized as an anti-zombie-virus cream.

Not only is the movie's social commentary thin and uncritical, aimed at getting a quick laugh from the audience, but its slapstick comedy is also fuelled by the usual ethnic, gender and class stereotypes. The school's discipline teacher, a loud and overweight Chinese woman who speaks Malay with an exaggerated Chinese accent, is constantly seen scolding two Malay students. An Indian ice-cream seller speaks in an exaggerated Indian accent and displays buffoonish mannerisms.

A wealthy, powerful and corrupt Malay man boasts about his cut of twenty trillion Malaysian ringgit, with which he plans to buy the whole of neighbouring Singapore and then level all its buildings to turn it into a giant golf course. These characters are among the first to be viciously attacked and killed by zombies. Thus, this movie starts off with zombies killing off minorities and the corrupt elite, a gesture that might satisfy an authoritarian populist desire. The infection is also linked somewhat to religiously or morally objectionable acts: petting a dog (which is '*haram*' or forbidden in Islam) and then getting bitten and infected by it; cheating on partners and passing the virus through kissing; and praying at a Chinese grave for lottery numbers.

The Indonesian zombie comedy *Reuni Z* (2018), directed by Monty Tiwa and Soleh Solihun, revolves round a zombie outbreak at a high school reunion party. Here also is a derivative treatment of the zombie comedy genre, filled with clichés, mindless jokes and slapstick humour. One stereotype was sustained throughout the movie in the character of Marina, a transgender woman whom her former classmates used to know as Mansur twenty years ago. Acting in a most affected manner and dressed voluptuously in a red dress and high heels, Marina is the butt of so many crude jokes, including the obligatory scene in which a man lusting after her is horrified to see her masculine body in a public toilet. The stereotypical performance of gender transgression can trigger transphobic attitudes, amplified in the movie by the assignment of zombification as a grotesque metaphor for sex change. The zombie terror resonates with conservative anxiety, repressed through laughter that ridicules.

Movies produced in Singapore are often critical of its authoritarian government and materialistic society. The comedies tend to be cheeky, ironic and thickly spread with a typically Singaporean brand of local humour expressed in the iconoclastic Singlish patois. In the zombie comedy movie *Hsien of the Dead* (2012), directed by Gary Ow and clearly inspired by *Shaun of the Dead* (2004), Edward is a high-flying civil servant in the fictional Ministry of Propaganda, whose job is to watch and censor pornography. One day, he finds that all his colleagues have turned into zombies. Hsien, a newly enlisted soldier in the Singapore army, also finds that everyone in his military camp has been zombified. 'Hsien' is pronounced 'sian', which in Singlish means to be bored, uninterested and disengaged. Hsien is also part of Singapore's current prime minister's name. Together with two other characters, the group tries to find ways to escape Singapore, which has been overrun by zombies. The movie is quite explicit about describing how Singaporeans are like zombies, responding predictably to stimuli like the proverbial Pavlovian dogs.

In a subplot, another character is also trying to escape Singapore, but for a different reason. Suspected of being a terrorist, he is a detainee who manages to escape via a window in the toilet. This actually happened in 2008, when Indonesia-born Singaporean Mas Selamat Kastari escaped through a toilet window after he had been detained for allegedly plotting to bomb Singapore's airport. His escape launched the country's largest manhunt and questioned the competence of a much-vaunted government.

Singapore's second zombie comedy movie *Zombiepura* (2018), directed by Jacen Tan, is set in a military camp, where Singaporean men are regularly called up to do compulsory military service. The word Zombiepura is a play on 'Singapura', which means Singapore in the Malay language. The movie makes the point that demoralized soldiers in an army camp are not dissimilar to zombies. They are forced to stand at attention every morning with minimal enthusiasm when the national anthem is played. They frequently report sick at the medical centre to avoid training. Emblazoned all over the campgrounds are meaningless slogans about organizational values. Out of this malaise, a virus spreads throughout the camp, turning the soldiers into zombies.

The movie, however, performs a conservative ideological role by allowing the protagonist—a lazy malingerer at first—to evolve into a hero, patriotic and true to the slogan 'leave no man behind'. He not only saves the girl and escapes to safety, but also returns to the zombie-infested camp so that he can rescue other survivors.

Backpackers, directed by Songyos Sugmakanan, is the third of five short movies that are part of the Thai anthology movie *Phobia 2* (2009). The zombies, in this case, are a group of smugglers who swallowed bags of drugs but then died while being transported in a truck across the country. A boy zombie escapes and finds his way into a rural market, presumably the start of an apocalypse. The symbolism is clear. Through the logic and attraction of the market, the exploitative practices of drug and human trafficking that are rampant in the region can no longer be contained, exploding into society in a violent way. This is the return of the repressed.

Probably the most commercially and critically successful Asian zombie movie to date is *Train to Busan* (2016), directed by Yeon Sang-ho. In the movie, a zombie apocalypse is breaking out in South Korea as a group of people travel in a train from Seoul to Busan. An infected woman, who manages to slip into the train, turns into a zombie and infects most of the passengers, who also turn. These zombies only attack those they can see and hear. And since they are unable to operate the train door handles, the survivors can hide from them and find their way along the carriages in search of their loved ones.

The movie presents the corporate world in a very negative light. Its main villain is Yon-suk, the Chief Operating Officer (COO) of a bus company. He is a caricature of absolute selfishness. He demands that the train depart from the station immediately even though the other survivors who stayed behind to help others have not yet returned to the train. And when they do return to the train, he refuses to let them in, fearing they might be infected. He keeps his carriage closed to the survivors from other carriages, leaving them exposed to the ravenous zombies. He makes false accusations about other survivors being infected, playing on the fear of those around him to preserve his personal safety in the most cowardly manner, just as demagogues often do when they manipulate the masses against immigrants and other outsiders. He has no qualms about pushing his loyal staff, a young girl, and then a train driver into a group of zombies to clear a way for his own escape. In the end, he is infected, turns into a zombie and is thrown off the train.

The lead protagonist, Gong Yoo, is also a representative of the corporate world. When he introduces himself as a fund manager, another passenger describes him as someone who 'leeches off others' and who is an 'expert at leaving useless people behind'. He is presented as a workaholic, always checking up on his staff. He is estranged from his wife and pays little attention to his young daughter, who asks him:

> Are you not tired of working all the time?

When his daughter gives up her seat to an elderly passenger, he advises her,

> At a time like this, you only watch for yourself.

He does not hesitate to ask for special favours. Gong Yoo's character and behaviour reflects his belief in the survival of the fittest and a sense of elite entitlement. His daughter, disappointed and in tears, tells him,

> Dad, you only care about yourself. That's why mommy left.

In a phone call with his staff, he learns that a biotech company, with which he does business, is responsible for the zombie outbreak. Distraught, his staff tries to minimize their responsibility by saying,

> We're only doing our jobs right?

This is the kind of reasoning that Hannah Arendt would have described as the banality of evil.

Gong Yoo, unlike Yon-suk, becomes a better person during the struggle against adversity. He eventually overcomes his selfishness and demonstrates self-sacrifice, leadership and teamwork. In the end, when he is infected, he jumps off the train to his death, images of his baby daughter the final thing on his mind. The movie gives him redemption and offers the audience a vision of how corporate capitalism can be transformed into a force for good.

#Alive (2020), directed by Cho Il-hyung, is another South Korean zombie movie, one that gels especially well with the sensibilities of a social-media generation in a time of pandemic isolation and danger. In the movie, a zombie outbreak starts in the wealthy and fashionable district of Gangnam in Seoul, and then spreads to the metropolitan

areas, which are hit hard because of the compact spacing of rental units within high-rise apartment complexes. The spatial injustice and inequality that this suggests are clear. The impact of the COVID-19 pandemic, in parallel with the movie, has also been vastly unequal for people in different socio-economic categories.

Oh Joon-woo and Kim Yoo-bin are the young male and female protagonists of a movie that draws heavily on youth subcultural style and tonality. But the movie also presents two opposite images of the older 'baby boomer' generation of South Koreans and their relationship with the younger generation. On the one hand, there is an older man who entraps Joon-woo and Yoo-bin in his apartment, with the aim of feeding them to his zombified wife. The man is part of a generation of men emasculated by the competitive capitalism of a developmental state. Made to feel like failures, especially in the context of more traditional family expectations of paternal masculinity, this frustrated older generation, the movie seems to suggest, will betray the younger generation to salve their own damaged egos.

On the other hand, there is Joon-woo's father, whose final message to him was,

> You must survive.

This keeps him going, even as he runs out of food and water and almost tries to kill himself in lonely desperation. The older generation of South Koreans was tough and resilient, working hard to survive in a country that rose from post-war poverty to one of the most economically successful developmental states in the 1980s. In the movie, this older spirit of survival and resilience inspires a younger generation that nations always worry about.

But what really saves them in the end are the culture and technology of their youth. Joon-woo and Yoo-bin are attracted to each other for being 'damn cool'. They can work together to find ingenious ways of surviving the outbreak. Often, their methods involve the use of technology, such as drones and social media. In fact, they are rescued in the end by a Korean military helicopter that picked up their location through Joon-woo's social media hashtag #I_MUST_SURVIVE. Soon, all over the city, young people are being rescued through their social media posting.

A Zombie Revolution and a New World Order

Depending on who the audience is, the cinematic zombie can suggest rather different things about how society needs to change.

Conservative critics of neoliberal globalization, especially if they have been persuaded by the nativist arguments of populist leaders and movements, may see in zombies a vision of their society being overrun by foreigners and their cultures, so easily let in by the market-driven globalization policies of a neoliberal elite. They may see that while globalization can increase overall economic growth and promote urban rejuvenation, the benefits do not necessarily go to them. They may lose their jobs to cheaper or more valued foreigners, or face salary cuts and poorer work conditions under foreign management and ownership. The repulsive image of zombies may reflect and reinforce their view of foreigners as strange, disgusting, unassimilable, entitled, rapacious, diseased and dangerous. Foreigners can seem to threaten their way of life in every sense. Similarly, in zombies they may see the 'others' within their society, such as racial and sexual minorities 'favoured' by the (neo) liberal elite, who have appeared to them as a threat to conservative values and norms. The cinematic world of the zombie is a world so radically different from their own. The rules are different. Human relationships are different. There is anarchy and a state of war. Individual self-defensive weaponry may be the only thing that can keep them alive.

More progressive critics of neoliberal globalization may see, reflected in the cinematic zombie, some of the most debased qualities of the neoliberal elite. Billionaires, who continue to accumulate vast amounts of wealth, not to better the economy and society, but for buying politicians who can make legislation and policies that benefit them. Corporate CEOs, who thoughtlessly exploit and harm ordinary people in nearly every possible facet of their lives, without any care for their interests and well-being, just to maximize profit. Wall Street bankers, who always seek the adrenaline rush of casino capitalism, to make a killing by gambling recklessly with other people's hard-earned money, oblivious to the immense suffering they cause. And politicians, who allow themselves to be bought and manipulated, taking the side of the wealthy and powerful, instead of standing up for the poor and the weak, who are most in need of political representation. The image of the zombie stands for the dangerously dehumanized billionaire, CEO, financier, politician and any other member of the elite who is so easily able to deny their conscience to do the right thing, and whose egoism, selfishness and thoughtless banality can lead to great suffering for others.

Progressive critics of neoliberal globalization may also regard our own mindless and uncritical behaviour in everyday life as a deep problem. The way we eat. The way we subject ourselves to the addiction and control of social media. The materialism and consumerism that define our values and choices. In some sense, the progressive expectation of personal responsibility for enlightenment and emancipation overlaps with neoliberal responsibilization and welfare.

While progressives may identify thoughtlessness in everyday behaviour with the figure of the mindless zombie, they may also associate the throng of flesh-eating zombies with the violence of a conservative populist backlash, especially in the manipulative context of authoritarian populism. Thus, while authoritarian populists may see foreigners and minorities in the figure of the zombie, progressives might see angry authoritarian populists themselves as the zombies.

Zombie comedy movies often end with adaptation and co-existence, rather than one species tragically wiping out the other. We don't have to fight with all our might the changes that we encounter in our lives. We need to accommodate them without necessarily having to make fundamental transformations to our world. With the more traditional zombie horror movies, however, we are instead confronted with apocalypse, the prospect of an end to humanity. We can struggle to save humanity if we think it is worth saving. Or we can allow apocalypse to happen if we think humanity has degraded to such a destructive level that a radically new post-human order is the only thing that can save our world. In this way, the zombie apocalypse stands for the most revolutionary change we can hope for in our world.

Chapter Seven

Can Movies Really Save Our World?

The world that we find ourselves in today is indeed more peaceful and more prosperous. Life is convenient. Lifestyle options are plenty.

But we may not have progressed as much as we might like to think. The technology we have today is exciting and opens new possibilities of living well, but these pose novel problems. The wealth that we have created through the productive ingenuity of capitalism and the boundary-breaking energy of globalization turns out to be concentrated in the hands of a small number of nations. Within those nations, wealth is further concentrated in the hands of a small economic and political elite. Since the end of the Cold War, the US has strategically exercised hard, soft and smart power (Nye, 2013) to retain its commanding position at the global centre of this wealth concentration and will no doubt continue to do that for the foreseeable future, even as contemporary China's prospects in the world continue to rise phenomenally. Vast sections of the world remain poor and unable to live in health and dignity. And large sections of wealthy countries, such as the US, similarly struggle to survive, much less prosper. As the world's billionaires continue to amass and hoard wealth, without necessarily making socially or even economically productive use of it, more and more people are unable to improve their lot in life. They become despondent, socially disengaged and politically disenfranchised, while technocratic governments align their interests with global and local capitalists who have the means to buy their support. In these conditions, populist demagogues opportunistically manipulate the disgruntled masses for political and economic gain, directing their fears, frustrations and fury towards the neoliberal elite and/or minority groups whose rights and interests the elite are said to protect and advance at the expense of the left-behind mainstream. Meanwhile, the relentless profit-maximizing production-consumption machinery of capitalism devours the world's natural resources, polluting land, air and oceans, making our habitat less and less habitable. The poor suffer the most, but in the long term the rich will too.

Why do so many people, including those who have the least to gain by it, put up with this situation? Is it because they are kept unaware of the full extent and harm caused by poverty, inequality and environmental degradation? Even if they did understand this, and believe it, are they made to think that there is nothing they or anyone can really do about it? Or are they conditioned to think that this is all someone else's problem, or a problem for some abstract faceless future generation that they simply do not have the time or energy to care about?

Movies—whether documentaries or features—might help to provide some answers to these questions. Movies are still a large part of people's lives, whether they are projected on to cinema screens, played from cassettes or discs, or streamed on to television screens and various other devices, legally or illegally, watched individually or in groups. They shape the way we think. They can mimic the best and the worst of our world, naturalizing the status quo and reinforcing our assumptions about it. But they can also jolt us into critical awareness of what is regressive, unjust, ugly and undesirable about our world and especially our assumptions about it. By explaining the big picture or the suppressed point of view with logical clarity, moral purpose, human and ecological empathy, persuasive rhetoric and imaginative artistry, movies can demand and provoke action directed at radical change, everything from the cumulative effects of small adjustments in daily life to mass activism that makes a big bang.

Moviemakers of the 21st century who want to change our world—indeed, to save it—are up against tremendous resistance and opposition.

The Fourth Industrial Revolution, Pandemic, Social Injustice and Autocratization

Amidst a 21st-century renaissance of zombie movies and less than a year after we watched movies such as *Downton Abbey*, *Joker*, *Parasite* and *The Platform*—which depict poverty, inequality and revolution in their many different forms—the world was hit by a new viral infection. In March 2020, the World Health Organization (WHO) declared COVID-19 a global pandemic. At the time of writing, the pandemic has infected hundreds of millions of people and taken millions of lives worldwide (Heng and Au, 2021). These numbers are concerning. New variants of the virus have emerged, highly infectious and resilient. The end of the pandemic is nowhere in sight.

Beyond its epidemiological implications, COVID-19 has transformed nearly every domain of human life, including the technological, economic, political, social, cultural, ecological, psychological and their various permutations and intersections. Some of these transformations have really been forceful accelerations of longer-term trends. Formalized future-oriented thinking about work, education and business many years ago already anticipated such practices as work-from-home, home-based learning, online deliveries and e-payments, so much a part of life in the COVID-19 pandemic. Many of these scenarios had already been imagined in preparation for the opportunities and threats of the 'Fourth Industrial Revolution', a powerful vision of the near future that Klaus Schwab (2015), the World Economic Forum's executive chairman, famously popularized. COVID-19 has accelerated commitments to implement technological solutions in anticipation of a protracted economic downturn, which has already affected the rich and the poor in vastly different ways. The wealthy and powerful are naturally better able to cope with, and perhaps even to profit by, the pandemic and technological developments. The disruptions that come with the integration of data analytics, artificial intelligence, automation and the internet of things point both to utopian as well as dystopian futures. In unequal societies, the privileged few will be liberated from routine labour, finding more time for satisfyingly creative and autonomous work, work-life balance, physically and mentally healthful lifestyles and an enriched life in the community and the public sphere. The many who are disadvantaged will be replaced by technology and, unable to 'reskill' or 'upskill', will be unemployable and stuck more deeply in poverty, perhaps a life of violence, crime and incarceration. Movies such as *3%*, *The Hunger Games*, *The Forever Purge* and especially *Elysium*—as discussed at the start of this book—are examples of critical dystopian science fiction that vividly project grossly undesirable futures that the persistence of neoliberal globalization, hyper-charged by crises and technological revolutions, might lead to.

As discussed in the previous chapter, one of the pleasures of zombie movies is the vicarious experience of an apocalyptic crisis, where we get to see humanity at its best and its worst, while learning how to survive in a world where human contact and relationships have been radically redefined because of the violent and rapid transmissibility of a fatal 'virus'. In many zombie movies, the causes of the outbreak are at least implied. Often, it starts with an accident, which is linked in some way or other to scientific-industrial hubris, corporate greed, political corruption or some combination of these. Thus, zombie movies can warn us about the dangers of unbridled authoritarian capitalism and thoughtless materialism taken to its logical extremes, predisposing us through the thrill of horror and terror to take a critical perspective on neoliberal globalization.

However, in the context of authoritarian populism, zombie movies might also reinforce regressive attitudes and behaviours of the disadvantaged masses such as racism, nativism and xenophobia. The idea of our mainstream society and its authentic way of life being invaded and overwhelmed by a throng of strange and dangerous people who are exaggeratedly different from ourselves resonates with the collective concern and hostility directed at the folk devils that are so much a part of moral panic. In the US, when the fatal effects of the COVID-19 pandemic were at their worst, President Trump used terms like 'China virus', 'Wuhan virus' and 'kung flu' to deflect culpability by blaming China for being the source of the global infection, even though this remains unproven. Repeated use of these terms by the president as well as Republican politicians and news media may have activated populist anxieties about Chinese immigrants, Chinese Americans and even Asian Americans, causing them emotional distress and, in widely reported cases in the media, even violence (Samson, 2021).

From a liberal standpoint, it is this kind of manipulated ultra-conservative backlash of the populist masses against globalization, technocratic elitism, liberal democratic institutions and tolerance of diversity that resonates with cinematic zombie behaviour as well as zombie-like behaviour in such movies as *The Forever Purge*. In the US, scenes of Trump followers storming the Capitol building to defy President Joe Biden's rightful victory in the 2020 presidential elections recall the violent throngs of cinematic zombies who have no understanding of and respect for the institutions of human civilization, which they destroy viciously and mechanically. Liberals also worry about the practical measures put in place to control the virus (in a pandemic or a zombie apocalypse) and their implications for civil rights, freedom, privacy, dignity, transparency and accountability. These measures can be quite draconian. And once put in place, will often be difficult to dislodge in the future. The V-Dem Institute's *Democracy Report 2021*, titled 'Autocratization turns viral', noted a steep ten-year global decline for liberal democracy, where only 14 per cent of the world's population live in only thirty-two countries that meet the criteria of liberal democracy. The pattern of autocratization begins with governments attacking the media and civil society, disrespecting political opponents, polarizing society, spreading false information and undermining formal institutions. The report noted that the impact of COVID-19 measures on democracy was not severe but warned that the final toll may be high if restrictions are not eliminated immediately after the pandemic.

In these times, when neoliberal globalization has been challenged, but also in many ways augmented, by authoritarian populist reactions, a severe pandemic crisis and radical technological disruptions, moviemakers who want to save the world have a lot to contend with.

Moviemaking as a Global Industry

But it also means that they have a lot of new material to work with.

For the most part, moviemaking is an industry, one that manufactures fantasies for mass consumption. Like any other industry, moviemaking needs raw materials, especially ideas and novel concepts for stories and characters. It needs to captivate audience-consumers who can identify with and learn something from these stories and characters. And it seeks to make a profit, or at least to cover costs. Media corporations, much like the big corporations criticized by many of the movies discussed in this book, are very much a part of the moviemaking world, if not essential to producing those blockbusters whose progressive influence may reach more global audiences. Thus, even progressive moviemaking is not specially insulated from the excesses of corporate capitalist profit maximization, and the over-commercialization, exploitative practices, socially unjust outcomes and authoritarian impulses associated with that.

Neoliberal globalization has made available a wider pool of resources to finance moviemaking, including progressive documentary-making. While this creates new possibilities for growth, the neoliberal obsession with key performance indicators—most pronounced in New Public Management values, practices and institutions—bureaucratically threatens movies that aim to break free of formal artistic conventions and to pursue an experimentally more radical progressive agenda. Funders often demand empirical measurement of social impact to ensure the documentaries they support contribute to the common good. But this, as Bill Nichols (2016) has argued, over-disciplines the field by privileging work that is tamer and more narrowly focused. A similar problem afflicts neoliberal-global universities whose research, teaching and outreach missions have been diminished by what historian Jerry Z. Muller (2018) has more broadly described as the 'tyranny of metrics'. Instead of facilitating more 'genuinely provocative' bodies of work whose social impact escapes rigid quantification, Nichols observes, external funding of this kind supports

> . . . forms of impact that are more ameliorative than transformative,

making these funders essentially the unquestioned conservative gatekeepers of the moviemaking world.

Secondly, documentaries that purport to advance the interests, rights and well-being of marginalized people and communities may end up exploiting them for commercial or artistic purposes. This is not always done intentionally, but the unwitting and insidious effect of it is to silence and disempower the subjects even further. In fact, even participatory documentaries, in which disenfranchised subjects are given the opportunity to represent themselves, may end up extending the practice of 'othering' not by exclusion, but by the performance of inclusion, participation and empowerment, as media scholar Pooja Rangan (2017) has argued. Rangan criticized what she called 'immediations', or the tropes of documentary immediacy such as the 'innocence' of non-Western children and the 'liveness' of disaster victims. These tropes rely on the truth effects of documentary and instrumentalize the dehumanized subjects to 'perform' their humanity for the documentary and its political purposes. Similar tropes may readily be found in the documentaries of Michael Moore, Morgan Spurlock and others discussed in this book. As much as they appear to want to defend the victims of neoliberal globalization, they do rely on artifice to produce documentary truth effects and, in doing so, may come dangerously close to being exploitative themselves.

In contrast, critical health communication scholar Mohan J. Dutta (2007) has advocated for a 'culture-centred approach' that engages with silenced communities through 'dialogical projects' designed so that their voice can be given a position of centrality in the collective process of understanding meanings, issues, and risks, and of constructing possible solutions. Filmmakers, artists and other cultural workers have a powerful role to play in such engagements.

Thirdly, there is the question of Hollywood. The criticism of Hollywood used to be based mainly on a model of cultural imperialism, where the internationally dominant cinema of the US was actively exported to the rest of the world for international box-office revenue. Hollywood movies had a strong impact on the arts and popular culture of importing countries, often displacing local work and providing cinematic genres and filmic vocabularies that were adopted or mimicked wholesale for their immediate entertainment value. American values, as well as America's image of the world that includes a system of national and ethnic stereotypes, were exported through Hollywood, as an instrument of US soft power. However, with neoliberal globalization, 'Hollywood' has become a much more transnational, even global, set of moviemaking practices and institutions. Hollywood studios have extended far beyond Los Angeles into other markets around the world to produce content that is local and directed mainly at local audiences. Hollywood is making 'Bollywood' movies in India. It is making movies in China, careful not to offend its heavy censorship rules. The Academy Awards, internationally the most prestigious recognition of moviemaking excellence given by the US-headquartered Academy of Motion Picture Arts and Sciences (AMPAS), have been increasingly recognizing non-US movies. *Parasite*, the first foreign-language movie to win Best Picture along with three other awards in 2020, is a much-celebrated example of this. Whether these developments signal a weakening of US cultural imperialism or a more complex manifestation of its neoliberally global cultural hegemony is debatable.

What is perhaps less debatable is the presence of inequality and exploitation within an insufficiently diverse Hollywood. Empirical data strongly suggests that there is institutionalized sexism, homophobia and racism. Over the decades, women, people from the LGBTQIA+ community and people of colour have been systematically under-represented in movies. And when they do appear, it is often for token or stereotypical and usually unflattering roles. A *Time* magazine report in 2016 noted that only 6.4 per cent of acting nominations since the Academy Awards began in 1929 had gone to non-white actors (Berman, 2016). A *Los Angeles Times* study in 2012 revealed the membership of AMPAS to be 94 per cent White and 77 per cent male, with a median age of sixty-two (Horn, Sperling and Smith, 2012). A vast majority of the most powerful creative decision-makers in the industry are White and cis male. In more recent years, the success of Hollywood movies such as *Black Panther* (2018), a superhero movie by a Black director and featuring a predominantly Black cast, and *Crazy Rich Asians* (2018), which had a majority ethnic Chinese cast, including Singaporean Chinese actors, was celebrated as a sign that Hollywood was finally taking diversity more seriously and showing results. Media scholars Sarah E. Turner and Sarah Nilsen (2019), however, cautioned against mistaking diversity on screen for diversity in the industry itself, which in many ways remains as patriarchal and White as ever. They explained how

> . . . neoliberal multiculturalism . . . celebrates incremental steps in screen visibility while leaving the structural inequality of the industry

> unchallenged. It accepts cultural visibility as a social good while erasing the reality of increasing poverty among ethnic and racial minorities in the United States . . . it rationalizes superficial evidence of diversity in terms of the language of market rather than based on the ethics and values of producing change for the common good.

Indeed, #MeToo, a high-profile social media movement fronted by female celebrities who had been sexually harassed and assaulted, exposed decades of egregious sexual misconduct by powerful and highly respected male moviemakers, actors, television journalists and even celebrity chefs in the entertainment industry. The most spectacular was the case of movie producer Harvey Weinstein, against whom multiple allegations of sexual abuse were made. He was eventually convicted as a sex offender. Many others experienced significant repercussions on their reputations and careers. The #MeToo movement quickly spread beyond the industry and has gone global (Hillstrom, 2018). In 2018, Korean director Kim Ki-duk was accused of multiple counts of sexual assault and harassment by actresses and university students. Investigators reported how Kim would say things to his students like,

> If you want a leading role in one of my films, it's simple. You just have to sleep with me . . . (Noh, 2018).

We have probably only seen the tip of the iceberg. The punishments meted out to these powerful men were not trivial, but they probably amounted to a kind of ritual cleansing, after which nothing fundamentally changes. It is hard to imagine that sexist and misogynistic behaviour in the moviemaking world, where power is hugely asymmetrical, has been eliminated because of this.

Perhaps more radical change might be possible when the mode of movie production also changes radically. We are in a post-cinematic age, which can mean many things including the way in which much of our movie watching happens on our personal devices via digital technology and streaming platforms such as Netflix and Hulu. Turner and Nilsen (2019) noted how these platforms are strategically targeting ethnic and racial minority audiences through the movies they curate and the original content they produce. This puts pressure on big-budget movie studios and networks that depend on advertisers. But the shifting of power structures that this can induce is slow and not guaranteed. Turner and Nilsen observed that the decision-makers of streaming platforms are also predominantly White men. They called for pressure on Hollywood gatekeepers to be exerted continuously by academics, social media activists and media activist organizations so that hegemonic change can happen.

Through a close analysis of more than seventy popular movies produced in these first two decades of the 21st century, we have explored the theme of poverty, inequality, ecological degradation and revolutionary change, all associated with a contemporary crisis of neoliberal globalization in a world where it has become so thoroughly pervasive. In such a world, profit rules, while poverty and inequality have made the political ground fertile for populist manipulation. By returning power to the people, populism can lead the way to progressive revolutionary change that enriches democracy and corrects for social injustice. However, through ideological and political manipulation, populism can also take more debased authoritarian forms that augment and entrench conformism, domination, exploitation, marginalization and degradation of humanity and its habitat.

We have discussed how neoliberal globalization and the more degraded forms of populism are reflected, supported or critiqued in the themes, narratives, characterization, socio-political settings and other formal aesthetic aspects of popular movies. We have discussed the socio-political implications of these movies as products of a profitable global culture industry, a major component of neoliberal globalization, which is itself highly susceptible to overcommercialization, exploitation, abuse, social injustice and authoritarianism.

With so much that is regressive in this world, we have looked for revolutionary possibilities, identifying ways in which movies may imagine with optimism alternatives to this world of poverty, inequality and environmental degradation, so that our world—confronted by so much adversity—may yet be saved.

Movies: Propaganda vs Deliberation

So now that we've come to the end of the book, what can you do?

Perhaps you think these more than seventy movies depicting a world in crisis are mere exaggerations, typical of the fame- and profit-seeking movie-industry that psychopathically relies on sensationalist fearmongering to mesmerize audiences for purely commercial benefit, all the while condoning or ignoring some of the worst practices of discrimination, exploitation, abuse and hypocrisy within the industry. Perhaps you also think the converging perspectives of a world in crisis, as represented so vividly in these movies, is a dangerous symptom of the closing of minds—a dogmatic, joyless, over-dramatic, apocalyptic and zombie-like inclination that, if left unchecked, can galvanize militant movements to suppress diversity, free speech, individual choice and the legitimate pleasures that we have become accustomed to in our modern lives. And you would not be entirely wrong to think in these ways. After all, the path from prophet to confidence trickster and then to tyrant is a very slippery slope. So, scepticism and a plurality of perspectives are important for our public sphere to prevent efforts to save the world from themselves becoming a new cause of its greater destruction.

But this should not mean that ignorance is bliss or that we should simply accept that everyone has a different perspective and so we should just get on with our own individual lives. The problems of the world, if or when they are real, will require coordination, difficult conversations and collective action. For this to happen, we need to learn how to talk to one another. We need to understand and appreciate why there are differences, particularly where moral intuitions are concerned, and what is at stake when someone gives up their position in an argument. We need good faith, the capacity to assume the best of one another, even if this grates on our sensibilities. We need to enrich the grammar and vocabulary of public discourse and deliberation, so impoverished over the last few decades by the polarizing dynamics of neoliberal globalization and authoritarian populism.

If the aim of movies were simply to get everyone on the same page, even if that turns out to be the correct page, then they would not have gone far enough to save our world. They would simply have deployed the techniques of brainwashing, as any other mode of propaganda would do.

Much more important and sustainable would be for movies to enrich our capacity for explanation, understanding, judgement and prediction, not just as individual and intellectual activities, but as a deliberative exercise of communication and collective thinking. Movies can help us understand and empathize with different positions, so that we can come to embrace higher-order knowledge instead of sticking stubbornly to our own points of view. Movies can help us appreciate the value of feelings and emotions that are just as significant as cerebral arguments, which tend to uphold facts and figures while disparaging lived experience and the stories we tell about our lives and the lives of others. By projecting alternative and yet often very familiar worlds, movies can fuel our imagination, freeing us from the shackles of daily necessities and the cynical tendency to say 'no, that's just not possible' or 'we've tried that before and it just doesn't work'. It is important to be able to imagine better worlds, to aspire to better things and not to limit ourselves to the small realities of the present. Movies can inspire, and they should.

So, if you are a moviemaker, and have not already done so, consider the power you have—especially with the availability of new digital technologies in a hyper-connected post-pandemic world—not only to get more people on the same page or the right page, but also to help expand and improve our deliberative capacities and to inspire optimism where many have found the situation to be hopeless.

And if you are an educator of any kind, teach with movies. When thoughtfully curated and properly scaffolded, they are an incredible resource for understanding difficult arguments; for appreciating different sides in every argument; for learning the skills and techniques of storytelling and deliberation; and for igniting ideas, feelings and energies that can inspire future generations to strive for changes that are informed, impactful and compassionate. So that if ever our world needed saving, we would be ready.

References

'False profits or false prophet? Michael Moore v capitalism', *The Economist*, 10 October 2009.

'Joe Biden is determined that China should not displace America', *The Economist*, 17 July 2021.

'Transforming our world: The 2030 agenda for sustainable development', Resolution adopted by the United Nations General Assembly on 25 September 2015.

'We can end poverty: Millennium Development Goals and beyond 2015', United Nations website, https://www.un.org/millenniumgoals/.

ABC News (2018) 'Michael Moore on Donald Trump and who Moore would love to see as the next president', *Popcorn with Peter Travers*, 21 September, https://youtu.be/mJlCMfAn3VU.

Adorno, Theodor W., Else Frenkel-Brunswik, Daniel Levinson and Nevitt Sanford (1950) *The Authoritarian Personality*, Harper & Row, Inc.

Adorno, Theodor W. and Max Horkheimer (trans. Edmund Jephcott) (2002/1944) *Dialectic of Enlightenment*, Stanford University Press.

Arendt, Hannah (1951) *The Origins of Totalitarianism*, Schocken Books.

Arendt, Hannah (1958) *The Human Condition*, University of Chicago Press.

Arendt, Hannah (1963) *Eichmann in Jerusalem: A Report on the Banality of Evil*, The Viking Press.

Aristotle (trans. C.D.C. Reeve) (1998) *Politics*, Hackett.

Ban, Cornel (2016) *Ruling Ideas: How Global Neoliberalism Goes Local*, Oxford University Press.

Bartle, John, David Sanders and Joe Twyman (2020) 'Authoritarian populist opinion in Europe', in *Authoritarian Populism and Liberal Democracy*, edited by Ivor Crewe and David Sanders, Palgrave Macmillan.

Beck, Bernard (2003) 'Moving targets: *Bowling for Columbine* and American gun play', *Multicultural Perspectives*, 5(3): 26–9.

Bell, Daniel A. and Li Chenyang (eds.) (2013) *The East Asian Challenge for Democracy: Political Meritocracy in Comparative Perspective*, Cambridge University Press.

Benson, Thomas W. and Brian J. Snee (2015) 'Michael Moore and the rhetoric of documentary: art, argument, affect', in *Michael Moore and the Rhetoric of Documentary*, edited by Thomas W. Benson, Brian J. Snee, Jennifer L. Borda, Christine Harold, Brian L. Ott and Susan A. Sci, Southern Illinois University Press.

Berlet, Chip and Matthew N. Lyons (2000) *Right-Wing Populism in America: Too Close for Comfort*, Guilford Press.

Berman, Eliza (2016) 'See the entire history of the Oscars diversity problem in one chart', *Time*, 20 January.

Brotherton, Rob (2015) *Suspicious Minds: Why We Believe Conspiracy Theories*, Bloomsbury.

Cadwalladr, Carole (2013) 'Inequality for All—another Inconvenient Truth?', *The Observer*, 2 February.

Callenbach, Ernest (2007) 'Sicko', *Film Quarterly*, 61(2): 18–20.

Channel 4 News (2018) 'Michael Moore on Trump, Brexit and his new film', *Ways to Change the World*, podcast, 18 October, https://youtu.be/FRRxG4L4upA.

Cohen, Stanley (1972) *Folk Devils and Moral Panics: The Creation of the Mods and Rockers*, MacGibbon and Kee.

Crewe, Ivor (2020) 'Authoritarian populism and Brexit in the UK in historical perspective', in *Authoritarian Populism and Liberal Democracy*, edited by Ivor Crewe and David Sanders, Palgrave Macmillan.

Crouch, Colin (2004) *Post-Democracy*, Polity.

Deleuze, Gilles and Félix Guattari (trans. Robert Hurley, Mark Seem and Helen R. Lane) (1983/1972) *AntiOedipus: Capitalism and Schizophrenia*, University of Minnesota Press.

Denzau, Arthur T. and Ravi K. Roy (2004) *Fiscal Policy Convergence from Reagan to Blair: The Left Veers Right*, Routledge.

Derrida, Jacques (trans. Peggy Kamuf) (1994/1993) *Specters of Marx: The State of the Debt, the Work of Mourning and the New International*, Routledge.

Douglas, Andrew J. (2010) 'Capitalism: A Love Story', *The Journal of American History*, 97(1): 281–2.

Douglas, Karen M., Robbie M. Sutton and Aleksandra Cichocka (2017) 'The psychology of conspiracy theories', *Current Directions in Psychological Science*, 26(6): 538–42.

Douthat, Ross (2020) *The Decadent Society: How We Became the Victims of Our Own Success*, Avid Reader.

Duignan, Brian (no date) 'What's the difference between a psychopath and a sociopath? And how do both differ from narcissists?', *Encyclopaedia Britannica*, https://www.britannica.com/story/whats-the-difference-between-a-psychopath-and-a-sociopath-and-how-do-both-differ-from-narcissists.

Dutta, Mohan J. (2007) 'Communicating about culture and health: theorizing culture-centered and cultural sensitivity approaches', *Communication Theory*, 17(3): 304–328.

Eatwell, Roger and Matthew Goodwin (2018) *National Populism: The Revolt Against Liberal Democracy*, Pelican.

Economopoulos, Spiro (2003) 'Burning down the house: Bowling for Columbine', *Senses of Cinema*, January.

Edin, Kathryn J. and H. Luke Shaefer (2015) *$2.00 a Day: Living on Almost Nothing in America*, Houghton Mifflin Harcourt.

Felperin, Leslie (2009) 'Capitalism: A Love Story', *Variety*, 5 September.

Floyd, Ife, Ashley Burnside and Liz Schott (2018) 'TANF reaching few poor families', Center on Budget and Policy Priorities.

Freud, Sigmund (1915) 'The Unconscious', in Volume XIV (On the History of the Psycho-Analytic Movement, Papers on Meta-psychology and Other Works [1914–16]), *The Standard Edition of the Complete Psychological Works of Sigmund Freud*, Hogarth Press.

Fukuyama, Francis (1992) *The End of History and the Last Man*, The Free Press.

Gabriel, Satya J. (2001) 'Oliver Stone's *Wall Street* and the market for corporate control', *Economics in Film Essay Series* (online papers), 21 November, http://www.crawfordsworld.com/rob/ape/APEFilms/APEWallStreet/WSGabriel.htm .

Gelles, David (2017) 'Robert Reich, a multiplatform gadfly, comes to Netflix', *The New York Times*, 20 November.

Giroux, Henry A. (2004) *The Terror of Neoliberalism: Authoritarianism and the Eclipse of Democracy*, Routledge.

Giroux, Henry A. (2014) *Neoliberalism's War on Higher Education*, Haymarket.

Giroux, Henry A. (2014) *Zombie Politics and Culture in the Age of Casino Capitalism*, 2nd Edition, Peter Lang.

Giroux, Henry A. (2019) *The Terror of the Unforeseen*, LARB Provocations.

Gleiberman, Owen (2019) 'Why "Joker" is about all of us', *Variety*, 20 October.

Good Morning Britain (2016) 'Michael Moore on guns, Trump and the EU with Piers Morgan—full interview', 14 June, https://youtu.be/wpBdKT8sL3M.

Goode, Erich and Nachman Ben-Yahuda (1994) *Moral Panics: The Social Construction of Deviance*, Wiley-Blackwell.

Goodnight, G. Thomas (2005) 'The Passion of the Christ meets Fahrenheit 9/11: A study in celebrity advocacy', *The American Behavioral Scientist*, 49(3): 410–35.

Gramsci, Antonio (eds. and trans. Quintin Hoare and Geoffrey Nowell Smith) (1971) *Selections from the Prison Notebooks*, International Publishers.

Greenstone, Michael, Adam Looney, Jeremy Patashnik and Muxin Yu (2013) 'Thirteen economic facts about social mobility and the role of education', The Hamilton Project, June, https://www.brookings.edu/research/thirteen-economic-facts-about-social-mobility-and-the-role-of-education/.

Greve, Bent (2020a) *Poverty: The Basics*, Routledge.

Greve, Bent (2020b) *Welfare, Populism and Welfare Chauvinism*, Bristol University Press.

Grierson, John (ed. Forsyth Hardy) (1966) *Grierson on Documentary*, University of California Press.

Grusky, David B. (2011) 'The stories about inequality that we love to tell', in *The Inequality Reader: Contemporary and Foundational Readings in Race, Class, and Gender*, edited by David B. Grusky and Szonja Szelenyi, Routledge.

Haidt, Jonathan (2012) *The Righteous Mind: Why Good People Are Divided by Politics and Religion*, Pantheon.

Hall, Stuart, Chas Critcher, Tony Jefferson, John Clarke and Brian Roberts (1978) *Policing the Crisis: Mugging, The State, and Law & Order*, Macmillan.

Harvey, David (2005) *A Brief History of Neoliberalism*, Oxford University Press.

HBO (2018) 'Michael Moore: Fahrenheit 11/9', *Real Time with Bill Maher*, 22 September, https://youtu.be/d79X7Udaa2c.

Hegel, Georg Wilhelm Friedrich (trans. A.V. Miller) (1807/1997), *Phenomenology of Spirit*, Oxford University Press.

Helliker, Kevin and Shirley Leung (2003) 'Judge dismisses obesity suit by 2 girls against McDonald's', *The Wall Street Journal*, 23 January.

Heng, Cheryl and Bonnie Au (2021) 'One year into COVID-19 pandemic, world marks anniversary of WHO's declaration on coronavirus', Video, *South China Morning Post*, 11 March, https://www.scmp.com/video/coronavirus/3125018/one-year-covid-19-pandemic-world-marks-anniversary-whos-declaration.

Hillstrom, Laurie Collier (2018) *The #MeToo Movement*, ABC-CLIO, LLC.

Horn, John, Nicole Sperling and Doug Smith (2012) 'Unmasking Oscar: Academy voters are overwhelmingly white and male', *Los Angeles Times*, 19 February.

Howard, Christopher, Amirio Freeman, April Wilson and Eboni Brown (2017) 'Poverty', *Political Opinion Quarterly*, 81(3): 769–89.

Hundt, David (2015) 'Neoliberalism, the developmental state and civil society in Korea', *Asian Studies Review*, 39(3): 466–82.

Ide, Wendy (2010) 'Capitalism: A Love Story', *The Times*, 26 February.

IPCC (2021) 'Summary for policymakers', in *Climate Change 2021: The Physical Science Basis* (Contribution of Working Group I to the Sixth Assessment Report of the Intergovernmental Panel on Climate Change).

Jones, Ellen E. (2011) 'Reel to real: can documentaries change the world?', *The Guardian*, 6 October.

Kapucu, Naim (2006) 'New Public Management: theory, ideology, and practice', in *Handbook of Globalization, Governance, and Public Administration*, edited by Ali Farazmand, Routledge.

Kelley, Sonaiya (2020) 'Netflix's class warfare movie "*The Platform*" has struck a chord', *LA Times*, 15 April.

Kellner, Douglas (2010) *Cinema Wars: Hollywood Film and Politics in the Bush-Cheney Era*, Wiley-Blackwell.

Kellner, Douglas (2016) *American Nightmare: Donald Trump, Media Spectacle, and Authoritarian Populism*, Sense.

Kim, Sam (2016) 'Brexit, Trump tide of populism swamps South Korea President Park', *Bloomberg*, 8 December.

King, Stephen (2010) *Danse Macabre*, Gallery Books.

Klees, Steven J. (2008) 'A quarter century of neoliberal thinking in education: misleading analyses and failed policies', *Globalisation, Societies and Education*, 6(4), 311–48.

Kristeva, Julia (1982) *Powers of Horror: An Essay in Abjection*, Columbia University Press.

Krzych, Scott (2015) 'The price of knowledge: hysterical discourse in anti-Michael Moore documentaries', *The Comparatist*, 39: 80–100.

Kyle, Jordan and Limor Gultchin (2018) 'Populists in power around the world', Report by the Tony Blair Institute for Global Change, 7 November, https://institute.global/policy/populists-power-around-world.

Lauro, Sarah Juliet (2017) 'Introduction' in *Zombie Theory: A Reader*, edited by Sarah Juliet Lauro, University of Minnesota Press.

Leistedt, Samuel J. and Paul Linkowski (2014) 'Psychopathy and the cinema: fact or fiction?', *Journal of Forensic Sciences*, 59(1): 167–74.

Lopez-Littleton, Vanessa and Arto Woodley (2018) 'Movie review of *13th* by Ava Duvernay: administrative evil and the prison industrial complex', *Public Integrity*, 20(4): 415–8.

Lyons, James (2019) *Documentary, Performance and Risk*, Routledge.

Mann, Keith (2012) 'Resistance to neo-liberalism: France, Greece, Spain, and the US', *Perspectives on Global Development and Technology*, 11(1): 182–91.

Marsh, David (2020) 'Populism and Brexit', in *Authoritarian Populism and Liberal Democracy*, edited by Ivor Crewe and David Sanders, Palgrave Macmillan.

Marx, Karl and Friedrich Engels (1848/1998) *The Communist Manifesto*, Monthly Review Press.

Mazin, Craig (2019) 'On "Joker"', *Variety*, 17 December.

McGrath, Matt (2021) 'Climate change: IPCC report is "code red for humanity"', BBC News, 9 August.

McIntosh, Peggy (1988) 'White privilege and male privilege: a personal account of coming to see correspondences through work in Women's Studies', Working Paper 189, Wellesley Centers for Women.

McNear, Claire (2021) '"Operation Varsity Blues" is light on new information, heavy on schadenfreude', *The Ringer*, 18 March.

Merry, Stephanie (2017) 'Michael Moore wants to take down a president', *The Washington Post*, 17 May.

Mijs, Jonathan J.B. and Mike Savage (2020) 'Meritocracy, elitism and inequality', *The Political Quarterly*, 91(2): 397–404.

Miliband, David (2007) 'The great climate change swindle?', blog on the website of the UK Department for Environment, Food and Rural Affairs, 14 March, https://web.archive.org/web/20070320212733/http://www.davidmiliband.defra.gov.uk/blogs/ministerial_blog/archive/2007/03/14/5960.aspx.

Mirrlees, Tanner and Isabel Pedersen (2016) 'Elysium as a critical dystopia', *International Journal of Media and Cultural Politics*, 12(3): 305–22.

Moore, Michael (2019) 'On "Joker"', *Variety*, 18 December.

Moore, Randy (1990) 'What's wrong with science education and how do we fix it?', *The American Biology Teacher*, 52(6): 330–7.

Muller, Jerry Z. (2018) *The Tyranny of Metrics*, Princeton University Press.

National Institute of Mental Health (no date) 'What is psychosis?', https://www.nimh.nih.gov/health/topics/schizophrenia/raise/what-is-psychosis.

Nestle, Marion (2013) *Food Politics: How the Food Industry Influences Nutrition and Health*, Revised and expanded tenth anniversary edition, University of California Press.

Nichols, Bill (2001) *Introduction to Documentary*, Indiana University Press.

Nichols, Bill (2016) *Speaking Truths with Film: Evidence, Ethics, Politics in Documentary*, University of California Press.

Noh, Jean (2018) 'Kim Ki-duk, Cho Jae-hyun accused of multiple sexual assaults', *Screen International*, 7 March.

Norris, Pippa and Ronald Inglehart (2019) *Cultural Backlash: Trump, Brexit and Authoritarian Populism*, Cambridge University Press.

Nye, Joseph S. (2013) 'Hard, soft, and smart power', in *The Oxford Handbook of Modern Diplomacy*, edited by A.F. Cooper, J. Heine and R. Thakur, Oxford University Press.

O'Dwyer, Davin (2007) 'Zeitgeist: the nonsense', the *Irish Times*, 8 August.

Orvell, Miles (1994) 'Documentary film and the power of interrogation: "American Dream" and "Roger & Me"', *Film Quarterly*, 48(2): 10–18.

Ott, Brian L. and Susan A. Sci (2015) 'The many moods of Michael Moore: aesthetics and affect in *Bowling for Columbine*', in *Michael Moore and the Rhetoric of Documentary*, edited by Thomas W. Benson, Brian J. Snee, Jennifer L. Borda, Christine Harold, Brian L. Ott and Susan A. Sci, Southern Illinois University Press.

Peterson, Janice (2020) 'Welfare policy and precarious lives: "welfare reform" revisited', *Journal of Economic Issues*, 54(2): 377–84.

Phillips, Kendall R. (2015) '"I'm sorry to see it go": nostalgic rhetoric in Michael Moore's *Capitalism: A Love Story*', in *Michael Moore and the Rhetoric of Documentary*, edited by Thomas W. Benson, Brian J. Snee, Jennifer L. Borda, Christine Harold, Brian L. Ott and Susan A. Sci, Southern Illinois University Press.

Piketty, Thomas (trans. Arthur Goldhammer) (2014/2013) *Capital in the Twenty-First Century*, Harvard University Press.

Pinker, Steven (2011) *The Better Angels of Our Nature: Why Violence Has Declined*, Viking.

Plato (trans. Francis M. Cornford) (1941) *The Republic of Plato*, Oxford University Press.

Porton, Richard (2016) 'Weapon of mass instruction: Michael Moore's *Fahrenheit 9/11* (2004)', in *The Documentary Film Reader: History, Theory, Criticism*, edited by Jonathan Kahana, Oxford University Press.

Potvin, Patrice and Abdelkrim Hasni (2014) 'Analysis of the decline in interest towards school science and technology from Grades 5 through 11', *Journal of Science Education and Technology*, 23: 784–802.

Purcell, Mark (2008) *Recapturing Democracy: Neoliberalization and the Struggle for Alternative Urban Futures*, Routledge.

Quiggin, John (2007) 'Denial lobby strikes again', *Australian Financial Review*, 29 March.

Rangan, Pooja (2017) *Immediations: The Humanitarian Impulse in Documentary*, Duke University Press.

Rawls, John (1971) *A Theory of Justice*, Belknap.

Rizzo, Sergio (2005) 'Why Less is Still Moore–Celebrity and the Reactive Politics of Fahrenheit 9/11', *Film Quarterly*, 59(2): 32–9.

Rodrik, Dani (2017) *Straight Talk on Trade: Ideas for a Sane World Economy*, Princeton University Press.

Samson, Carl (2021) 'Trump SUED for Saying "China Virus", "Kung Flu" While He Was in Office', *Yahoo!News*, 22 May.

Sandel, Michael (2012) *What Money Can't Buy: The Moral Limits of Markets*, Farrar, Straus and Giroux.

Scholte, Jan A. (2005) 'The sources of neoliberal globalization', Overarching Concerns Paper No. 8, October, UNRISD, https://www.unrisd.org/80256B3C005BCCF9/search/9E1C54CEEB19A314C12570B4004D0881?OpenDocument=

Schram, Sanford F. (2019) 'Neoliberal relations of poverty and the welfare state', in *The Relational Nordic Welfare State*, edited by Sakari Hänninen, Kirsi-Marja Lehtelä and Paula Saikkonen, Edward Elgar Publishing.

Schwab, Klaus (2015) 'The Fourth Industrial Revolution: what it means and how to respond', *Foreign Affairs*, 12 December.

Scott, James C. (1985) *Weapons of the Weak: Everyday Forms of Peasant Resistance*, Yale University Press.

Sennett, Richard (1977) *The Fall of Public Man*, Knopf.

Singer, Ross (2011) 'Anti-Corporate Argument and the Spectacle of the Grotesque Rhetorical Body in *Super Size Me*', *Critical Studies in Media Communication*, 28(2): 135–52.

Spiegel, Alix (2011) 'Creator Of Psychopathy Test Worries About Its Use', *NPR*, 27 May.

Stanley, Anya (2021) 'Let's pray that *The Forever Purge* is the last Purge', *A.V. Club*, 1 July.

Strange, Susan (1986) *Casino Capitalism*, Blackwell.

Stroud, Natalie Jomini (2007) 'Media Effects, Selective Exposure, and Fahrenheit 9/11', *Political Communication*, 24(4): 415–32.

Sunstein, Cass R. and Adrian Vermeule (2009) 'Conspiracy theories: Causes and Cures', *Journal of Political Philosophy*, 17(2): 202–27.

Sutherland, Jean-Anne and Kathryn M. Feltey (eds.) (2012) *Cinematic Sociology: Social Life in Film*, Sage.

Tan, Kenneth P. (2008) 'Meritocracy and Elitism in a Global City: Ideological Shifts in Singapore', *International Political Science Review*, 29(1): 7–27.

The Late Show (2018) 'Extended interview: Michael Moore talks with Stephen Colbert', 10 July, https://youtu.be/ojgum7H7g8w.

The World Bank (2020) 'Poverty and shared prosperity 2020: reversals of fortune', Published report, https://www.worldbank.org/en/publication/poverty-and-shared-prosperity.

Toplin, Robert B. (2006) *Michael Moore's Fahrenheit 9/11: How One Film Divided a Nation*, University Press of Kansas.

Turner, Sarah E. and Sarah Nilsen (2019) *The Myth of Colorblindness: Race and Ethnicity in American Cinema*, Palgrave Macmillan.

V-Dem Institute (2021) 'Autocratization turns viral: Democracy Report 2021', University of Gothenburg.

Waugh, Thomas (2011) *The Right to Play Oneself: Looking Back on Documentary Film*, University of Minnesota Press.

Whiteley, Paul, Harold D. Clarke, and Marianne C. Stewart (2020) 'Populism plus: voting for Donald Trump and Hillary Clinton in the 2016 US presidential election', in *Authoritarian Populism and Liberal Democracy*, edited by Ivor Crewe and David Sanders, Palgrave Macmillan.

Winston, Brian, Gail Vanstone and Wang Chi (2017) *The Act of Documenting: Documentary Film in the 21st Century*, Bloomsbury.

Wolf, Martin (2017) 'The economic origins of the populist surge', *Financial Times*, 28 June.

Appendix

List of Movies Discussed

#Alive (2020), directed by Cho Il-hyung

3% (2016), directed by César Charlone, Daina Giannecchini, Dani Libardi, Jotagá Crema and Philippe Barcinski

13th (2016), directed by Ava DuVernay

28 Days Later (2002), directed by Danny Boyle

28 Weeks Later (2007), directed by Juan Carlos Fresnadillo

A Plastic Ocean (2016), directed by Craig Leeson

American Psycho (2000), directed by Mary Harron

An Inconvenient Sequel: Truth to Power (2017), directed by Bonni Cohen and Jon Shenk

An Inconvenient Truth (2006), directed by Davis Guggenheim

Backpackers (2009), directed by Songyos Sugmakanan, in anthology movie *Phobia 2*

Before the Flood (2016), directed by Fisher Stevens

Black Panther (2018), directed by Ryan Coogler

Capitalism: A Love Story (2009), directed by Michael Moore

Cargo (2017), directed by Ben Howling and Yolanda Ramke

City of God (2002), directed by Fernando Meirelles and Kátia Lund

Crazy Rich Asians (2018), directed by Jon M. Chu

Dark Victory (1939), directed by Edmund Goulding

Dawn of the Dead (1978), directed by George A. Romero

Dawn of the Dead (2004), directed by Zack Snyder

Don't Look Up (2021), directed by Adam McKay

Downton Abbey (2019), directed by Michael Engler

Elysium (2013), directed by Neill Blomkamp

Everything's Cool (2007), directed by Daniel B. Gold and Judith Helfand

Fahrenheit 9/11 (2004), directed by Michael Moore

Fahrenheit 11/9 (2018), directed by Michael Moore

How to Change the World (2015), directed by Jerry Rothwell

Hsien of the Dead (2012), directed by Gary Ow

Inequality for All (2013), directed by Jacob Kornbluth

Inside Job (2010), directed by Charles Ferguson

Ivory Tower (2014), directed by Andrew Rossi

Joker (2019), directed by Todd Phillips

KL Zombie (2013), directed by Woo Ming Jin

Little Monsters (2019), directed by Abe Forsythe

Margin Call (2011), directed by J.C. Chandor

Merchants of Doubt (2014), directed by Robert Kenner

Modern Times (1936), directed by Charles Chaplin

Operation Varsity Blues: The College Admissions Scandal (2021), directed by Chris Smith

Parasite (2019), directed by Bong Joon-ho

Park Avenue: Money, Power and the American Dream (2012), directed by Alex Gibney

Ravenous (2017), directed by Robin Aubert

Reuni Z (2018), directed by Monty Tiwa and Soleh Solihun

Roger & Me (1989), directed by Michael Moore

Saving Capitalism (2017), directed by Jacob Kornbluth and Sari Gilman

Shaun of the Dead (2004), directed by Edgar Wright

Sicko (2007), directed by Michael Moore

Slacker Uprising (2008), directed by Michael Moore

Super Size Me (2004), directed by Morgan Spurlock

Super Size Me 2: Holy Chicken! (2017), directed by Morgan Spurlock

The 11th Hour (2007), directed by Nadia Conners and Leila Conners

The Big Short (2015), directed by Adam McKay

The Birth of a Nation (1915), directed by D.W. Griffith

The Bleeding Edge (2018), directed by Kirby Dick

The Cured (2017), directed by David Freyne

The Day After Tomorrow (2004), directed by Roland Emmerich

The Dead Don't Die (2019), directed by Jim Jarmusch

The End of Poverty? (2008), directed by Philippe Diaz

The Forever Purge (2021), directed by Everardo Gout

The Girl with all the Gifts (2016), directed by Colm McCarthy

The Great Global Warming Swindle (2007), directed by Martin Durkin

The Great Warming (2006), directed by Michael Taylor

The Hunger Games (2012), directed by Gary Ross

The Matrix (1999), directed by the Wachowskis

The Platform (2019), directed by Galder Gaztelu-Urrutia

The Purge (2013), directed by James DeMonaco

The Social Dilemma (2020), directed by Jeff Orlowski

The Texas Chainsaw Massacre (1974), directed by Tobe Hooper

The Wolf of Wall Street (2013), directed by Martin Scorsese

Time To Choose (2016), directed by Charles Ferguson

Too Big to Fail (2011), directed by Curtis Hanson

Train to Busan (2016), directed by Yeon Sang-ho

Twister (1996), directed by Jan de Bont

Waiting For 'Superman' (2010), directed by Davis Guggenheim

Wall Street (1987), directed by Oliver Stone

Wall Street: Money Never Sleeps (2010), directed by Oliver Stone

World War Z (2013), directed by Marc Forster

Zeitgeist: Addendum (2008), directed by Peter Joseph

Zeitgeist: Moving Forward (2011), directed by Peter Joseph

Zeitgeist: The Movie (2007), directed by Peter Joseph

Zombieland (2009), directed by Ruben Fleischer

Zombieland: Double Tap (2019), directed by Ruben Fleischer

Zombiepura (2018), directed by Jacen Tan